Appalachian Trail Guide to Central Virginia

Dedicated to John S. Albright

*For his devotion to the Trail, and for
his work as field editor of the first
edition of this guidebook and its
earlier incarnation as the guide to
Central and Southwest Virginia*

Appalachian Trail Guide to Central Virginia

Bob Ellinwood
Field Editor

Appalachian Trail Conference
Harpers Ferry

Acknowledgments

Robert Ellinwood of Bedford, Va., did much research for sections 17 through 26 of this edition. Also contributing: Nancy Anthony, Bill Austin, Bill Baggett, Carolyn Bates, Dave Benavitch, Bruce Benedict, Malcolm Black, Dot Bliss, Jim Carico, Roger Clifton, Pee Wee Crowell, Mike Dawson, Faye and Bill Dawson, Celia Demers, Alice Denney, Jaqueline Dennis, John Doyle, Rosemary Dunn, Cecil Eby, Sandra Elder, Michelle Ellinwood, Ralph and Barbara Etherington, Eugenia Farrar, Bill and Laurie Foot, Jim Fox, Burleigh and Phyllis Gilliam, Bill Gordge, Linda Granger, Bob Giffin, Charles Hansrote, Wayne Hash, T. Gibson Hobbs, Harold E. Howard, Taft Hughes, Julie Hulslander, Tommy Jamerson, Don Johnson, Haynie Kabler, Brian Kelley, Mary J. Layne, Fran Leckie, Len Lennard, Doug MacLeod, Fred Mann, Lisa McCown, Tom Morgan, Jacob Morrill, Ed Page, Gene Parker, Rufus Parker, Charles Parry, Dave Pierce, Laurie Potteiger, Mary and Roy Quick, Gywnn Ramsey, Wayne Rhodes, Guy and Verma Rivers, Ron Ross, Frank Smith, Brewster Snow, Connie Sparrow, Al Summerville, Norman Sykora, Ed Talone, Pete Tansill, Jim Tennant, William Trout, Peter Viemeister, Ed Warehime, Jimmy Whitney, Vogt Wilcher, Dave Wilcox, Louise Williams, Andrew Woody.

Cover photograph: View along the Blue Ridge Parkway
© 1994, David Muench

ISBN 1-889386-23-5

First Edition, Revised
Printed in the United States of America on recycled paper.

Contents

Contents

Notice To All Trail Users

The information contained in this publication is the result of the best effort of the publisher, using information available to it at the time of printing. Changes resulting from maintenance work and relocations are constantly occurring, and, therefore, no published route can be regarded as precisely accurate at the time you read this notice.

Notices of pending relocations are indicated. Maintenance of the Trail is conducted by volunteers and maintaining clubs listed in the guidebooks, and questions about the exact route of the Trail should be addressed to the maintaining clubs or to the Appalachian Trail Conference, 799 Washington Street, P.O. Box 807, Harpers Ferry, W. Va. 25425-0807; telephone, (304) 535-6331; or e-mail, <info@appalachiantrail.org>. On the Trail, please pay close attention to—and follow—the white blazes and any directional signs.

Responsibility for Safety

It is extremely important to plan your hike, especially in places where water is scarce. Purify water drawn from any source. Water purity cannot be guaranteed. The Appalachian Trail Conference and the various maintaining clubs attempt to locate good sources of water along the Trail but have no control over these sources and cannot, in any sense, be responsible for the quality of the water at any given time. You must determine the safety of all water you use.

Certain risks are inherent in any Appalachian Trail hike. Each A.T. user must accept personal responsibility for his or her safety while on the Trail. The Appalachian Trail Conference and its member maintaining clubs cannot ensure the safety of any hiker on the Trail, and, when undertaking a hike on the Trail, each user thereby assumes the risk for any accident, illness, or injury that might occur on the Trail.

Enjoy your hike, but please take all appropriate precautions for your safety and well-being.

The Appalachian Trail

The Appalachian Trail (A.T.) is a continuous, marked footpath extending more than 2,160 miles from Katahdin, a granite monolith in the central Maine woods, south to Springer Mountain in Georgia, along the crest of the Appalachian mountain chain.

The Trail traverses mostly public land in fourteen states. Virginia has the longest section, with 523 miles, while West Virginia has the shortest, a short 2.4-mile swing into Harpers Ferry at the Maryland border and another 23.4 miles that straddle the Virginia–West Virginia border. The highest elevation along the Trail is 6,643 feet at Clingmans Dome in the Great Smoky Mountains. The Trail is 124 feet above sea level near its crossing of the Hudson River in New York.

Trail History

Credit for establishing the Trail belongs to three leaders and countless volunteers. The first proposal for the Trail to appear in print was an article by regional planner Benton MacKaye of Shirley Center, Massachusetts, entitled, "An Appalachian Trail, a Project in Regional Planning," in the October 1921 issue of the *Journal of the American Institute of Architects*. He envisioned a footpath along the Appalachian ridgeline where urban people could retreat to nature.

MacKaye's challenge kindled considerable interest, but, at the time, most of the outdoor organizations that could participate in constructing such a trail were east of the Hudson River. Four existing trail systems could be incorporated into an A.T. The Appalachian Mountain Club (AMC) maintained an excellent series of trails in New England, but most ran north-south; the Trail could not cross New Hampshire until the chain of huts built and operated by the AMC permitted an east-west alignment. In Vermont, the southern 100 miles of the Long Trail, then being developed in the Green Mountains, were connected to the White Mountains by the trails of the Dartmouth Outing Club.

In 1923, a number of area hiking clubs that had formed the New York–New Jersey Trail Conference opened the first new section of the A.T. in Palisades Interstate Park, near Bear Mountain.

The Appalachian Trail Conference (ATC) was formed in 1925 to stimulate greater interest in MacKaye's idea and coordinate the clubs' work in choosing and building the route. The Conference remains a nonprofit educational organization of individuals and clubs of volunteers dedicated to maintaining, managing, and protecting the Appalachian Trail.

Although interest in the Trail spread to Pennsylvania and New England, little further work was done until 1926, when retired Judge Arthur Perkins of Hartford, Connecticut, began persuading groups to locate and cut the footpath through the wilderness. His enthusiasm provided the momentum that carried the Trail idea forward.

The southern states had few trails and even fewer clubs. The "skyline" route followed by the A.T. in the South was developed largely within the new national forests. A number of clubs were formed in various parts of the southern Appalachians to take responsibility for the Trail there.

Perkins interested Myron H. Avery in the Trail. Avery, chairman of the Conference from 1931 to 1952, enlisted the aid and coordinated the work of hundreds of volunteers who completed the Trail by August 14, 1937, when a Civilian Conservation Corps crew opened the last section (on the ridge between Spaulding and Sugarloaf mountains in Maine).

At the eighth meeting of the ATC, in June 1937, Conference member Edward B. Ballard successfully proposed a plan for an "Appalachian Trailway" that would set apart an area on each side of the Trail, dedicated to the interests of those who travel on foot.

Steps taken to effect this long-range protection program culminated first in an October 15, 1938, agreement between the National Park Service and the U.S. Forest Service for the promotion of an Appalachian Trailway through the relevant national parks and forests, extending one mile on each side of the Trail. Within this zone, no new parallel roads would be built or any other incompatible development allowed. Timber cutting would not be permitted within 200 feet of the Trail. Similar agreements, creating a zone one-quarter mile in width, were signed with most states through which the Trail passes.

After World War II, the encroachments of highways, housing developments, and summer resorts caused many relocations, and the problem of maintaining the Trail's wilderness character became more severe.

In 1968, Congress established a national system of trails and designated the Appalachian Trail and the Pacific Crest Trail as the initial components. The National Trails System Act directs the Secretary of the Interior, in consultation with the Secretary of Agriculture, to administer the Appalachian Trail primarily as a footpath and protect the Trail against incompatible activities and the use of motorized vehicles. Provision was also made for acquiring rights-of-way for the Trail, both inside and outside the boundaries of federally administered areas.

In 1970, supplemental agreements under the act—among the National Park Service, the U.S. Forest Service, and the Appalachian Trail Conference—established the specific responsibilities of these organizations for initial mapping, selection of rights-of-way, relocations, maintenance, development, acquisition of land, and protection of a permanent Trail. Agreements also were signed between the Park Service and the various states, encouraging them to acquire and protect a right-of-way for the Trail outside federal land.

Slow progress of federal efforts and lack of initiative by some states led Congress to strengthen the National Trails System Act. President Jimmy Carter signed the amendment, known as the Appalachian Trail Bill, on March 21,1978.

The new legislation emphasized the need for protecting the Trail, including acquiring a corridor, and authorized $90 million for that purpose. With fewer than eighteen miles unprotected by the end of 2000, this project is close to completion.

In 1984, the Interior Department delegated the responsibility of managing the A.T. corridor lands outside established parks and forests to the Appalachian Trail Conference. The Conference and its clubs retain primary responsibility for maintaining the footpath, too. A new, more comprehensive ten-year agreement was signed in 1994.

The Appalachian Trail Conference

As an organization, the Conference is governed by a volunteer Board of Managers, consisting of a chair, three vice chairs, a treasurer, a secretary, an assistant secretary, and twenty members—six from each of the three regions of ATC (New England, mid-Atlantic, and southern) and two at large. It publishes information on constructing and maintaining hiking trails, official A.T. guides, and general information on the Appalachian Trail.

ATC membership consists of organizations and individuals that maintain the Trail or contribute to the Trail project. Members receive a subscription to *Appalachian Trailway News*, published six times a year, and discounts on publications. The Conference also issues three newsletters: *The Register*, for Trail maintainers; *Trail Lands*, for contributors to its land-trust program, the Appalachian Trail Conference Land Trust; and *Inside ATC*, for major donors. Annual membership dues range from $25 to $100, with life memberships available for $600 (individual) or $900 (couple).

Membership forms and a complete list of publications are available from the Appalachian Trail Conference, P.O. Box 807, Harpers Ferry, WV 25425; (304) 535-6331. The office is open from 9:00 a.m. to 5:00 p.m. (Eastern Time), Monday through Friday, year-round and 9:00 a.m. to 4:00 p.m. on weekends from mid-May through October. ATC's Internet site is: <*www.appalachiantrail.org*>.

The Appalachian Trail Conference, as part of its charter to serve as the clearinghouse of official information on the Trail, publishes a number of books other than guides and also sells books from other publishers. ATC members receive a discount on publications sold through the Conference. Proceeds from sales help underwrite the costs of A.T. maintenance and Trail-corridor management.

A complete list of the publications and merchandise available from ATC can be obtained by writing ATC at P.O. Box 807, Harpers Ferry, WV 25425, calling (304) 535-6331, or (888) AT STORE, or by e-mail, at <*info@appalachiantrail.org*>.

Maintaining Clubs

Five member clubs of the Appalachian Trail Conference maintain the Trail in central Virginia. The clubs, their areas of responsibility, and total mileages maintained are:

Old Dominion Appalachian Trail Club
Rockfish Gap to Reeds Gap, 19.4 miles

Tidewater Appalachian Trail Club
Reeds Gap to Tye River, 10.5 miles

Natural Bridge Appalachian Trail Club
Tye River to Black Horse Gap, 89.9 miles

Roanoke Appalachian Trail Club
Black Horse Gap to Pine Swamp Branch Shelter, 85.9 miles

The Outdoor Club at Virginia Tech
 Pine Swamp Branch Shelter to New River, 19.1 miles

Route of the Appalachian Trail
in Central Virginia

From Rockfish Gap, where this guide begins, heading south, the Trail shares a narrow ridge with the Blue Ridge Parkway. As the ridge widens into a broader band of peaks, the Trail diverges from the parkway and crosses a number of outlying peaks.

From Rockfish Gap to the James River, the lowest point in the central–Virginia Blue Ridge, the Trail passes through the Pedlar District of the George Washington National Forest.

South of the James River, the Trail enters the Glenwood District of the Jefferson National Forest but, for about nine miles, traverses Blue Ridge Parkway land. Ten miles north of Roanoke, it leaves the ridge and descends into the geologic region known as the Great Valley of Virginia, between the Blue Ridge and the Allegheny Plateau to its west.

The route then traverses the Jefferson National Forest's New Castle District and ends at the New River in Pearisburg, about halfway through the Jefferson's New River District.

The sections of the Appalachian Trail in northern Virginia are covered in two other guides. The first five sections in the state are described in the *Appalachian Trail Guide to Maryland and Northern Virginia*. Sections six through fourteen are described in the *Appalachian Trail Guide to Shenandoah National Park*. Both guides are published by the Potomac Appalachian Trail Club and sold by that club and ATC (see "Important Addresses," page 273).

Much of the A.T. in central Virginia is graded to avoid steep ascents and descents, although, in places, the route is rugged and more varied. The Trail sometimes follows fire roads, old woods roads, and old railroad beds. The route is primarily located on ridges, bypassing some minor summits that do not have viewpoints in summer.

The Mountains of Virginia

At the Potomac River on the Virginia–Maryland border, the Blue Ridge Mountains are a narrow crestline of peaks, with spurs on either side and high intervening gaps. Many outlying mountains are found fifty miles farther south and throughout the Shenandoah National Park.

North of Rockfish Gap, just south of the park, the Blue Ridge is a jumbled mass of mountains separated by high gaps and 3,000-foot drops to the intervening valleys. For some fifty miles, the eastern-most area of this mountain region is dominated by "The Religious Range"—The Priest, Little Priest, The Cardinal, and The Friar.

South of the James River, to the east, are the well-known Peaks of Otter: Flat Top, Sharp Top, and Harkening Hill, accessible from the A.T.

Most of this mountainous region was home to Indians since prehistoric times. At every broad saddle and around every spring in the Blue Ridge, one can find evidence of the prehistoric inhabit-ants in the chips of the quartzite, chert, and quartz used by the Indians to make tools and projectile points. The area was then occupied more than two hundred years ago by settlers from Penn-sylvania, who followed the Warriors' Path down the Cumberland and Shenandoah valleys, or settlers from Tidewater Virginia to the east. They found virgin stands of pine, red cedar, oak, and many other varieties of trees, streams teeming with fish, and a variety of game. Unfortunately, most of the grants of land were for one hundred and two hundred acres; after a few generations had lived on them, the trees were all cut, the streams fished out, and the game killed or driven away. Nearly all settlers then moved west or south.

A flurry of prospecting and mining for copper, saltpeter, and similar minerals and, later, the tanbark industry brought renewed activity temporarily. Afterwards, the land was again abandoned. Since the establishment of national forests in Virginia in 1918 and their subsequent protection, the hills have had a remarkable recov-ery.

Many of the mountains are heavily forested, but some cliffs and balds reveal wide vistas.

Flowers carpet the route in spring. Summer brings a profusion of azalea and rhododendron blossoms. The fall-color displays of the southern hardwoods are well known.

Snow and very low temperatures are common in the winter.

The Blue Ridge Parkway

The Blue Ridge Parkway begins at the southern end of Skyline Drive in Rockfish Gap and extends to Cherokee, North Carolina, just southeast of the Great Smoky Mountains National Park. It is a two-lane road through a strip of park varying in width from 500 to 1,200 feet on either side. It was built for recreational purposes and is limited to passenger vehicles. The parkway lands are left as natural as possible.

For much of its course in Virginia, the Blue Ridge Parkway follows the original route of the Appalachian Trail. The Trail was relocated, usually onto national forest lands on either side of the parkway, often crossing or coming close to provide easy access.

Along the parkway are several picnic areas with water, toilet facilities, and, in the summer, concessions selling meals, light refreshments, and gasoline. The Peaks of Otter area has a motel, restaurant, and campground. Otter Creek, just north of the James River, has a campground and seasonal restaurant.

A newspaper, *The Milepost*, with items of interest along the parkway, is available from the Management Assistant, Virginia Blue Ridge Parkway, Rural Route 3, Box 39D, Vinton, VA 24179. A map keyed to mileposts along the parkway is available from staffed visitors' centers for a small fee. The Blue Ridge Parkway has adopted the convention of referring to all mileage locations along it as "mileposts," even when no physical milepost exists. This guide follows that convention.

Public pay telephones are at the following points: milepost 0.0 (Metelson Restaurant), milepost 5.5 (Humpback Rocks Recreation Area), milepost 29.0 (Whetstone Ridge), milepost 60.8 (Otter Creek Campground), milepost 85.6 (Peaks of Otter Lodge), and milepost 86.0 (Peaks of Otter Visitors' Center).

Hikers are urged to observe the following regulations: No hitchhiking is allowed on the parkway; no camping allowed along the Appalachian Trail on Blue Ridge Parkway land except at designated locations; park in paved overlooks when possible; do not block gates; please notify rangers if you plan to park overnight.

In case of emergencies, dial (828) 298-0281 or (800) PARKWATCH.

General Information

Trail Marking

The Appalachian Trail is marked for daytime travel in both directions. The marks are white-paint blazes about two inches wide and six inches high on trees, posts, and rocks. Occasionally, on open ledges, stone cairns identify the route. In some areas, diamond-shaped A.T. metal markers or other signs mark the Trail. Two blazes, one above the other, signal an obscure turn, a change in route, or a warning to check blazes carefully.

When the route is not obvious, normal marking procedure is to position the blazes so that anyone standing at one blaze will always be able to see the next. When the footway is unmistakable, blazes frequently are farther apart. If you have gone a quarter-mile without seeing a blaze, retrace your steps until you locate one, and then check to ensure that you did not miss a turn. Since the Trail is marked for both directions, a glance back may locate blazes for travel in the opposite direction.

Side trails from the A.T. to water, viewpoints, and shelters usually are blazed in blue paint. Intersecting trails not part of the A.T. system are blazed in a variety of colors.

At trail junctions or near important features, the Trail route is often marked by signs. Some list mileages and detailed information. The Virginia Department of Highways and Transportation has erected signs where the Trail crosses major roads.

Trail Relocations

Always follow the marked Trail. If it differs from the guidebook's Trail description, it is because the Trail was relocated recently in the area, probably to avoid a hazard or undesirable feature or to remove it from private property. If you use the old Trail, you may be trespassing and generating ill-will toward the Trail community.

Information on Trail relocations between guidebook revisions often is available from the ATC information department. Check the ATC Web site at *<www.appalachiantrail.org>* for updates. Every effort has been made in this guide to alert you to relocations that may occur. Do not follow new trails that are not blazed, because they may not be open to the public yet.

Water

Water sources along the Trail's high ridgecrests in central Virginia are limited. Carrying one or more water containers is necessary; a two-quart minimum capacity is recommended. The exertion of hiking, combined with water shortages, could lead to dehydration and increase fatigue, thus marring an otherwise enjoyable experience.

Although the A.T. may have sources of clean, potable water, any water source can become polluted. Most water sources along the Trail are unprotected and consequently very susceptible to contamination. All water should be boiled, chemically treated, and/or filtered (with a filter claiming to be effective against *giardia*) before use.

Avoid contaminating the water supply and the surrounding area. Dishes, clothes, and hands should never be washed in the water supply. Draw water from the supply, and wash elsewhere. Make sure food and human wastes are buried well away from any water source.

Weather

Heavy rainstorms are common in Virginia. Tents should be thoroughly waterproof. A full-length poncho or rainsuit and pack cover are recommended.

In midsummer, many open summits expose travelers to the direct rays of the sun, and the heat can be extreme. Avoid overexertion and protect your face, shoulders, and legs from the sun.

Do not assume that winter weather in Virginia will be mild. It can suddenly become extremely cold, with temperatures as low as zero degrees Fahrenheit for extended periods, especially at higher elevations. Considerable snowfall can occur. Although the Trail in Virginia usually can be traversed throughout the year, winter weather makes travel and camping particularly difficult.

Equipment

Never carry more than you need. Some items should be with you on every hike: the *A.T. Data Book* and/or guidebook and maps; water; flashlight, even on day trips; whistle; emergency food; matches and fire starter; multipurpose knife; compass; rain gear; proper shoes and socks; warm, dry spare clothes; and a first-aid kit (see page 25).

Take the time to consult periodicals, books, employees of outfitter stores, and other hikers before choosing the equipment that is best for you.

Navigation

The compass variation, or declination, in central Virginia varies from 6 degrees at Rockfish Gap to 3.5 degrees at New River at Pearisburg. This means that true north is 6 to 3.5 degrees to the right of the compass pointer, depending upon your location.

If You Get Lost

Stop, if you have walked more than a quarter-mile (1,320 feet or roughly five minutes of hiking) without noticing a blaze or other Trail indicator (see page 9). If you find no indication of the Trail, retrace your path until one appears. The cardinal mistake behind unfortunate experiences is insisting on continuing when the route seems obscure or dubious. Haste, even in a desire to reach camp before dark, only complicates the difficulty. When in doubt, remain where you are to avoid straying farther from the route. The Trail is marked for daylight use only and can be difficult to follow after dark, even in good conditions. In the dark, especially on moonless nights or in foggy conditions, it is easy to become disoriented.

Hiking long distances alone should be avoided. If undertaken, it requires extra precautions. A lone hiker who suffers a serious accident or illness might be risking death if he has not planned for the remote chance of disability in an isolated spot. Your destinations and estimated times of arrival should be known to someone who will initiate inquiries or a search if you do not appear when expected. On long trips, reporting your plans and progress every few days is a wise precaution.

A lone hiker who gets lost and chooses to bushwhack toward town runs considerable risks if an accident occurs. If the accident occurs away from a used trail, the hiker might not be discovered for days or even weeks. Lone hikers are advised to stay on the Trail (or at least on a trail), even if it means spending an unplanned night in the woods in sight of a distant electric light. As part of your prehike preparations, make sure your pack contains enough food and water to sustain you until daylight, when a careful retracing of your steps might lead you back to a safe route.

Distress Signals

An emergency call for distress consists of three short calls—audible or visible—repeated at regular intervals. A whistle is particularly good for audible signals. Visible signals may include, in daytime, light flashed with a mirror, or smoke puffs; at night, a flashlight or three small bright fires.

Anyone recognizing such a signal should acknowledge it with two calls—if possible, by the same method—then go to the distressed person and determine the nature of the emergency. Arrange for more aid, if necessary.

Most of the A.T. is busy enough that, if you are injured, you can expect to be found. However, if an area is remote and the weather bad, fewer hikers will be on the Trail. In that case, it might be best to study the guide for the nearest place people are likely to be and attempt to move in that direction. If it is necessary to leave a heavy pack behind, be sure to take essentials, in case rescue is delayed. In bad weather, a night in the open without proper covering could be dangerous.

Pests

Rattlesnakes and copperheads are found in central Virginia. See page 24 for the recommended treatment of snakebites.

Ticks, chiggers, no-see-ums, mosquitoes, and other insects are often encountered. Carry repellent.

Poison ivy, stinging nettle, and briars grow along many sections of the Trail in Virginia. Long pants are recommended. Trailside plants grow rapidly in spring and summer, and, although volunteers try to keep the Trail cleared, some places may be filled by midsummer with dense growth, especially in clearings and where gypsy moths have destroyed the overstory vegetation.

Parking

Park in designated areas. For regulations regarding parking along the Blue Ridge Parkway, see page 8. If you leave your car parked overnight unattended, you may be risking theft or vandalism, even in designated areas. Please do not ask Trail neighbors for permission to park your car near their homes. Often, however, a nearby business will be willing to let you park in its lot for a fee. Ask first.

Hunting

Hunting is allowed along many parts of the A.T. Though prohibited in many state parks and on National Park Service lands—whether acquired specifically for protection of the Appalachian Trail or as part of another unit of the national park system—many of the boundary lines that identify those lands have yet to be surveyed or marked with signs. It may be very difficult for hunters to know that they are on Park Service lands. Hunters who approach the A.T. from the side, and who do not know that they are on Trail lands, also may have no idea that the Trail is nearby. The Trail traverses lands of several other types of ownership, including national forest lands and state gamelands, on which hunting is allowed as part of a multiple-use management plan (national forests) or specifically for game (state gamelands).

Some hunting areas are marked by permanent or temporary signs, but any sign is subject to vandalism and removal. The prudent hiker, especially in the fall, makes himself aware of local hunting seasons and wears "blaze orange" during them. ATC's Web site, <*www.appalachiantrail.org*>, posts hunting seasons for various parts of the Trail, as do state governments' sites.

Trail Ethics

As more and more people use the Trail and other backcountry areas, it becomes more important to learn to enjoy wild places without ruining them. The best way to do this is to understand and practice the principles of Leave No Trace, a seven-point ethic for enjoying the backcountry that applies to everything from a picnic outing to a long-distance expedition. Leave No Trace is also a nonprofit organization dedicated to teaching the principles of low-impact use. For more information, contact Leave No Trace at: <*www.lnt.org*>, or call (800) 332-4100.

The seven Leave No Trace principles are:

1. *Plan ahead and prepare.* When you don't have the facts about where you are going or what to expect, you're more likely to cause problems in the backcountry.
2. *Travel and camp on durable surfaces.* Stay on the trail and don't cut switchbacks. Keep off fragile trailside areas, such as alpine zones. Camp in designated spots.
3. *Dispose of waste properly.* Bury or pack out excrement. Pack out all trash and food waste, including that left behind by others. Do not bury trash or food, and do not try to burn packaging materials in campfires.
4. *Leave what you find.* Don't take flowers or other sensitive natural resources. Don't disturb historical artifacts such as cellar holes and arrowheads.
5. *Minimize campfire impacts.* Know local regulations, which may prohibit fires.
6. *Respect wildlife.* Don't feed or disturb wildlife. Store food properly to avoid attracting bears and rodents. If you bring a pet, keep it leashed.
7. *Be considerate of other visitors.* Limit overnight groups to ten or fewer, twenty-five on day trips. Minimize noise and intrusive behavior. Share shelters and other facilities. Be considerate of Trail neighbors.

Group Hikes and Special Events

Special events, group hikes, or other group activities that could degrade the Appalachian Trail's natural or cultural resources or social values should be avoided. Examples of such activities include publicized spectator events, commercial or competitive activities, or programs involving large groups.

The policy of the Appalachian Trail Conference is that groups planning to spend one or more nights on the Trail should not exceed ten people, and day-use groups should not exceed twenty-five people at any one location, unless the local maintaining organization or state agency has made special arrangements to both accommodate the group and protect Trail values.

First Aid Along the Trail

By Robert Ohler, M.D., and the
Appalachian Trail Conference

Hikers encounter a wide variety of terrain and climatic conditions along the Appalachian Trail. Prepare for the possibility of injuries. Some of the more common Trail-related medical problems are briefly discussed below.

Preparation is key to a safe trip. If possible, every hiker should take the free courses in advanced first aid and cardiopulmonary resuscitation (CPR) techniques offered in most communities by the American Red Cross.

Even without this training, you can be prepared for accidents. Emergency situations can develop. Analyses of serious accidents have shown that a substantial number originate at home, in the planning stage of the trip. Think about communications. Have you informed your relatives and friends about your locations, schedule, and time of return? Has all of your equipment been carefully checked? Considering the season and altitude, have you provided for water, food, and shelter?

While hiking, set your own comfortable pace. If you are injured or lost or a storm strikes, stop. Remember, your brain is your most important survival tool. Inattention can start a chain of events leading to disaster.

If an accident occurs, treat the injury first. If outside help is needed, at least one person should stay with the injured hiker. Two people should go for help and carry with them notes on the exact location of the accident, what has been done to aid the injured hiker, and what help is needed.

The injured will need encouragement, assurances of help, and confidence in your competence. Treat him gently. Keep him supine, warm, and quiet. Protect from the weather with insulation below and above him. Examine him carefully, noting all possible injuries.

General Emergencies

Back or neck injuries: Immobilize the victim's entire body where he lies. Protect head and neck from movement if the neck is injured,

16

and treat as a fracture. Transportation must be on a rigid frame such as a litter or a door. The spinal cord could be severed by inexpert handling. This type of injury must be handled by a large group of experienced personnel. Obtain outside help.

Bleeding: Stop the flow of blood by using a method appropriate to the amount and type of bleeding. Exerting pressure over the wound with the fingers, with or without a dressing, may be sufficient. Minor arterial bleeding can be controlled with local pressure and bandaging. Major arterial bleeding might require compressing an artery against a bone to stop the flow of blood. Elevate the arm or legs above the heart. To stop bleeding from an artery in the leg, place a hand in the groin, and press toward the inside of the leg. Stop arterial bleeding from an arm by placing a hand between the armpit and elbow and pressing toward the inside of the arm.

Apply a tourniquet only if you are unable to control severe bleeding by pressure and elevation. *Warning:* This method should be used only when the limb will be lost anyway. Once applied, a tourniquet should only be removed by medical personnel equipped to stop the bleeding by other means and to restore lost blood. The tourniquet should be located between the wound and the heart. If there is a traumatic amputation (loss of hand, leg, or foot), place the tourniquet two inches above the amputation.

Blisters: Good boot fit, without points of irritation or pressure, should be proven before a hike. Always keep feet dry while hiking. Prevent blisters by responding early to any discomfort. Place adhesive tape or moleskin over areas of developing redness or soreness. If irritation can be relieved, allow blister fluid to be reabsorbed. If a blister forms and continued irritation makes draining it necessary, wash the area with soap and water, and prick the edge of the blister with a needle that has been sterilized by the flame of a match. Bandage with a sterile gauze pad and moleskin.

Dislocation: Dislocation of a leg or arm joint is extremely painful. Do not try to put it back in place. Immobilize the entire limb with splints in the position it is found.

Exhaustion: Exhaustion is caused by inadequate food consumption, dehydration and salt deficiency, overexertion, or all three. The victim may lose motivation, slow down, gasp for air, complain of weakness, dizziness, nausea, or headache. Treat by feeding, especially carbohydrates. Slowly replace lost water (normal fluid intake should be two to four quarts per day). Give salt dissolved in water (one teaspoon per cup). In the case of overexertion, rest is essential.

Fractures: Fractures of legs, ankles, or arms must be splinted before moving the victim. After treating wounds, use any available material that will offer firm support, such as tree branches or boards. Pad each side of the arm or leg with soft material, supporting and immobilizing the joints above and below the injury. Bind the splints together with strips of cloth.

Shock: Shock should be expected after all injuries. It is a potentially fatal depression of bodily functions that is made more critical with improper handling, cold, fatigue, and anxiety. Relieve the pain as quickly as possible. Do not administer aspirin if severe bleeding is present; Tylenol or other nonaspirin pain relievers are safe to give. Look for nausea, paleness, trembling, sweating, or thirst. Lay the hiker flat on his back, and raise his feet slightly, or position him, if he can be safely moved, so his head is down the slope. Protect him from the wind, and keep him as warm as possible. A campfire will help.

Sprains: Look or feel for soreness or swelling. Bandage, and treat as a fracture. Cool and raise joint.

Wounds: Wounds (except eye wounds) should be cleaned with soap and water. If possible, apply a clean dressing to protect the wound from further contamination.

Chilling and Freezing Emergencies

Every hiker should be familiar with the symptoms, treatment, and methods of preventing the common and sometimes fatal condition of *hypothermia.* Wind chill and/or body wetness, particularly aggravated by fatigue and hunger, can rapidly drain body heat to dangerously low levels. This often occurs at temperatures well above freezing. Shivering, lethargy, mental slowing, and confusion are early symptoms of hypothermia, which can begin without the victim's realizing it and, if untreated, can lead to death.

Always keep dry spare clothing and a water-repellent windbreaker in your pack, and wear a hat in chilling weather. Wet clothing loses much of its insulating value, although polypropelene, synthetic pile, and wool are warmer than other fabrics when wet. Always, when in chilling conditions, suspect the onset of hypothermia.

Wind Chill Chart

					Actual Temperature (°F)						
	50	**40**	**30**	**20**	**10**	**0**	**-10**	**-20**	**-30**	**-40**	**-50**
					Equivalent Temperature (°F)						
0	50	40	30	20	10	0	-10	-20	-30	-40	-50
5	48	37	27	16	6	-5	-15	-26	-36	-47	-57
10	40	28	16	4	-9	-21	-33	-46	-58	-70	-83
15	36	22	9	-5	-18	-36	-45	-58	-72	-85	-99
20	32	18	4	-10	-25	-39	-53	-67	-82	-96	-110
25	30	16	0	-15	-29	-44	-59	-74	-88	-104	-118
30	28	13	-2	-18	-33	-48	-63	-79	-94	-109	-125
35	27	11	-4	-20	-35	-49	-67	-82	-98	-113	-129
40	26	10	-6	-21	-37	-53	-69	-85	-100	-116	-132

Wind Speed (mph) labels the rows.

This chart illustrates the important relationship between wind and temperature.

To treat this potentially fatal condition, immediately seek shelter and warm the entire body, preferably by placing it in a sleeping bag and administering warm liquids. The addition of another person's body heat may aid in warming.

A sign of *frostbite* is grayish or waxy, yellow-white spots on the skin. The frozen area will be numb. To thaw, warm the frozen part by direct contact with bare flesh. When first frozen, a cheek, nose, or chin can often be thawed by covering with a hand taken from a warm glove. Superficially frostbitten hands sometimes can be thawed by placing them under armpits, on the stomach, or between the thighs. With a partner, feet can be treated similarly. Do not rub frozen flesh.

Frozen layers of deeper tissue beneath the skin are characterized by a solid, "woody" feeling and an inability to move the flesh over bony prominences. Tissue loss is minimized by rapid rewarming of the area in water slightly below 105 degrees Fahrenheit (measure accurately with a thermometer).

Thawing of a frozen foot should not be attempted until the patient has been evacuated to a place where rapid, controlled thawing can take place. Walking on a frozen foot is entirely possible and does not cause increased damage. Walking after thawing is impossible.

Never rewarm over a stove or fire. This "cooks" flesh and results in extensive loss of tissue.

Treatment of a deep freezing injury after rewarming must be done in a hospital.

Heat Emergencies

Exposure to extremely high temperatures, high humidity, and direct sunlight can cause health problems.

Heat Cramps: Heat cramps are usually caused by strenuous activity in high heat and humidity, when sweating depletes salt levels in blood and tissues. Symptoms are intermittent cramps in legs and the abdominal wall and painful spasms of muscles. Pupils of eyes may dilate with each spasm. The skin becomes cold and clammy. Treat with rest and salt dissolved in water (one teaspoon of salt per glass).

Heat Exhaustion: Heat exhaustion is caused by physical exercise during prolonged exposure to heat, is a breakdown of the body's heat-regulating system. The circulatory system is disrupted, reducing the supply of blood to vital organs, such as the brain, heart, and lungs. The victim can have heat cramps and sweat heavily. Skin is moist and cold with face flushed, then pale. The pulse can be unsteady, and blood pressure low. He may vomit and be delirious. Place the victim in shade, flat on his back, with feet eight to twelve inches higher than his head. Give him sips of salt water—half a glass every fifteen minutes—for about an hour. Loosen his clothes. Apply cold cloths.

Heat Stroke and *Sun Stroke:* These are caused by the failure of the heat-regulating system to cool the body by sweating. They are emergency, life-threatening conditions. Body temperature can rise to 106 degrees or higher. Symptoms include weakness, nausea, headache, heat cramps, exhaustion, body temperature rising rapidly, pounding pulse, and high blood pressure. The victim may be delirious or comatose. Sweating will stop before heat stroke becomes apparent. Armpits may be dry and skin flushed and pink, then turning ashen or purple in later stages. Move victim to cool place immediately. Cool the body in any way possible (*e.g.*, sponging). Body temperature must be regulated artificially from outside of the body until the heat-regulating system can be rebalanced. Be careful not to overchill once temperature goes below 102 degrees.

Heat Weakness: Symptoms are fatigue, headache, mental and physical inefficiency, heavy sweating, high pulse rate, and general weakness. Drink plenty of water, find as cool a spot as possible, keep quiet, and replenish salt loss.

Sunburn: This causes redness of the skin, discoloration, swelling, and pain. It occurs rapidly and can be severe at higher elevations. It can be prevented by applying a commercial sun screen; zinc oxide is the most effective. Treat by protecting from further exposure and covering the area with ointment and a dressing. Give the victim large amounts of fluids.

Artificial Respiration

Artificial respiration might be required when an obstruction constricts the air passages or after respiratory failure caused by air being depleted of oxygen, such as after electrocution, by drowning, or because of toxic gases in the air. Quick action is necessary if the victim's lips, fingernail beds, or tongue have become blue, if he is unconscious, or if the pupils of his eyes become enlarged.

If food or a foreign body is lodged in the air passage and coughing is ineffective, try to remove it with the fingers. If the foreign body is inaccessible, grasp the victim from behind, and with one hand hold the opposite wrist just below the breastbone. Squeeze rapidly and firmly, expelling air forcibly from the lungs to expel the foreign body. Repeat this maneuver two to three times, if necessary.

If breathing stops, administer artificial respiration, as air can be forced around the obstruction into the lungs. The mouth-to-mouth or mouth-to-nose, method of forcing air into the victim's lungs should be used. The preferred method is:

1. Clear the victim's mouth of any obstructions.
2. Place one hand under the victim's neck and lift.

3. Place heel of the other hand on the forehead, and tilt head backwards. (Maintain this position during procedure.) Use thumb and index finger to pinch nostrils.
4. Open your mouth, and make a seal with it over the victim's mouth. If the victim is a small child, cover both the nose and the mouth.
5. Breathe deeply, and blow out about every five seconds, or twelve breaths a minute.
6. Watch victim's chest for expansion.
7. Listen for exhalation.

Lyme Disease

Lyme disease is contracted from bites of certain infected ticks. Hikers should be aware of the symptoms and monitor themselves and their partners for signs of the disease. When treated early, Lyme disease usually can be cured with antibiotics.

Inspect yourself for ticks and tick bites at the end of each day. The four types of ticks known to spread Lyme disease are smaller than the dog tick, about the size of a pin head, and not easily seen. They are often called "deer ticks" because they feed during one stage of their life cycle on deer, a host for the disease.

The early signs of a tick bite infected with Lyme disease are a red spot with a white center that enlarges and spreads, severe fatigue, chills, headaches, muscle aches, fever, malaise, and a stiff neck. However, one-quarter of all people with an infected tick bite show none of the early symptoms.

Later effects of the disease, which may not appear for months or years, are severe fatigue, dizziness, shortness of breath, cardiac irregularities, memory and concentration problems, facial paralysis, meningitis, shooting pains in the arms and legs, and other symptoms resembling multiple sclerosis, brain tumors, stroke, alcoholism, mental depression, Alzheimer's disease, and *anorexia nervosa*.

It may be necessary to contact a university medical center or other research center if you suspect you have been bitten by an infected tick. It is not believed people can build a lasting immunity to Lyme disease. For that reason, a hiker who has contracted and been treated for the disease should still take precautions.

Lightning Strikes

Although the odds of being struck by lightning are low, two hundred to four hundred people a year are killed by lightning in the United States. Respect the force of lightning, and seek shelter during a storm.

Do not start a hike if thunderstorms are likely. If caught in a storm, immediately find shelter. Hard-roofed automobiles or large buildings are best; tents and convertible automobiles offer no protection. When indoors, stay away from windows, open doors, fireplaces, and large metal objects. Do not hold a potential lightning rod, such as a metal trekking pole. Avoid tall structures, such as ski lifts, flagpoles, powerline towers, and the tallest trees or hilltops. If you cannot enter a building or car, take shelter in a stand of smaller trees. Avoid clearings. If caught in the open, crouch down, or roll into a ball. If you are in water, get out. Spread out groups, so that everyone is not struck by a single bolt.

If a person is struck by lightning or splashed by a charge hitting a nearby object, the victim will probably be thrown, perhaps a great distance. Clothes can be burned or torn. Metal objects (such as belt buckles) may be hot, and shoes blown off. The victim often has severe muscle contractions (which can cause breathing difficulties), confusion, and temporary blindness or deafness. In more severe cases, the victim may have feathered or sunburst patterns of burns over the skin or ruptured eardrums. He may lose consciousness or breathe irregularly. Occasionally, victims stop breathing and suffer cardiac arrest.

If someone is struck by lightning, perform artificial respiration (see page 21) and CPR until emergency technicians arrive or you can transport the injured to a hospital. Lightning victims may be unable to breathe independently for fifteen to thirty minutes but can recover quickly once they can breathe on their own. Do not give up early; a seemingly lifeless individual can be saved if you breathe for him promptly after the strike.

Assume that the victim was thrown a great distance; protect the spine, treat other injuries, then transport him to the hospital.

Snakebites

Hikers on the Appalachian Trail may encounter copperheads and rattlesnakes on their journey. These are pit vipers, characterized by triangular heads, vertical elliptical pupils, two or less hinged fangs on the front part of the jaw (fangs are replaced every six to ten weeks), heat-sensory facial pits on the sides of the head, and a single row of scales on the underbelly by the tail.

The best way to avoid being bitten by venomous snakes is to avoid their known habitats and reaching into dark areas (use a walking stick to move suspicious objects). Wear protective clothing, especially on feet and lower legs. Do not hike alone or at night in snake territory; always have a flashlight and walking stick. Do not handle snakes. A dead snake can bite and envenomate you with a reflex action for twenty to sixty minutes after its death.

Not all snakebites result in envenomation, even if the snake is poisonous. The signs of envenomation are one or more fang marks in addition to rows of teeth marks, burning pain, and swelling at the bite (swelling usually begins within five to ten minutes of envenomation and can become very severe). Lips, face, and scalp may tingle and become numb thirty to sixty minutes after the bite. (If those symptoms are immediate and the victim is frightened and excited, then they are most likely due to hyperventilation.) Thirty to ninety minutes after the bite, the victim's eyes and mouth may twitch, and he may have a rubbery or metallic taste in his mouth. He may sweat, experience weakness, nausea, and vomiting, or faint one to two hours after the bite. Bruising at the bite usually begins within two to three hours, and large blood blisters may develop within six to ten hours. The victim may have difficulty breathing, have bloody urine, vomit blood, and collapse six to twelve hours after the bite.

If someone you are with has been bitten by a snake, act quickly. *The definitive treatment for snake-venom poisoning is the proper administration of antivenin. Get the victim to a hospital immediately.*

Keep the victim calm. Increased activity can spread the venom and the illness. Retreat out of snake's striking range, but try to identify it. Check for signs of envenomation.

Immediately transport the victim to the nearest hospital. If possible, splint the body part that was bitten, to avoid unnecessary motion. If a limb was bitten, keep it at a level below the heart. Do not apply ice directly to the wound. If it will take longer than two hours to reach medical help, and the bite is on an arm or leg, place a 2" x 2.5"-thick cloth pad over the bite and firmly wrap the limb (ideally, with an elastic wrap) directly over the bite and six inches on either side, taking care to check for adequate circulation to the fingers and toes. This wrap may slow the spread of venom.

Do not use a snakebite kit or attempt to remove the poison. This is the advice of Maynard H. Cox, founder and director of the Worldwide Poison Bite Information Center. He advises medical personnel on the treatment of snakebites. If you hike in fear of snakebites, carry his number, (904) 264-6512, and when you're bitten, give the number to the proper medical personnel. Your chances of being bitten by a poisonous snake are very, very slim. Do not kill the snake; in most Trail areas, it is a legally protected species.

First-Aid Kit

The following kit is suggested for those who have had no first aid or other medical training. It costs about $20, weighs about a pound, and occupies about a 3" x 6" x 9" space.

Eight 4" x 4" gauze pads
Four 3" x 4" gauze pads
Five 2" bandages
Ten 1" bandages
Six alcohol prep pads
Ten large butterfly closures
One triangular bandage (40")
Two 3" rolls of gauze
Twenty tablets of aspirin-free pain killer
One 15' roll of 2" adhesive tape
One 3" Ace bandage
Twenty salt tablets
One 3" x 4" moleskin
Snake-bite kit
Three safety pins
One small scissors
One tweezers
Personal medications as necessary

Shelters and Campsites

Few public accommodations are available near the Trail in central Virginia. Major highways cross mountain ranges traversed by the Trail at intervals of two to three days' hiking time. Hikers who make transportation arrangements can secure public lodging by leaving the Trail route, usually for a considerable distance. The general locations of such lodgings are listed in each Trail section, but most hikers should plan to camp for much of their trip.

With some exceptions, shelters (or lean-tos, as they are sometimes called in other states) have been built at regular intervals along the Trail, many separated by one day's hike. Some areas, particularly where recent relocations have taken place, may not have shelters. A few designated campsites are available, as well as several U.S. Forest Service (USFS) campgrounds. (USFS campgrounds usually charge a fee and are not open year-round but may provide such amenities as hot showers.) Each section lists shelters, campgrounds, designated campsites, and, often, undeveloped trailside campsites.

Shelters are generally three-sided, with open fronts, and have a wooden floor serving as a sleeping platform. They may be fitted with bunks. Water, a privy, a fireplace, and, in some cases, a table and benches are usually nearby. Hikers should bring their own sleeping equipment, cooking utensils, and a stove. When camping at both shelters and campsites, it is important for all hikers to observe Leave No Trace camping techniques, for both the sake of the environment and the enjoyment of others.

Shelters along the Trail are provided primarily for the long-distance hiker who may have no other shelter. People planning overnight hikes are asked to consider this and carry tents. This is good insurance in any case, since the Trail is heavily used, and shelters are usually crowded during the summer. Organizations should keep their groups small (eight to ten people, including leaders), carry tents, and not monopolize the shelters (see page 15). Although shelter use is on a first-come, first-served basis, please cooperate, and consider the needs of others.

If a shelter has a register, please sign it.

Shelters are for overnight stays only, and, except for bad weather, injury, or other emergency, hikers should not stay more than one or two nights. Hunters, fishermen, and other non-Trail hikers should not use the shelters as bases of operation.

Use facilities with care and respect. Do not carve initials or write on shelter walls. Do not use an ax on any part of the shelter or use benches or tables as chopping blocks. The roofing material, especially if it is corrugated aluminum, is easily damaged; do not climb on it. Avoid putting excess weight or strain on wire bunks; breaking one wire endangers air mattresses and sleeping bags.

Be considerate of the rights of others, especially during meal times. Keep noise to a minimum between 9 p.m. and 7 a.m. for the sake of those attempting to sleep.

Preserve the surroundings and the ecological integrity of the site. Vandalism and carelessness mar the site's pristine nature and cause maintenance problems. Never cut live trees. Keep to trodden paths. Be conservative and careful with the environment.

Leave the shelter in good condition. Do not leave food in the shelter; this may cause damage by animals. Remove unburned trash from the fireplace, including aluminum foil, and pack out food and refuse.

Campfires

All travelers in central Virginia should be extremely careful with campfires or cigarettes. Individuals responsible for fire damage to a national forest or park are liable for the cost of the damage. No matter how many people use a fire, all share in responsibility for it. Be especially alert for sparks blowing from fires during periods of high wind.

Because of the decreasing availability of firewood for cooking fires, it is wise to carry a camping stove, which has the added advantage of causing less environmental harm.

Fires within Blue Ridge Parkway boundaries are illegal, except in the fireplaces provided.

Fires at shelters should be built in the fireplaces provided. If building a fire elsewhere, kindle it only in a cleared, open area, keep the burning area minimal, and, upon leaving, remove traces of the campfire. Fires should be attended at all times.

Use wood economically. Use dead or downed wood only, even if this requires searching some distance away. Many campsites have suffered visible deterioration from hikers cutting wood from trees within the site. The effective cooking fire is small. Do not build bonfires. If you use wood stored in a shelter, replenish the supply.

Upon leaving the campsite, even temporarily, ensure that your fire—to the last spark—is out. Douse it with water, and overturn the ashes until all underlying coals have been thoroughly extinguished.

Access to the Appalachian Trail in Central Virginia

Road Access

All sections of the A.T. in central Virginia end on roads. Most of these roads are paved or gravel and are easily passable by car in spring, summer, and fall. However, in winter, road access to many sections may be difficult.

The official Virginia state highway map, available free from the Virginia Department of Transportation and Highways, shows all major highways and many of the secondary roads. The maps included with this guide show adjacent parts of most roads providing access to the Trail. Road approaches to section ends are described in detail in each guidebook section.

Under the Virginia highway system, all rights-of-way for public roads are designated by highway numbers. Those not included in the primary highway system are numbered in the 600 and 700 series. These secondary roads may be hard-surfaced or rough, narrow, pitted, and impassable by vehicles. Roads maintained by the USFS are in similar condition. U.S. Geological Survey (USGS) seven-and-one-half-minute topographic quadrangles, district maps for the George Washington and Jefferson National Forest, ATC, and Virginia county maps generally show all roads in detail.

Bus Lines

Daily bus service is available to a number of cities and towns near the Trail. By using connecting bus lines, hikers can arrange bus transportation from most points in the United States to the Trail. Contact bus companies for route schedules.

Railroads

Call Amtrak (800) USA-RAIL for passenger-service schedules in central Virginia. By connecting with other Amtrak routes, hikers can arrive in the vicinity of the Trail by train from most parts of the country.

Air Service

Roanoke, Lynchburg, Staunton, Waynesboro, and Charlottesville, Virginia, and Bluefield, West Virginia, have daily commercial service. Routes, schedules, and carriers change frequently, so check with your local travel agent for current information.

Taxi Service

A number of cities in central Virginia have taxi service, which may be the only convenient way to reach certain sections of the Trail, particularly from airports or railroad stations. Check telephone directories or directory assistance for taxi companies in the area. The Appalachian Trail Conference also maintains a list of persons who provide shuttle service in certain areas.

Hitchhiking

In Virginia, it is illegal to hitchhike on interstates, limited-access highways, and the Blue Ridge Parkway.

Suggestions for Extended Trips

In the Pedlar District of the George Washington National Forest, the Tye River Valley is accessible by car from Va. 56 and is a good beginning for a 46-mile trip, ending at the highway along the James River (sections 17-21). The trip provides views of the Piedmont from The Priest or the high bald of Cold Mountain, a panoramic view from Spy Rock, and a view of the James River Valley from Fullers Rocks on Little Rocky Row. The trip could be divided in the middle into two shorter hikes by using U.S. 60 as a starting or ending point.

The Glenwood District of the Jefferson National Forest provides a similar trip, of some 57 miles (sections 22–27). It is primarily a forest walk. The rhododendron and laurel there bloom in June. The section has good views, especially from the top of Apple Orchard Mountain, which is the highest point on the Appalachian Trail between Chestnut Knob in southwest Virginia and Mt. Moosilauke in New Hampshire. Side trails lead to Apple Orchard Falls and Devils Marbleyard.

The New Castle and New River districts of the Jefferson National Forest provide many opportunities for extended scenic trips. An eight-day trip of 91 miles from the Valley of Virginia to the New River includes the cliffs of Tinker Mountain, the rocky rims of Cove Mountain and Dragon's Tooth, and the deep woods, rock outcrops, and grassy fields with floral displays and far-reaching views of Sinking Creek Mountain (see sections 28–33).

Shorter trips along the Trail can be planned by using the information in the individual Trail sections. Note especially the circuit hikes listed in the introduction to some sections.

Pedlar District of the
George Washington National Forest
Rockfish Gap (U.S. 250) to
James River (U.S. 501)

The following seven sections of the A.T. trace the northeast- to southwest-trending, central-Virginia Blue Ridge from Rockfish Gap to the James River. Except for several stretches that cross Blue Ridge Parkway land, the route travels through the Pedlar District of the George Washington National Forest. The George Washington National Forest is administered jointly with the Jefferson National Forest from a central headquarters in Roanoke. (If you are north of the James River, you are in the George Washington National Forest. South of the James, you are in the Jefferson National Forest.)

At the northern end, the Trail closely follows the same ridge as the Blue Ridge Parkway. It then diverges to the east, crossing a series of 4,000-foot peaks, including The Priest. After descending to Pedlar Lake, the Trail route rises westward and crosses the Blue Ridge Parkway. It then traverses Bluff Mountain and Big Rocky Row and descends steeply to 659 feet at the James River, the lowest point between Springer Mountain and the Potomac River.

The Trail route in the Pedlar District offers many good views from high peaks, rock outcrops, and open meadows. It crosses through mature timberland, old farmland (much of which is now wooded), one stand of virgin timber, and across several balds with views in all directions. The route is rugged, frequently ascending and descending steeply, and subject to summer growth that sometimes partially obscures the footway.

The Trail originally followed the water divide, a low-lying range to the west of the high, single peaks in this area. The Blue Ridge Parkway took much of this original route, and the Trail was relocated to cross a series of peaks to the east. The relocation began in 1940 but was interrupted by World War II, disrupting the continuity of the whole Trail. Work resumed after the war, and, in June 1951, the last 9.5 miles, between Three Ridges and The Priest, were opened to provide a continuous A.T. again.

Minor relocations are still made, with better views or treadway as a result.

Three clubs are responsible for the Trail in this area (see page 4). The USFS helps manage and maintain the Trail throughout the area in a partnership with the clubs and the Appalachian Trail Conference.

Except for the section between Rockfish Gap and Reeds Gap, shelters are located at frequent intervals along the Trail in the Pedlar District. Few commercial accommodations are available; those known are listed in individual sections.

The Pedlar District of the George Washington National Forest begins in the north at Rockfish Gap, where U.S. 250 and I-64 cross the Blue Ridge, passing under the parkway. The Trail proceeds south, traversing Elk Mountain, the same ridge followed by the parkway.

The route swings away from the parkway, descends through Mill Creek Valley, then climbs Humpback Mountain (3,600 feet), where a side trail to Humpback Rocks leads to a superb view west. The Trail leaves this peak and descends to the west, crossing the parkway at Dripping Rock. The Trail parallels the parkway for about four miles and recrosses it at Three Ridges Overlook.

The Trail then crosses a meadowed knoll on its way to Reeds Gap. At Reeds Gap, the parkway swings west, and the Trail veers south, avoiding the parkway for more than 30 miles. It enters the Three Ridges Wilderness and crosses the summits of Three Ridges (3,970 feet), where ledges provide views north and south of Tye River Valley and The Priest. It drops some 3,000 feet from Three Ridges to the Tye River, crossing it on a suspension bridge.

Entering the Priest Wilderness, the Trail climbs 3,000 feet above the river again and traverses The Priest (4,063 feet). Outlooks have views of the Tye River and Silver Creek valleys. The route descends the west side of the mountain, passing a side trail to Crabtree Falls. The falls, a five-part cascade and the highest falls on the Virginia Blue Ridge, drop 1,500 feet to the Tye River. Ancient hemlocks and rhododendron grow on the levels between the cascades.

The A.T. then passes over the wooded summit of Main Top Mountain (4,040 feet). It passes Spy Rock, a rock outcrop with a panoramic view of the Religious Range—The Priest, Little Priest, The Friar (originally Bald Friar), The Cardinal, and the Mt. Pleasant area. The Trail continues over Porters Ridge with views of many peaks in the area.

The Trail climbs and crosses two summits similar to the balds of the southern Appalachians: Tar Jacket Ridge (3,847 feet) and Cold Mountain (4,022 feet). Once grazed by cattle and hogs, the fields on the summits are still clear, with striking panoramic views. Twelve miles of old stone walls that were built in the early 1800s and once fenced livestock are visible throughout the area. The 6,700-acre Mt. Pleasant National Scenic Area offers spectacular views from both Cold Mountain and Mt. Pleasant.

The Trail continues through Cow Camp Gap and over Bald Knob (4,059 feet), the highest peak in the area, once cleared for farming but now densely wooded. Then, it descends and crosses U.S. 60 on Long Mountain. From the highway, it drops into Brown Mountain Creek Valley and, for about 3 miles, gradually descends along the creek, bordered by old Canadian hemlocks. Ruins of old homesteads are marked by stone chimneys and crumbling walls, remains of farms that once existed in many of the coves of the Blue Ridge. Scare Rock can be seen below the Trail.

After leaving the valley, the Trail travels along the hillside above Pedlar Lake, one of the few lakes on the Blue Ridge, and passes the base of Pedlar Dam, which was built to create the lake as a water supply for the city of Lynchburg, 20 miles away. The Trail climbs westward from the lake, past a tract of virgin forest of pine and hemlock preserved by the USFS; crosses the wooded summit of Rice Mountain (2,208 feet); and meets the Blue Ridge Parkway again on the shoulder of Punchbowl Mountain (2,157 feet).

The Trail climbs across the wooded summits of Punchbowl Mountain (2,848 feet), Bluff Mountain (3,372 feet), Big Rocky Row (2,992 feet), and Little Rocky Row (2,448 feet), then descends to the James River. From Fullers Rocks, on the south end of Little Rocky Row, hikers can see the course of the James River through the Blue Ridge and into the Piedmont in the east. The James River marks the southern end of the Pedlar District of the George Washington National Forest.

The northern part of the Pedlar Ranger District contains 30,000 acres of wilderness and near-wilderness areas in the Sherando-Big Levels-Saint Marys River complex, which is not traversed by the A.T. The area has fourteen marked trails, totalling more than 45 miles, and is accessible on the east and south from Mt. Torry Furnace on Va. 664, 4.5 miles north of Reeds Gap, and from Va. 814 north of milepost 16 of the Blue Ridge Parkway. It can be reached by foot from White Rock Gap, Bald Mountain parking area, and Fork Mountain Overlook, mileposts 18.5, 22.3, and 23, respectively, of the parkway. The area can be approached on the north and west sides from Stuarts Draft on Va. 608 and from Vesuvius on Va. 56.

More detailed information is available from the recreation staff officer of the George Washington and Jefferson National forests (see "Important Addresses," page 273).

Rockfish Gap (U.S. 250 and I-64) to Reeds Gap (Va. 664)
Section Fifteen
19.4 miles

Brief Description of Section

The Old Dominion Appalachian Trail Club, responsible for this section, and the Konnarock A.T. Crew have relocated all but 3 miles of this section since 1984.

The elevation at Rockfish Gap, at the northern end of the section, is 1,902 feet; at Reeds Gap, the southern end, 2,645 feet. The high point of the section is Humpback Mountain (3,600 feet), and its lowest elevation (1,680 feet) is at the crossing of Mill Creek.

Points of Interest

Rockfish Gap: Thomas Jefferson called the view to the east one of the best in the world. Swannanoa Mansion, situated in the gap, is a replica of an Italian villa with an outstanding stained-glass window. It is open to the public.

Mill Creek: a wild, remote valley.

Blue Ridge Parkway Visitor Center and reconstructed mountain farm: an introduction to the parkway and a display of mountaineer living that was once common in the region (on a 1.5-mile side trail).

Humpback Rocks: an outstanding viewpoint west.

Humpback Mountain: a high plateau with good views north and south.

Cedar Cliffs: outstanding views to the north and west.

Road Approaches

The northern end of the section (with ample parking) is on the Blue Ridge Parkway where it crosses I-64 and U.S. 250 in Rockfish Gap. The gap is 21 miles west of Charlottesville *via* I-64, 4 miles east of Waynesboro on U.S. 250, and 40 miles south of Swift Run Gap (U.S. 33) on Skyline Drive.

The parkway parallels the Trail throughout the section and crosses the Trail two times (14.6 miles south at Dripping Rock and 18.9 miles south at Three Ridges Overlook). Humpback Rocks parking area and the northern side of the picnic area (water and toilets, May to November) provide access to the A.T. *via* a 0.2-mile blue-blazed trail.

The section's southern end is on Va. 664 (ample parking on road shoulders), 100 yards east of its intersection with the Blue Ridge Parkway, milepost 13.6, and 6 miles west of its intersection with Va. 151.

Maps

For route navigation, refer to ATC Pedlar District Map or Potomac Appalachian Trail Club (PATC) Map 12. For additional area detail, refer to the following USGS topographic quadrangles: Sherando, Waynesboro East, and Waynesboro West.

Shelters and Campsites

This section has one shelter:

Paul C. Wolfe Shelter: built by members and friends of the Old Dominion Appalachian Trail Club, with help from the Konnarock A.T. Crew in 1991; 5.0 miles from the northern end of the section; accommodates ten; water available from Mill Creek.

Next shelter: north 12.0 miles (Calf Mountain); south 16.1 miles (Maupin Field).

Several good tentsites are along Mill Creek.

Regulations

Camping is permitted along the A.T. except within sight of the parkway, picnic area, or visitors center.

Supplies, Services, and Public Accommodations

Accessible from the northern end of the section in Rockfish Gap are restaurants, motels, a Rockfish Gap Visitors Center, and a gas station with a limited selection of groceries. It is 2.1 miles east to Afton (ZIP Code 22920) on Va. 151, 3.5 miles east to a grocery store on U.S. 250, and 21 miles east to Charlottesville (all supplies and services, including a backpacking store). From the gap, it is 4.5 miles west to Waynesboro (ZIP Code 22980, supermarkets, motels, restaurants, shoe store, shoe repair, coin laundry, sports store, and bus stop). Greyhound bus lines servicing Waynesboro pass through Rockfish Gap.

At the southern end of the section, Sherando Lake Campground (all services) is 1 mile west of Reeds Gap on Va. 664. Open April 1 through October 31.

Trail Description, North to South

Miles	Data
0.0	At southern end of I-64 overpass, the Trail turns left (east) in guardrail opening, descends grassy berm of the Blue Ridge Parkway, then enters woods. Avoid road going steeply downhill. Trail and parkway are roughly parallel.
0.9	Cross marshy area, with small streams, and ascend.
1.9	A.T. turns sharp left, crossing stream; blue-blazed trail right goes steeply uphill. In 0.1 mile, ascend rock steps.
3.2	Cross rocky area with small stream, and ascend gradually.
3.4	Pass remnants of old cabin. In 0.1 mile descend old road.
4.0	Trail ascends right. Rock piles are from efforts of farmers in an earlier time to clear land to grow crops.
4.1	Pass remnants of old cemetery on left. Begin gradual descent of Elk Mountain over long switchbacks.
5.0	Reach **Paul C. Wolfe Shelter**. Privy is uphill, behind the shelter. Water is from Mill Creek. Swimming hole with waterfall is just downstream.
5.1	Cross old road, then Mill Creek, and ascend to left.

5.7   Trail passes cleared overlook with excellent views of the locally named Southwest Mountains, Rockfish Valley, and the southern summits of Shenandoah National Park.

6.0   Turn sharp right onto woods road and, in 300 feet, turn sharp left, ascending on second woods road. Blue-blazed trail straight ahead ascends to west side of Dobie Mountain.

6.6   Side trail leads 1.0 mile to Humpback Gap parking area (milepost 6.1).

6.8   Reach side trail on left leading 0.2 mile to Glass Hollow overlook.

7.6   Bear left on Howardville Turnpike (old woods road). A right turn here leads 0.2 mile to parkway.

8.1   Old turnpike bears right toward Humpback Ridge.

8.7   Begin ascending eight switchbacks.

9.0   Bear Spring on right. Ascend switchbacks.

9.8   Pass spring on left.

10.4   Reach rock staircase, "Stairway to Heaven."

10.6   At saddle of Humpback Mountain, pass side trail on right leading 0.3 mile to Humpback Rocks and 0.8 mile farther to parkway.

11.6   Reach northern crest of Humpback Mountain. Excellent view from narrow cliff to north and east. Continue south across flat top of Humpback Mountain (3,600 feet).

12.7   Bear right along top of cliff, with views to south.

13.3   Trail turns left. Blue-blazed trail right 0.3 mile to picnic area (milepost 8.5; seasonal water, restrooms).

13.7   Cross cliff, and descend steeply.

14.2   Pass Laurel Springs (unreliable) on left, and ascend gradually.

14.4   Trail ascends sharply to right toward crest of small knoll. Straight ahead is Wintergreen Ski Resort.

14.6   Cross parkway at Dripping Rock parking area (milepost 9.6). Small, undeveloped spring is right of Trail.

15.1   Trail crosses grassy top of Cedar Cliffs. Spectacular views north and west.

15.8   Reenter woods. Blue-blazed trail to right leads 400 feet to rocky outcrop, with views to north and west. Ridge across valley is Big Levels Wildlife Management Area and Sherando Lake Campground.

16.1   Descend on log steps.

16.7   Cross stream as it cascades down steep hillside; usually a reliable water source.

18.5   Cross rocky area, slippery in wet weather, and begin gradual ascent.

18.8   Cross parkway at southern end of Three Ridges Overlook (milepost 13.1; picnic area, parking) and enter woods.

19.0   Ascend through meadow, with fence on left.

19.1   Reach wooded crest of small hill.

19.2   Leave woods, and descend gradually through meadow with fence on left.

19.4   Reach Va. 664 in Reeds Gap (2,645 feet) and end of section. Parkway milepost 13.6 is 100 yards right. Va. 151 is 6 miles left. To continue on Trail, cross Va. 664, and proceed across meadow, with woods on left (see Section 16).

Trail Description, South to North

Miles   **Data**

0.0   From Va. 664, 100 yards east of milepost 13.6 (2,645 feet), follow Trail along fence on east side of cleared field, and ascend to small, wooded knoll.

0.3   Reach wooded crest, and begin descent along fence.

0.6   Cross parkway at southern end of Three Ridges Overlook (milepost 13.1; picnic area, parking) and descend west into woods.

0.9   Cross first of several large rocky area. *Be extremely cautious on the rocks in wet weather.*

2.7   Cross cascading stream (usually reliable) as Trail traverses steep sidehill.

3.3   Ascend on log steps.

3.6   Blue-blazed trail to left leads 400 feet to rocky outcrop with views to north and west. Sherando Lake Campground is on far side of valley, with Big Levels Wildlife Management Area rising above it.

4.3   Trail leaves woods and passes across grassy top of Cedar Cliffs. Spectacular views north and west.

4.4   Turn right, and enter woods. Ascend gradually.

4.8   Cross parkway at Dripping Rock parking area (milepost 9.6), and ascend. Small spring (undeveloped) is on east side of parkway, just left of Trail.

5.0   Descend east side of small knoll, and turn sharply left.

5.2   Pass Laurel Springs (unreliable), on right and begin gradual ascent.

5.7   Reach top of small cliff and overlook. Views in winter.

6.1   Trail turns right. Blue-blazed trail ahead leads 0.3 mile to Humpback Rocks picnic area (milepost 8.5; seasonal water and restrooms).

6.7   Pass along top of cliff with views to south and east. Turn left, and cross flat top of Humpback Mountain (3,600 feet).

7.8   Reach northern summit of Humpback Mountain. Views to north and east. Begin descent.

8.8   At saddle of Humpback Mountain (sign), pass blue-blazed trail on left leading 0.3 mile to Humpback Rocks and 0.8 mile farther to parkway.

9.0   Reach rock staircase, "Stairway to Heaven."

9.6   Pass spring on right.

10.4   After descending switchbacks, reach Bear Spring on left. Descend eight switchbacks ahead in 0.3 mile.

11.3   Bear left on Howardville Turnpike (old woods road).

11.8   Bear right off Howardville Turnpike, which continues as side trail leading to parkway in 0.2 miles.

12.6   Reach side trail on right leading 0.2 mile to Glass Hollow Overlook.

12.8   Side trail on left leads 1.0 mile to Humpback Rocks parking area (milepost 6.1).

13.4   Reach woods road with blue-blazed trail coming from the left. A.T. turns sharply right and, in 300 feet, turns sharply left onto a graded trail before descending gradually over a series of switchbacks.

13.7   Trail passes overlook with views to the north and east.

14.3   Cross Mill Creek, and reach old road. A.T. continues straight ahead and ascends Elk Mountain.

14.4   **Paul C. Wolfe Shelter** with privy is to the left of the Trail. Water is available here; privy is uphill, behind (west) of the shelter. Swimming hole with waterfall downstream.

15.3   Pass old cemetery on right. Trail bears right and descends gradually on remains of old woods road. Large rock cairns in the area are the result of former inhabitants' efforts to clear fields in order to grow crops.

15.4   Trail bears left and ascends gradually on old road.

16.0   Trail levels and begins to descend gradually. Remains of old cabin are to the left of the Trail.

16.2   Cross rocky area with small stream, and continue north over nearly level Trail.

17.4   Descend over switchbacks and rock steps.

17.5   Cross small stream, turn left uphill, and then immediately take a hard right. The path going uphill is a maintenance-access trail that reaches the parkway in about 0.4 mile.

18.5   Cross broad, marshy area with several small streams.

19.3   Ignore road going downhill to right, and follow A.T. straight ahead on grassy berm of Blue Ridge Parkway.

19.4   Reach southern end of Blue Ridge Parkway I-64 overpass and the end of the section at Rockfish Gap (1,902 feet). The Trail north is covered in the *Appalachian Trail Guide to Shenandoah National Park.* (Skyline Drive begins north of I-64 in Shenandoah National Park.)

Reeds Gap (Va. 664)
to Tye River (Va. 56)
Section Sixteen
10.5 miles

Brief Description of Section

The outstanding feature of this section is Three Ridges (3,970 feet), a flat, wooded dome trending north and south to form the northern wall of the Tye River Valley. Ledges north of the crest provide spectacular views north and south of the valley and The Priest, which forms the southern wall of the valley.

This section includes the 4,608-acre Three Ridges Wilderness Area, established in 2000, and is, at times, steep and rocky, passing through many rocky areas as it ascends Three Ridges. Northbound hikers climb a total of 3,000 feet in elevation from the Tye River to the summit of Three Ridges. Southbound hikers climb 1,320 feet. Although the mileage is short, the ascent of Three Ridges and descent into the Tye River Valley make this a strenuous section.

The blue-blazed Mau-Har Trail, a three-mile side trail, makes a weekend loop hike possible. Beginning at either Reeds Gap or Tye River, hikers can follow the A.T. over Three Ridges, then return on the Mau-Har Trail along Campbells Creek, passing a 40-foot waterfall 1.5 miles from Maupin Field Shelter. This section of Appalachian Trail is the responsibility of the Tidewater Appalachian Trail Club.

Points of Interest

Three Ridges (3,970 feet) *and Three Ridges Wilderness:* see above.
Bridge over Tye River: 100-foot-long suspension bridge built by USFS over scenic river.
Mau-Har Trail: see above.
Hanging Rock Overlook: broad top of a sheer cliff that offers outstanding views of The Priest, Three Ridges, Harpers Creek Valley, and points south and east.

43

Chimney Rocks: views to the west of Hanging Rock and the Tye River Valley.

Road Approaches

The northern end of the section is on Va. 664 (parking for twenty cars), 100 yards east of Blue Ridge Parkway milepost 13.6, in Reeds Gap. I-64 and U.S. 250 are 16.4 miles north, *via* the parkway, in Rockfish Gap.

The southern end of the section is on Va. 56, 11.3 miles east of the parkway near parkway milepost 27 and 6.8 miles west of Va. 151 in the Tye River Valley. Parking is available for twenty cars in a lot on the southern side of the highway at the Trail crossing. Vandalism has been a problem here. Do not block the driveway on the northern side of road.

Maps

For route navigation, refer to ATC Pedlar District Map or PATC Map 12. For area detail, refer to the following USGS topographic quadrangles: Vesuvius, Horseshoe Mountain, Massies Mill, and Sherando.

Shelters and Campsites

This section has two shelters:

Maupin Field Shelter: (1961) 1.7 miles from northern end of section; accommodates six; several tentsites; water from spring 50 feet behind shelter. Blue-blazed Mau-Har Trail begins behind shelter and rejoins A.T. 3 miles to the south.

Next shelter: north 16.1 miles (Wolfe); south 6.2 miles (Harpers Creek).

Harpers Creek Shelter: (1961) built by USFS; 2.6 miles from southern end of section; accommodates 6; several tentsites; water from Harpers Creek 75 feet in front of shelter.

Next shelter: north 6.2 miles (Maupin Field); south 7.4 miles (The Priest).

Camping is permitted anywhere in the George Washington National Forest, unless specifically prohibited. Camping is not permitted at Reeds Gap, because it is Blue Ridge Parkway property.

Two private campgrounds are on Va. 56. Crabtree Falls Campground is 5 miles west of the Trail crossing. Montebello Campground (all services) is 9.5 miles west.

Regulations

Most of the section lies within the George Washington National Forest. Cutting or damaging living trees is prohibited. Carry out all trash and garbage.

Supplies, Services, and Public Accommodations

From the Trail crossing of Va. 56 at the southern end of the section, it is 1.4 miles east to Tyro (small grocery store just beyond) and 1.1 miles west to a small grocery store. The stores are sometimes closed on Sundays or holidays.

At the northern end of the section, Sherando Lake Campground (all services) is 1 mile west of Reeds Gap on Va. 664. Open April 1 through October 31.

Trail Description, North to South

Miles	Data
0.0	From Va. 664 (2,650 feet), head southwest over meadow, with woods on left.
0.2	Enter woods, and begin ascent of Meadow Mountain.
0.4	Pass through rocky area, and, after 0.1 mile, turn sharp left, reaching northern end of ridge in another 0.1 mile. Enter Three Ridges Wilderness.
0.8	Pass overlook 75 feet to right with views west. A **campsite** is 30 feet to left (no water).
1.0	Begin descent through sparse woods with occasionally heavy undergrowth.
1.7	Enter fire road. Trail on right leads 300 feet to **Maupin Field Shelter** and privy, and Mau-Har Trail. Mau-Har

Trail follows Campbells Creek and leads southwest 1.5 miles to a 40-foot waterfall; in 3 miles, it rejoins A.T. 4.6 miles south of Three Ridges summit.

1.8	Trail turns left from road and leads uphill over Bee Mountain. (Road ahead ends in 0.1 mile.)
2.1	Reach top of Bee Mountain (3,304 feet), with limited view to east. Descend through sag, and begin gradual ascent across west slope of knob.
3.2	Pass through rocky area (intermittent water). Ascend gradually into mature forest, then steeply in rhododendron thicket.
3.7	Cross rock crest on Hanging Rock. To the right are views of Harpers Creek drainage, Three Ridges, and The Priest.
4.2	Reach top of Three Ridges (3,970 feet) in mature woods with no views. Continue ahead on broad, level ridge.
4.4	Turn right, and begin descent—at times, steep, rocky, and on switchbacks. Overlook with views north, east, and south is 200 feet to left.
5.8	Pass overlook 50 feet to right, with view west.
5.9	Cross top of second ridge of Three Ridges. Just beyond is overlook to left, with views east and south. Beyond overlook, on right, is Chimney Rocks, a series of upright, projecting boulders.
6.2	Cross top of third ridge of Three Ridges.
6.3	Pass flat-rock overlook on right with excellent views of The Priest and Harpers Creek Valley. Beyond, descend, sometimes steeply, passing through four rocky areas.
7.9	Turn left onto old road, and descend gradually. Road to right leads 400 feet to **Harpers Creek Shelter** and privy.
8.0	Cross Harpers Creek. (Crossing can be difficult during high water.) Begin moderate ascent of east slope of mountain.
8.8	The southern end of blue-blazed Mau-Har Trail enters on right, just before A.T. reaches top of ridge. A.T. continues ahead, descending moderately.
9.8	Pass through overgrown clearing, and descend on switchbacks. Leave Three Ridges Wilderness.
10.4	Cross suspension bridge over Tye River. **Campsites** at both ends of bridge.

10.5   Reach Va. 56 (997 feet) and end of section. Trail continues
        south, directly across Va. 56 (see Section 17).

Trail Description, South to North

Miles   **Data**

0.0   From Va. 56 (997 feet), enter woods, and descend briefly.
0.1   Cross suspension bridge over Tye River. Begin moderate-
       to-steep ascent on switchbacks. Enter Three Ridges Wil-
       derness.
0.7   Pass through overgrown clearing, and continue moderate
       ascent.
1.7   Just over top of ridge, Mau-Har Trail leads left 1.5 miles to
       40-foot waterfall and 3 miles to **Maupin Field Shelter**,
       with privy, where it rejoins Trail. A.T. continues ahead.
2.5   Cross Harpers Creek (difficult crossing in spring, due to
       high water). Continue uphill, and, in 200 feet, turn left
       onto old road.
2.6   Turn sharp right uphill onto graded trail. Side trail ahead
       leads 400 feet to **Harpers Creek Shelter** and privy.
3.1   Ascend moderately to steeply, passing through four rocky
       areas.
4.2   Pass flat-rock overlook on left, with views of The Priest
       and Harpers Creek Valley. Trail continues ahead, gradu-
       ally ascending ridge.
4.3   Cross top of lowest ridge of Three Ridges. Soon, begin
       ascent of next ridge.
4.6   Pass Chimney Rocks, a series of upright, projecting boul-
       ders on left. Just beyond to right is overlook with views
       east and south. Beyond overlook, reach top of second
       ridge of Three Ridges.
4.7   Pass overlook 50 feet to left with view west. Ascend
       highest ridge of Three Ridges on sometimes steep, rocky
       trail.
6.1   Turn left, and climb gradually along broad ridge in ma-
       ture woods. Straight ahead 200 feet is overlook with views
       north, east, and south.

6.3   Reach highest ridge of Three Ridges (3,970 feet) in mature woods (no views). Begin gradual-to-moderate descent.

6.8   Cross rocky crest of Hanging Rock. Overlook to left provides views of The Priest, Three Ridges, and Harpers Creek Valley. Descend steeply through rhododendron thicket for short distance, then gradually across western slope of mountain.

7.3   Pass through rocky area with intermittent water. Beyond, pass through sag; begin moderate ascent of Bee Mountain.

8.4   Reach top of Bee Mountain (3,034 feet) with limited view to east. Begin descent, rocky in places.

8.7   Trail turns right onto old road.

8.8   Turn right on Trail, leaving road. Side trail on left leads 300 feet to **Maupin Field Shelter** and privy, and northern end of Mau-Har Trail.

10.1   Pass overlook 75 feet to left with views west. A **campsite** is 30 feet to right (no water). Cross ridge of Meadow Mountain, descending through rocky area. Leave Three Ridges Wilderness.

10.3   Leave woods, with meadow on left.

10.5   Reach Va. 664 at Reeds Gap (2,650 feet). Blue Ridge Parkway milepost 13.6 is 300 feet to left. To continue on Trail, cross road into pasture (see Section 15).

Tye River (Va. 56) to Fish Hatchery Road
Section Seventeen
9.4 miles

Brief Description of Section

This section traverses two peaks of more than 4,000 feet: The Priest, an imposing massif of the Religious Range, with adjoining ridges and spurs between the Piney and Tye rivers, and Main Top, with Spy Rock prominent on its south spur.

The Priest, on the southern side, and Three Ridges, on the northern side, form the portal of the Tye River Valley between the Blue Ridge and the Piedmont. A largely unspoiled natural environment, the area between the Tye River and Crabtree Farm Road contains the 5,963-acre Priest Wilderness Area, established in 2000. This begins the area of Trail responsibility of the Natural Bridge Appalachian Trail Club (NBATC), which extends from the Tye River south to Black Horse Gap in the Jefferson National Forest.

On the northern slope of The Priest, the Trail follows sidehill footway and rocky switchbacks, with a strenuous elevation change of 3,100 feet in the four miles from the Tye River to the summit (4,063 feet). On the southern side, the elevation change is less than 750 feet in 1.4 miles, from the summit to Crabtree Farm Road at Shoe Creek Hill (3,319 feet), and the Trail follows an old road. Overlooks provide views of the Tye River and Silver Creek valleys and adjacent mountains.

At the southern end of the section, the Trail gradually climbs over a distance of three miles to the wooded summit of Main Top Mountain (4,040 feet), passing Cash Hollow Rock with excellent views to the south. There are spectacular views from the rocky outcrop near the Main Top summit, and especially from Spy Rock, a favorite destination of hikers.

A number of spring wildflowers can be found along this section of the Trail. In April, look for trillium, early saxifrage, fire pink, rock twist, wild geranium, cut-lead toothwort, Dutchman's breeches, star chickweed, and several kinds of violets. Also seen on The Priest are a lily called Turk's cap, moss pink or creeping phlox, large cow parsnip, and goat's beard. Trees on The Priest summit consist mainly of chestnut oak, shortened and gnarled by the high elevation and harsh environment. The forest generally is deciduous, with some apple orchards nearby at lower elevations. From The Priest to Shoe Creek Hill (Crabtree Farm Road), look for the bird or fire-cherry tree (wild cherry), also the red-berried elder, and mountain ash.

The Priest can also be reached by Crabtree Falls Trail (see below) and the Crabtree Farm Road, which intersects the Trail 3.7 miles from the southern end of the section.

Crabtree Falls Trail

This 2.9-mile blue-blazed trail extends from the Crabtree Meadows parking area, 0.5 mile from the A.T. on Crabtree Farm Road (Va. 826), to the Crabtree Falls parking area on Va. 56, 4.6 miles from the northern end of the section. It follows Crabtree Creek, with scenic overlooks at the five major cascades, which, with a number of smaller ones, have a total fall of 1,200 feet. The trail drops 1,500 feet from the meadows to the South Fork of the Tye River, crossing it on a 100-foot, wooden-arch bridge.

This trail route is especially rich in wildflowers—from bloodroot, trillium, wake robin, and bleeding heart in April, through Solomon's seal, and Solomon's plume, showy orchis, pink lady's-slipper, Indian pipe, bellwort, and jack-in-the-pulpit in May, through a summer display of jewelweed, monkey-flower, lobelia, and cone-flower, to an early-fall showing of turtlehead, horse-balm, and goldenrod. Rhododendron, azalea, and dogwood are even more impressive in their blooming seasons.

Water (hand pump) and a telephone are available at the lower end of the trail. Crabtree Creek water is at the upper end. Pit toilets are at both ends. The entire trail is well-graded. *Caution: Stay on the trail. For the sake of your safety and the environment, do not take short cuts. The cliffs and paths near the creek are steep, and the rocks slippery. Fatal falls have occurred here.*

Some Local History

The Tye River is named for an explorer of this region in the 1730s, Allen Tye.

Several stories try to explain the naming of The Priest, a landmark since the early 1700s and shown on the 1751 Jefferson and Fry map of Virginia. A family named DuPriest lived in the region and may have owned the mountain. It also has been speculated that Pastor Robert Rose, prominent in the early history of the area, may have named the Religious Range, including The Bald Friar and The Cardinal. A legend holds a small monastery had been (a) not far from Tyro or (b) near the Amherst–Nelson County line, and traces of the foundations are said to exist today. One version placed a solitary priest living on the mountain.

Cash Hollow may have been named for Howard Cash, an area surveyor in the mid-18th century.

The original name of Main Top Mountain was Maidenhead Mountain. A stream that flows northwest from the flanks of Main Top still carries that name.

During the last two years of the Civil War, the road along the Tye River was a frequent Confederate supply and escape route.

More recently, this area was famous for moonshine. In one raid in 1928, officers found 11 stills, 9,100 gallons of mash, 1,155 gallons of whiskey, huge copper kettles with a total capacity of 1,750 gallons, and 258 fermenters. They "poured their contents into Shoe Creek, making it appear like hog slop for several hundred yards."

Much of the original A.T. route in this region was taken by the construction of the Blue Ridge Parkway. In 1951, the huge relocation task, which had taken 13 years of hard work, was completed with the opening of the new Trail section from the Tye River to the summit of The Priest.

In August 1969, Hurricane Camille devastated the Tye River Valley, causing more than 100 deaths in Nelson County alone. Nine hundred buildings and more than 100 bridges were destroyed. More than a mile of the Appalachian Trail was washed away. Hiker Alfred Bishop, descending north off The Priest toward Va. 56, was shocked to discover before he reached Cripple Creek that the Trail had simply disappeared, with the mountainside "washed white" to bedrock and trees lying everywhere.

Points of Interest

The Priest: massif dominating the area, with outstanding viewpoints from the A.T. and a challenging, 3,100-foot elevation change in 4.3 miles to the Tye River.

Tye River and Valley: a wild and attractive stream gorge, in which a catastrophic flood from Hurricane Camille in 1969 exposed rock that had been covered for 350 million years.

Lesesne State Forest: Within 5 miles of the A.T. Tye River crossing, near Ramsey's Gap *via* Va. 56 and 699, is the largest chestnut planting and research program in the United States, managed by the University of Virginia. On land donated by the DuPont family, Asian and blight-resistant chestnuts gathered from many states are being grafted and seeds irradiated in the search for a mutation free of blight.

Little Priest: 3,700-foot peak on south spur of The Priest, with views of Piney River Valley and a legend about a Revolutionary-war fortified dwelling for colonists.

Pinnacle Ridge: a sharp, rocky, narrow ridge, known historically as Cone Mountain, visible and accessible from The Priest and considered as a route for the Appalachian Trail when the huge relocation due to the Blue Ridge Parkway was in process.

Crabtree Falls: cited as Dwight's Falls on a 1863 map. Other than the Peaks of Otter, perhaps the most popular attraction for dayhikers in the NBATC section of the Blue Ridge. See description above.

Cash Hollow Rock: a large rock slab on the A.T. between Cash Hollow Road and Main Top; a fine viewpoint overlooking Cash Hollow. Nice lunch spot, with Little Priest, The Friar, High Peak of Tobacco Row, and The Cardinal in the distance.

Main Top Mountain: a rocky outcrop with spectacular views. Combined with Spy Rock and reached from Fish Hatchery Road, it provides a superb day hike.

Spy Rock: a spur of Main Top and many hikers' favorite—a large rock dome with 360-degree views and easy access.

The Religious Range: Several mountains—The Priest, Little Priest, The Cardinal, The Friar—viewed best from Cash Hollow Rock, Spy Rock, Tar Jacket Ridge, and Cold Mountain. The Friar was named Bald Friar from at least 1751 to mid-1900s.

Montebello State Fish Hatchery: large trout for visitors to see, 1.1 miles north of A.T. at south end of section and 0.7 mile from Montebello. Trailhead parking 0.1 mile uphill toward A.T.

Circuit Hikes

1. Crabtree Meadows: A fairly easy forest hike is possible after driving *via* Va. 56 and Va. 826, near Montebello, to Crabtree Meadows, the site of an old sawmill with several dwellings as late as the 1930s. After parking in the parking area (with latrines) for the Crabtree Falls Trail, hike 0.5 mile on Va. 826 up to Shoe Creek Hill and the A.T. Turn right onto the A.T. for 1.8 miles to Cash Hollow Road (USFS 596). Turn right for 0.5 mile on USFS 596 to Va. 826, where you turn right to return 0.8 mile to your car, for a total hike of 3.6 miles.

2. Main Top/Cash Hollow: A more strenuous walk with spectacular views is possible with a long dirt-roadwalk and 0.3 mile along Va. 56. Park beyond the Montebello State Fish Hatchery at the USFS Trailhead parking (Va. 56, then Va. 690, near Montebello), and climb the gated dirt road to the ridge, where you turn left on the A.T. At the grassy saddle, leave time for a lengthy stay on Spy Rock, immediately on your right. Continue on the A.T. over Main Top (rocky outcrop on left with view), and pause at Cash Hollow Rock for more views. At Cash Hollow Road (USFS 596), turn left 0.5 mile to Va. 826. Turn left and mostly descend for 3.3 miles to Va. 56, where you turn left. After 0.3 mile, turn left on Va. 690 to the fish hatchery, for a total of 8.8 miles. A truly outstanding noncircuit hike, possible with two cars, is to follow this hike to Cash Hollow Road, then continue north on the A.T. to Crabtree Farm Road. There, descend left 0.5 mile to the Crabtree Falls Trail parking area, turn right, and descend 2.9 miles along beautiful Crabtree Falls (see separate trail description) to reach Trailhead parking on Va. 56 after 8.4 miles.

3. Crabtree/Main Top Combination: It is possible to combine circuit hikes 1 and 2, above, for a total of 11.9 miles, eliminating the 0.5-mile segment on Cash Hollow Road.

Road Approaches

The northern end of this section is on Va. 56, 11.3 miles east of the Blue Ridge Parkway near parkway milepost 27 and 6.8 miles west of Va. 151 in the Tye River Valley. Parking is available for twenty cars in a lot on the southern side of the highway at the Trail crossing. Vandalism has been a problem here. Please do not block driveway on the northern side of the road.

Crabtree Falls and The Priest also can be approached from Va . 56 on Va. 826 (unpaved Crabtree Farm Road), 14.6 miles west of Va. 151. After 3.3 miles on Va. 826, pass Cash Hollow Road, a dirt road not passable by car that leads the hiker right 0.5 mile to meet the Appalachian Trail. Continuing on Va. 826 0.8 mile, reach parking area (with latrines) for Crabtree Falls Trail, upper end. A half-mile farther on Va. 826 takes one to Shoe Creek Hill, where the A.T. crosses, and The Priest can be reached by hiking north (left).

The southern end of this section can be reached *via* Va. 56, turning onto Va. 690 (sign for Montebello State Fish Hatchery) 0.4 miles southeast of Montebello. At the fish hatchery, continue ahead on dirt road to a Forest Service Trailhead parking area on left. On foot, ford tiny stream, continue uphill, past gate in road (at 0.8 mile), for 1.0 mile to the ridgecrest and A.T. crossing.

Maps

For route orientation, refer to ATC Pedlar District Map or PATC Map 13. For more area detail, refer to USGS Massies Mill and Montebello topographic quadrangles.

Shelters and Campsites

This section has one shelter:
The Priest Shelter: built in 1960 by USFS, maintained jointly with the Natural Bridge Appalachian Trail Club; on 0.1-mile side trail 4.8 miles from the northern end of the section; accommodates eight; ample spring water (unprotected source) at site. This shelter is often full, but tent spaces are available nearby.

Next shelter: north 7.4 miles (Harpers Creek); south 6.9 miles (Seeley-Woodworth).

Camping (see regulations below) is permitted at the USFS primitive campground at Crabtree Meadows, 0.5 mile from A.T. at Va. 826 (creek water and pit toilets).

Regulations

Generally, in the George Washington National Forest, camping and campfires are at the hiker's discretion, except for the Crabtree Falls Recreation Area. Camping and campfires are prohibited 500 feet on either side of the Crabtree Falls Trail and parking area. Camping is permitted in Crabtree Meadows, on the opposite side of the road from the parking area. Specific areas where camping is prohibited are signed. Read the bulletin board at the Crabtree Meadows parking area, or contact the office of the Pedlar District of the George Washington National Forest, (540) 291-2189. *Note:* All water is untested.

Supplies, Services, and Public Accommodations

Tyro, with a small grocery store just beyond, is 1.4 miles east of the northern Trailhead. Nearest lodging on the east side is at Lovingston, which also has a bus stop, about 18 miles away on U.S. 29. Nearest lodging to the west is at Raphine, near I–81 about 15 miles west of Montebello on Va . 56. Orchards near the northern end of the section sell apples and cider in the fall. Commercial camp-grounds (closed in winter) are 4.1 miles west of the A.T. and at Montebello, 8.2 miles west of the A.T. and 3.1 miles east of the Blue Ridge Parkway, on Va. 56.

Montebello (ZIP Code 24464), with post office and Montebello Campground (campsites, cabins, laundry, limited groceries, gas station, and restaurant), is 1.8 miles from A.T. *via* Fish Hatchery Road, Va. 690, and Va. 56 (west).

In emergencies, contact the Nelson County sheriff's office in Lovingston, by calling 911 or (804) 263-4242.

Trail Description, North to South

Miles   **Data**

0.0   From Va. 56, at Tye River (970 feet), begin 3,100-foot, 37-switchback ascent of The Priest, west on Trail past Trail-head parking lot. Enter the Priest Wilderness.

0.2   Switch back right, avoiding distinct path straight ahead. In 60 yards, switch back left, joining old road for 10 yards before ascending bank left.

0.6   Switch back right onto old road. In 70 yards, switch back sharply left onto another old road, and, in 20 yards, bear right.

0.7   Bear left, joining old road, and, in 25 yards, keep left as old road ascends right.

1.0   Sixty yards after ascending right off old road, cross branch of Cripple Creek, and switch back up bank. In 80 yards, cross another small branch of Cripple Creek.

1.3   Reach log bridge over Cripple Creek (last water for 3.6 miles); ascend steeply on northern spur by switchbacks.

1.7   Swing right across ridge, with saddle on left.

2.7   After short, steep stretch on ridgeline, reach rocky outlook on left (2,891 feet).

Expansive views to east of Tye River and Silver Creek valleys, now 2,000 feet below, and a winter view of Three Ridges to left.

2.8   After three more switchbacks, briefly join narrow ridgecrest, with winter views to rear of Three Ridges and Tye River Valley.

3.2   Seven switchbacks later and 360 yards beyond 10-yard-long level step in ridge, leave ridgeline, and begin to skirt left side of ridge, passing 3,623-foot knob on right. Continue ascent along crest of spur.

Winter view ahead of The Priest summit.

3.6   Reach 35-yard-long level spot in narrow saddle, and begin steep ascent.

4.1   After 0.4 mile of steep ascent, including 270 yards of very narrow ridge, bear right, and reach dry **campsite** in clearing to right at first high point.

4.3   Reach wooded summit of The Priest (4,063 feet). Begin 743-foot descent to Crabtree Farm Road.

4.4   Seventy yards after path on right to dry **campsite,** reach path to right leading 150 feet to boulders with the best views from the top of The Priest.

Prominent ridge in foreground (Pinnacle Ridge) was Cone Mountain historically and in late 1940s, considered as possible A.T. route. On far left are Elk Pond Mountain, Spy Rock, and Main Top. On far right are Devil's Knob, Humpback, and

Three Ridges. Ahead on Trail, three more paths lead right to limited views.

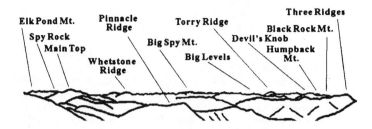

4.7   Reach junction with unmarked path leading left 1.3 yards to **shelter** and unprotected spring. Path to right leads to dry **campsite.**

4.8   Turn sharp right at junction and campsite. Blue-blazed side trail left leads 0.1 mile to **The Priest Shelter** and privy, unprotected spring, and tent spaces.

5.0   Unmarked trail goes left to Little Priest summit (3,733 feet), with view of Piney River gorge.

    This trail first drops 600 feet to 3,200-foot col and then rises 533 feet in 1.5 miles to summit. In Revolutionary times, British Army Major Thomas Massie, who sympathized with the colonists, supposedly built a fortified residence in the saddle between Big and Little Priest mountains, which he intended to occupy if the British were victorious.

5.1   Reach sag in ridge, and, in 130 yards, cross to northeast (right) side of ridge, with occasional views to right of The Priest.

5.4   Pass to left of saddle leading to Pinnacle Ridge (Cone Mountain).

5.6   Pass through barrier fence, and bear right off old road.

5.7   Reach Crabtree Farm Road (Va. 826) at 3,319-foot sag called Shoe Creek Hill. Exit the Priest Wilderness. A.T. crosses road and 50-yard open area before ascending spur.

    *Va. 826 leads right across Crabtree Creek 0.5 mile to Crabtree Meadows (**camping**) and upper end of blue-blazed Crabtree Falls Trail. From meadows, it is 0.8 mile along Crabtree Falls*

Road to Cash Hollow Road and 3.3 miles to Va . 56. For circuit hikes here, see section introduction.

5.9   Pass two dry **campsites** on right.

6.1   Reach high point of spur, then descend with winter views ahead of Main Top, with Spy Rock to its left.

6.3   Join old lumber road entering from right.

6.5   Thirty-three yards after woods road enters from left, reach dirt Cash Hollow Road in sag (3,280 feet) at head of hollow. Cross road, and, in 35 yards, pass through barrier fence, and begin 772-foot ascent of Main Top Mountain.

 To right on Cash Hollow Road, it is 0.5 mile to Va. 826 which leads right 0.8 mile to head of Crabtree Falls Trail at Crabtree Meadows (camping) or left 3.3 miles to Va. 56. For circuit hikes here, see section introduction.

7.2   After three switchbacks and two flat sections in ridge, pass side trail on right to dry **campsite.**

7.5   Trail climbs over 14-foot rock.

7.6   After two switchbacks, pass side trail right to another dry **campsite**. In 100 yards, bear left where old trail ascends straight ahead.

7.8   Ascend rock and log steps, and reach Cash Hollow Rock, a large rock face (3,512 feet) with an excellent view.

 Left to right over Cash Hollow are Little Priest, The Friar, High Peak of Tobacco Row (in distance), and The Cardinal. Much of the Piney River area between The Friar and The Cardinal, including the north and east slopes of The Cardinal, was ravaged by fire in 1894.

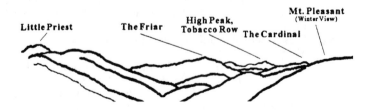

8.0 Pass old trail back to right.

8.2 After short, rocky ascent, pass rock overhang on left (possible emergency shelter except during electrical storms), and reach side trail, which leads 30 feet right to rock with winter view north.

8.6 Reach wooded summit of Main Top Mountain (4,040 feet), and begin 586-foot descent to Fish Hatchery Road. In 70 yards, pass dry **campsite** on left.

The original name of Main Top was Maidenhead Mountain, the name still used for a stream flowing from its northwest side.

8.7 Bear left around shoulder, passing rocky outcrops to right with views.

These rocks and Spy Rock supposedly were used as Confederate lookouts during the Civil War.

8.9 Reach grassy saddle and dry **campsite** (3,862 feet). The A.T. turns sharp right.

Side trail straight ahead goes 400 feet to Spy Rock with outstanding views. Main Top Mountain lies directly north. Clockwise from Main Top are Pinnacle Ridge, The Priest, Little Priest, The Friar, The Cardinal, Mt. Pleasant, Pompey Mountain, Cold Mountain, Tar Jacket Ridge, Rocky Mountain, Elk Pond Mountain, and Whetstone Ridge. Among plants found in the Spy Rock area are silver whitlowort, mountain sandwort, three-leafed cinquefoil, blue cohosh, wild geranium, michaux saxifrage, black chokeberry, and lily-of-the-valley.

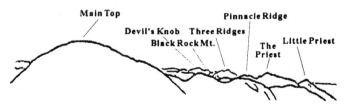

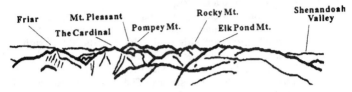

9.3   One hundred twenty yards after passing through barrier fence, leave old road, and bear to right.

9.4   At dirt-road junction, reach Fish Hatchery Road (3,454 feet) and end of section. To continue on A.T., cross road, and enter woods (see Section 18).

Road to right leads downhill 1.1 miles to Montebello State Fish Hatchery, with water and a Trailhead parking lot available, and 0.3 mile farther to Va. 56, 0.4 mile southeast of Montebello. For circuit hikes here, see section introduction.

Trail Description, South to North

Miles   **Data**

0.0   From Fish Hatchery Road (3,454 feet) at junction with intersecting road, enter woods, and begin 586-foot ascent of Main Top Mountain.

For circuit hikes here, see section introduction.

0.1   Reach old road, and follow it uphill to left. In 120 yards, pass through barrier fence.

0.5   Reach grassy saddle and dry **campsite** (3,862 feet). A.T. turns sharp left.

Side trail to right leads 400 feet to Spy Rock with outstanding views. Main Top Mountain lies directly north. Clockwise from Main Top are Pinnacle Ridge, The Priest, Little Priest, The Friar, The Cardinal, Mt. Pleasant, Pompey Mountain, Cold Mountain, Tar Jacket Ridge, Rocky Mountain, Elk Pond Mountain, and Whetstone Ridge. Plants found in the Spy Rock area include silver whitlowort, mountain sandwort, three-leafed cinquefoil, blue cohosh, wild geranium, michaux saxifrage, black chokeberry, and lily-of-the-valley.

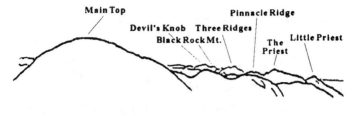

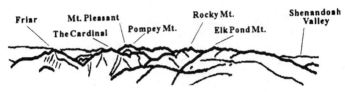

0.7   Bear right around shoulder, passing rocky outcrops to left
      with views.
          These rocks and Spy Rock supposedly were used as Confeder-
          ate lookouts during the Civil War.
0.8   Seventy yards after dry **campsite** on right, reach wooded
      summit of Main Top Mountain (4,040 feet). Begin 772-foot
      descent to Cash Hollow Road.
          The original name of Main Top was Maidenhead Mountain,
          a name still used for a stream flowing from its northwest side.
1.2   Side trail left leads 30 feet to rock with winter views north.
      Pass overhanging rock (possible emergency shelter except
      during lightning storms).
1.4   Bear right where old trail continues straight.
1.6   Reach Cash Hollow Rock, a large rock face (3,512 feet)
      with an excellent view.
          Left to right over Cash Hollow are Little Priest, The Friar,
          High Peak of Tobacco Row (in distance), and The Cardinal.
          Much of the Piney River area between The Friar and The
          Cardinal, including the north and east slopes of The Cardinal,
          was ravaged by a fire in 1894.

1.8   Pass old trail descending on left, and, in 100 yards, reach side trail left to dry **campsite.**

1.9   After two switchbacks, Trail climbs over 14-foot rock.

2.2   Pass side trail to left to another dry **campsite.**

2.9   After three switchbacks, pass through barrier fence, and reach dirt Cash Hollow Road in sag (3,268 feet) at head of hollow. Cross Cash Hollow Road, and follow old road.

*To left on Cash Hollow Road 0.5 mile is Va. 826, which leads right 0.8 mile to Crabtree Meadows (**camping**) and upper end of Crabtree Falls Trail or left 3.3 miles to Va. 56. For circuit hikes here, see section introduction.*

3.1   Old road enters on left.

3.3   Reach high point of spur, and descend.

3.5   Pass two dry **campsites** on left.

3.7   Emerging from timber, cross 50-yard cleared field, and reach unpaved Crabtree Farm Road (Va. 826) in sag called Shoe Creek Hill (3,319 feet). A.T. crosses road, enters the Priest Wilderness and begins 743-foot ascent of The Priest along worn road.

*Va. 826 leads left across Crabtree Creek 0.5 mile to Crabtree Meadows (**camping**) and upper end of Crabtree Falls Trail. From meadows, it is 0.8 mile along Crabtree Falls Road to Cash Hollow Road, 0.5 mile from southern end of section, and another 3.3 miles to Va. 56. For circuit hikes here, see section introduction.*

3.8   Pass through barrier fence.

4.0   Pass to right of saddle leading to Pinnacle Ridge (Cone Mountain).

4.2   After occasional views of The Priest, ahead to left, reach ridgecrest, and, in 130 yards, cross sag in ridge.

4.4   Unmarked trail leads right to summit of Little Priest (3,733 feet), with view of Piney River gorge.

This trail drops 600 feet through 3,200-foot col and then rises 533 feet to summit in 1.5 miles. In Revolutionary times, British Army Major Thomas Massie, who sympathized with the colonists, supposedly built a fortified residence in the saddle between Big and Little Priest mountains, to occupy if the British were victorious.

4.6   Pass interesting rock formation on right; in 65 feet, turn sharp left (north) on crest at **campsite** and junction. Blue-blazed side trail leads straight ahead 0.1 mile to **The Priest Shelter** and privy, unprotected spring and tent spaces.

4.7   Reach junction, with unmarked path leading right 130 yards to **shelter** area and unprotected spring and path left leading to dry **campsite.**

5.0   After three paths left to limited views, reach path left leading 150 feet to boulders; best views from the top of The Priest.

*Prominent ridge in foreground (Pinnacle Ridge) was Cone Mountain, historically considered in late 1940s as possible A.T. route. On far left are Elk Pond Mountain, Spy Rock, and Main Top. On far right are Devil's Knob, Humpback, and Three Ridges. Seventy yards ahead is path left to dry **campsite.***

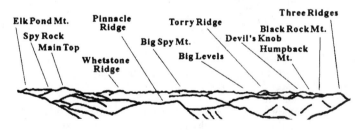

5.1   Reach wooded summit of The Priest (4,063 feet). Begin descent of 3,100 feet and thirty-seven switchbacks to Tye River.

5.3   Reach dry **campsite,** to left in clearing at end of narrow ridge, and, in 80 yards, bear left, descending knife-edge ridge for 270 yards. Very steep for 0.4 mile. Partial views of Tye River Valley to east, 3,200 feet below.

5.8   Reach 35-yard-long level spot in narrow saddle, and descend right, more gradually.

6.2   After passing 3,623-foot knob on left, rejoin descending ridgecrest. In 360 yards, cross a 10-yard-long level step in ridge, and then begin seven switchbacks, with occasional views of Three Ridges ahead and valleys to north and east.

6.6   Briefly rejoin narrow ridgecrest, and begin three more switchbacks.

6.7   Reach rocky outlook (2,891 feet) on right. Descend steeply for 130 yards before resuming switchbacks.

Here are expansive views to east of Tye River and Silver Creek valleys, now 2,000 feet below, and winter view of Three Ridges to left.

7.6   Swing left across ridge, with saddle on right.

8.1   Reach log bridge over Cripple Creek. Main series of switchbacks ends.

8.3   Cross small branch of Cripple Creek.

8.4   After short switchback down bank, cross another branch of Cripple Creek, and, in 60 yards, bear left on old road.

8.7   Old road descends from left. In 25 yards, bear right downhill, leaving old road.

8.8   Join old road, and, in 20 yards, switch back sharply right on another old road.

8.9   Switch back left off old road.

9.1   Descend bank, join old road for 10 yards, and switch back right. In 60 yards, switch back left where distinct path descends from right.

9.4   Leaving the Priest Wilderness, reach Trailhead parking lot and end of section (970 feet) at Va. 56 at Tye River. To continue, cross highway, and enter woods (see Section 16).

Tyro is 1.4 miles right; Montebello 8.2 miles left.

Fish Hatchery Road
to Salt Log Gap (USFS 63)
Section Eighteen
7.8 miles

Brief Description of Section

This section offers a feeling of remote isolation within the George Washington National Forest. The Trail averages 3,640 feet in elevation. Many old logging roads and traces of former logging railroads are evident, with the A.T. crossing old railroad beds several times. Several springs near the Trail, and Lovingston Spring on a blue-blazed side trail, afford good camping areas.

After crossing Porters Ridge, the Trail crosses the 1749 route of an exploration party at Porters Field and begins to flank Elk Pond Mountain. Sadly, neither the elk nor the pond on the level portion of the ridge-like mountain can be seen today. The route of 1749 is crossed again at the North Fork of Piney River (Amherst–Nelson County line) as the Trail ascends to Wolf Rocks, the finest viewpoint from the A.T. in the section.

Side trails reach the summits of Elk Pond Mountain (4,034 feet) and Rocky Mountain (4,072 feet). Rocky Mountain has a sweeping view from its western edge, but Elk Pond is heavily wooded.

The forest is mostly deciduous, with a scattering of conifers. Shagbark hickory can be found, and the high-elevation springs are sites of hemlock and yellow birch, as well as rhododendron and mountain laurel. Hundreds of herbaceous plants bloom in the understory during the spring and summer. Among the showiest are Canada lily, columbine, black cohosh, fly poison, and Indian pipe. In the fall, lobelias, asters, and gentians bloom, and the fruits of jack-in-the-pulpit, doll's eyes, and pokeweed appear.

Lovingston Spring

This wonderful spring (also known historically as Campbell Shanty Spring and Livingstone Spring) is a fine camping spot. It can be reached *via* a blue-blazed side trail that leaves the current A.T. at

Greasy Spring Road. Immediately west of the spring (an unprotected water source) and ridgeline lies private property.

Some Local History

In the 1740s, Parson Robert Rose owned 33,000 acres in the area and, in 1747, built his house, "Bear Garden," at the confluence of the Tye and Piney rivers. On December 6, 1749, Rose, accompanied by John Blyre, who had built a cabin "on top of the [Blue] Ridge near a pond," and Henry Bunch, a surveyor, explored this section for three days. They followed the north bank of the North Fork of Piney River to Elk Pond Branch, which they ascended, passing through the gap between Porters Ridge and Elk Pond Mountain (this would be Porters Field, where the A.T. crosses their route). They camped that night at the head of Mill Creek ("the Head Spring of the So Branch of Tye River") and, backtracking the next day, "Traveled all this day thro the Mountains" to the North Fork of Piney River and followed it to its source and Lovingston Spring. They camped, and "Blyre killed a bear at Night." On December 8, "Left our lodging place where the Earth had been our Bed and the Heavns our Canopy." The men then "traveld southerly along a Ridge of Rich land (Rocky Mountain and Tar Jacket Ridge) to the Head Spring of the So Branch of Piney River (the spring at Hog Camp Gap)." They then went "cross a Mountain" (Pompey) to Little Piney River, hence downstream back to "Bear Garden."

From Rocky Mountain (see "Circuit Hikes"), one can see Wigwam Mountain, the campsite in the early 1800s of a band of Cherokee Indians banished from Lexington, Va., because some had smallpox. One can also see Yankee Horse Ridge, named for a hard riding Yankee's exhausted horse that died on the ridge during the Civil War.

The term "Salt Log" comes from notches cut in a fallen log where handfuls of salt were placed for livestock—the forerunner of the modern salt block.

The forest here was largely stripped of timber before World War II. The South River Lumber Company, of Cornwall, Va., built fifty-seven miles of railroad track in an operation that extended from 1916 to 1938. Timberlands of profitable trees "of good size" were estimated to contain 60 percent chestnut, 10 percent yellow poplar, and the remainder oak and various softwoods. Accidents were a part of the work. Minutes after saying, "We will either be in hell or in Cornwall in fifteen minutes," Charles Floyd, engineer, was crushed in a wreck. The chestnut blight and the Depression caught the company, which had brought 100 million board feet from these woods, with 13 million board feet to be sold at a loss. Devastating floods in 1920 and 1929 washed out bridges. The final cutting occurred near Crabtree Falls. The Leftwich Timber Co., later the Woodson Lumber Co., of the Piney River area also built many miles of track in this area. Eventually, the cut-over timberlands were sold to the Forest Service. The A.T. joins an old railroad bed 1.2 miles from Fish Hatchery Road, crosses one at midsection at the North Fork of the Piney River, and another 1.6 miles north of Salt Log Gap. Greasy Spring, 0.25 mile east of the A.T., was supposedly named because cooks for a lumber crew polluted its waters with dishwater.

Points of Interest

Wolf Rocks: excellent views of Rocky Mountain, Elk Pond Mountain, Lovingston Spring area, Main Top, Spy Rock, Three Ridges, and The Priest.

Porters Field: spring and campsite near the path of the 1749 Rose, Blyre, and Bunch trek, and the South River Lumber Company railroad bed.

North Fork of Piney River: The A.T. again crosses the course that Rose, Blyre, and Bunch followed in 1749, near the headwaters of this tributary of the Tye River. Earlier this century, logging railroad tracks came uphill here.

Montebello State Fish Hatchery: large trout for visitors to see, 1.1 miles north of A.T. at end of section and 0.7 mile from Montebello. Trailhead parking 0.1 mile uphill toward A.T.

Lace Falls (pronounced "Lacey") or Statons Creek Falls: beautiful cascades on Statons Creek, 4.7 miles west of A.T. in Salt Log Gap *via* Va. 634 and 633. Falls are next to Va. 633 but best viewed down the steep path into the stream gorge. Avoid dangerous, wet rocks.

Rocky Mountain: outstanding views from this highest peak in the Pedlar District, especially from an outcropping on west side. Accessible from blue-blazed loop from A.T. at Greasy Spring Road. See "Circuit Hikes."

Circuit Hikes

1. Rocky Mountain: A 4.4-mile loop takes you to the summit of Rocky Mountain (4,072 feet) for outstanding views in all directions. From Salt Log Gap, hike north on A.T. for 1.7 miles, and turn left on blue-blazed trail 25 yards beyond Greasy Spring Road. Ascend 0.6 mile, reaching Rocky Mountain crest. Take unmarked side trail (old road) left for 300 feet to USFS 1176, which leads another 0.3 mile right to Rocky Mountain summit. At top, take short road to right, then path to outcropping with view west. Descend access road back to Salt Log Gap, bearing right downhill at saddle.

2. Porters Field: This pleasant woods walk could be combined with a side visit to Spy Rock. From USFS parking area just beyond Montebello Fish Hatchery, cross shallow stream, and ascend blue-blazed road for 0.6 mile to junction of several roads. Turn right off blue-blazed road onto old, unblazed railroad bed. Gradually ascend. In 0.2 mile, pass a gate across road, an old railroad bed. Cross a creek in 1.1 mile, followed by Mill Creek 0.4 mile later. In another 0.1 mile, switch back sharply left onto another old railroad bed, and in 0.7 mile, reach A.T. in Porters Field. Turn left on A.T. for 1.2 miles to Fish Hatchery Road, where a side trip to Spy Rock (ahead on A.T.) would add 1.2 miles to your hike. Descend left on Fish Hatchery Road, passing gate in 0.2 mile and reaching parking lot in 1.0 mile, for a total of 5.1 miles (or 6.3 miles including Spy Rock).

3. Greasy Spring Road: Greasy Spring Road and USFS 246 afford three variations, with distances of 5.9, 7.3, and 8.7 miles. From Salt Log Gap, hike north on the A.T. for 1.7 miles, then descend right on unmarked Greasy Spring Road (identified by a trail junction and sign 25 yards beyond). After 1 mile and 24 berms, ignore road ascending left, and descend 0.1 mile to junction in saddle. Here, Greasy Spring Road descends left. Option A takes right fork 0.2 mile through old clear-cut with views to USFS 246, where you turn right and follow USFS 246 1.7 miles back to A.T. crossing. Turn left on A.T. for 1.2 miles to Salt Log Gap, for a total of 5.9 miles. Options B and C follow Greasy Spring Road left from the junction in the saddle and, in 0.4 mile, reach junction where road curves left and ascends. Here, Option B takes older road to right, which curves left below clear-cut and descends ravine to reach USFS 246 in 0.1 mile. Turn right on USFS 246 for 2.8 miles to A.T., then left on A.T. for 1.2 miles to Salt Log Gap, for a total of 7.3 miles. Option C curves left uphill and follows the road 0.8 mile, past a creeklet and cabin, to a major junction at gap on Wolf Ridge. Turn sharp right on USFS 246, and follow it 3.5 miles to A.T., then left on A.T. for 1.2 miles to Salt Log Gap, for a total of 8.7 miles.

4. *Lovingston Spring:* The rewards of this hike are Lovingston Spring (nice camping) and a walk along Elk Pond Mountain—a former section of the Appalachian Trail first designated in the 1940s—with a possible side trip to the top of Rocky Mountain. Tall weeds may make summer a less desirable time for this loop. From Salt Log Gap, proceed north on A.T. for 1.7 miles, and turn left on blue-blazed trail 25 yards beyond Greasy Spring Road. In 0.6 mile, reach Rocky Mountain crest. (Here, unmarked side trail and old road left lead 300 feet to USFS 1176, which leads another 0.3 mile right to Rocky Mountain summit, 4,072 feet. A rocky outlook 0.1 mile west from summit has sweeping view across valley, with Yankee Horse Ridge about 1 mile away and Wigwam Mountain north about 2 miles.) At Rocky Mountain crest, blue-blazed trail bears right 0.6 mile to Lovingston Spring (unprotected water source) and 2.2 miles farther along Elk Pond Mountain to former A.T. at Twin Springs, where you turn right. After 4.1 miles, reach Greasy Spring Road; 1.7 miles farther brings you to Salt Log Gap and your vehicle, after a total of 10.9 miles. The Rocky Mountain side trip would add 0.8 mile.

Road Approaches

The northern end of this section can be reached *via* Va. 56, turning onto Va. 690 (sign for Montebello State Fish Hatchery) 0.4 mile southeast of Montebello. At the fish hatchery, continue ahead on dirt road to a Forest Service Trailhead parking area on left. On foot, cross shallow stream, continue uphill, past gate in road (at 0.8 mile), for 1.0 mile to the ridgecrest and A.T. crossing.

The southern end of this section is at Salt Log Gap (Lowmans Gap), 7.1 miles northeast of U.S. 60. One mile west of Long Mountain Wayside on U.S. 60, take Va. 634, which becomes USFS 63. There is ample parking near the Trail crossing. Do not confuse this Salt Log Gap with the Saltlog Gap 22.2 miles south, in Section 21.

From Salt Log Gap, USFS 1176 leads uphill 2.6 miles to Rocky Mountain. After 1.2 miles, USFS 246 bears right off USFS 1176 at a saddle, and unmarked Greasy Spring Road (USFS 1167A) immediately descends far side of saddle beyond a large berm. Limited parking. It is 0.2 mile on Greasy Spring Road to the A.T.

The southern end also can be approached from Piney River on Va. 151, *via* Va. 778 to Lowesville, or from U.S. 60 *via* Va. 778 to Lowesville. Then, follow Va. 666, turn left on Va. 827 and left on Va. 745, which becomes USFS 63; scenic approach not recommended in winter.

Maps

For route orientation, refer to ATC Pedlar District Map or PATC Map 13. For more area detail, refer to Montebello USGS topographic quadrangle.

Shelters and Campsites

This section has one shelter:
Seeley-Woodworth Shelter: built in 1984 and maintained by Natural Bridge Appalachian Trail Club and USFS; 2.3 miles from northern end on a 120-yard side trail; water from unprotected spring 0.1 mile beyond shelter on blue-blazed trail; accommodates six. A new privy is nearby.

Next shelter: north 6.9 miles (The Priest); south 10.2 miles (Cow Camp Gap), on a 0.6-mile side trail.

Campsites with convenient water (unprotected sources) are 1.2 miles from northern end of section at Porters Field, near Greasy Spring, and at the North Fork of Piney River. Hikers wishing to camp at Lovingston Spring (which is close to private property and should be used with respect) should take blue-blazed trail 1.2 miles from point near Greasy Spring Road.

Regulations

This section lies within the Pedlar District of the George Washington National Forest, (540) 291-2189, and camping is permitted. Attend fires at all times. *Note:* All water is untested.

Supplies, Services, and Public Accommodations

Montebello (ZIP Code 24464), with post office and Montebello Campground (campsites, cabins, laundry, limited groceries, and gas station) is 1.8 miles from A.T. *via* Fish Hatchery Road, Va. 690 and Va. 56 (west). Crabtree Falls Campground is 3.8 miles east of Va. 690 and 0.5 mile east of Crabtree Falls. Both campgrounds are closed in the winter.

Raphine, on I-81 12.5 miles from the A.T. *via* Va. 56 and Va. 690, has lodgings.

Whetstone Ridge Restaurant (open April through October), at milepost 29 on the parkway near the ranger station, is 4 miles from the A.T. *via* Fish Hatchery Road, Va. 690, Va. 56, Va. 603, and Va. 813.

The only supply source near the southern end is a small country store at the intersection of Va. 634 (USFS 63) and U.S. 60, 7.1 miles from Salt Log Gap.

In the event of emergencies north of the North Fork of the Piney River, contact the Nelson County sheriff's office in Lovingston by calling 911 or (804) 263-4242. South of that point, contact the Amherst County sheriff's office in Amherst, (804) 946-9300.

Trail Description, North to South

Miles	Data

0.0   From Fish Hatchery Road (8,454 feet), immediately turn right off intersecting dirt road into woods. *For circuit hike here, see section introduction.*

0.5   Ascend through shagbark hickory and hemlock, and, in 0.2 mile, switch back left.

0.8   Reach blazed post at Trail bend on open Porters Ridge. More hemlock and shagbark hickory ahead.

Left to right, view behind (north) Main Top, Spy Rock, The Priest, and Little Priest, with The Cardinal to far right.

1.2 After old road joins from left, reach Porters Field and junction with old road on left
     One hundred yards down the first of two roads to the right is unprotected spring and **campsite**. *Second road here is an old logging railroad bed (in service 1916–1938). Look for many haw bushes and some wild crabapple trees. For circuit hike here, see section introduction.*

1.6 Bear right uphill, leaving old railroad bed.

2.3 Blue-blazed trail left leads 120 yards to **Seeley-Woodworth Shelter** and privy. Unprotected spring 0.1 mile beyond shelter.

2.7 Swing right, crossing broad shoulder.

3.0 Cross Elk Pond Branch.

3.4 Just before cresting ridge, turn sharp right.

3.6 Unmarked spring (unprotected) 75 yards left in basin.

4.2 Cross old road and bed of the old logging railroad. In 50 yards, reach first branch of North Fork of the Piney River in hemlock and beech grove. Cross second branch 50 yards farther, and pass **campsite** on left.
     The A.T. crosses the Nelson–Amherst county line here.

4.6 Make wide swing right onto ridge.

5.1 Pass Wolf Rocks (3,893 feet) 50 yards on right.
     Excellent view left to right of Rocky Mountain, Elk Pond Mountain, Main Top, Spy Rock, Three Ridges, and The Priest.

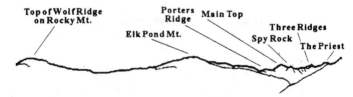

5.2 Reach high point on ridge, near large boulders at left.

5.9 Unmarked spring (unprotected) 20 yards to left.

6.1 Reach blue-blazed trail junction, and, in 25 yards, cross Greasy Spring Road (USFS 1176A).

The name Greasy Spring comes from logging-company cooks supposedly throwing greasy dishwater into spring branch. To find spring, go left on road 285 yards, following faint old A.T. blazes. Beyond fifth berm, at double blaze, turn right, and go 130 yards to unmarked, unprotected spring. In dry weather, get water farther downstream. Right 0.2 mile on Greasy Spring Road is USFS 1176 which connects Rocky Mountain summit with Salt Log Gap (USFS 63). Blue-blazed trail leads right to Rocky Mountain, Lovingston Spring, and Elk Pond Mountain. For circuit hikes here, see section introduction.

6.2 After crossing old woods road and, in 50 yards, crossing another old road, reach abandoned logging railroad bed.

6.6 After another old road, switch back left, and, in a saddle, reach USFS 246. Cross diagonally left.
For circuit hikes here, see section introduction.

7.3 After climbing several rock steps, bear right around gentle ridgecrest.

7.7 Pass within 15 yards of bend in old road (open) to right.

7.8 Reach USFS 63 (extension of Va. 634) in Salt Log Gap (Lowmans Gap, 3,257 feet) and end of section. To continue on Trail, cross road, and begin ascent of Tar Jacket Ridge (see Section 19).
Right on USFS 63, it is 7.1 miles to U.S. 60 (1.1 miles north of A.T. crossing) via Va. 634.

Trail Description, South to North

Miles   **Data**

0.0 From USFS 63 (extension of Va. 634, 7.1 miles north of U.S. 60) in Salt Log Gap (Lowmans Gap, 3,257 feet), A.T. ascends north in mixed conifers and hardwoods. In 200 feet, reach old apple orchard, overshadowed by forest.
For circuit hike here, see section introduction.

0.1 Pass within 15 yards of bend in old road (open area) to left.

0.5 Bear left around gentle ridgecrest; descend rock steps.

1.2 Cross USFS 246 in saddle.
For circuit hike here, see section introduction.

1.3 After right switchback, cross old road.

1.6   Descend to cross distinct abandoned logging railroad bed. In 100 yards, cross an old woods road, and, in 50 yards, another old road.

1.7   Cross Greasy Spring Road (USFS 1176A), and, in 25 yards, pass blue-blazed trail junction.

The name, Greasy Spring, comes from logging-company cooks supposedly throwing greasy dishwater into spring branch. To find spring, go right on road 285 yards, following faint old A.T. blazes. Beyond fifth berm, at double blaze, turn right, and go 130 yards to unprotected, unmarked spring. In dry weather, get water farther downstream. To left on Greasy Spring Road, 0.2 mile is USFS 1176 which connects Rocky Mountain summit with Salt Log Gap (USFS 63). Blue-blazed trail leads left to Rocky Mountain, Lovingston Spring, and Elk Pond Mountain. For circuit hike here, see section introduction.

1.9   Unmarked spring (unprotected) 20 yards to right.

2.6   After gentle ascent, reach high point on ridge, near large boulders on right.

2.7   At second height of land, reach Wolf Rocks (3,893 feet), 50 yards to the left.

View left to right of Rocky Mountain, Elk Pond Mountain, Main Top, Spy Rock, Three Ridges, and The Priest.

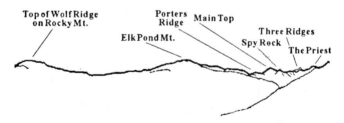

3.2   Make wide swing left off ridge.

3.6   Thirty yards before road ends, take left fork in Trail. Pass **campsite** to right, and, in 60 and 110 yards, cross two branches of the North Fork of the Piney River in hemlock and beech groves. Cross old road and bed of old logging railroad (in service from 1916 to 1938), 50 yards beyond the streams.

The A.T. crosses the Amherst–Nelson county line here.

4.2   Unmarked spring (unprotected) 75 yards right in basin.

4.4   After cresting ridge, turn sharp left.

4.8   Cross Elk Pond Branch.

5.1   Swing left, crossing broad shoulder.

5.5   Blue-blazed trail right leads 120 yards to **Seeley-Wood-worth Shelter** and privy, with unprotected spring another 0.1 mile beyond shelter.

6.2   Descending, join old railroad bed again.

6.6   Cross old road at Porters Field. In 25 yards, bear left at fork and ascend through hemlock and shagbark hickory, with views ahead of Main Top and Spy Rock.

*One hundred yards down the first of two roads to the left is unprotected spring and **campsite**. The other road was the logging railroad bed. Look for many haw bushes and some wild crabapple here.*

7.0   Reach blazed post at Trail bend on open Porters Ridge.

Left to right, view north of Main Top, Spy Rock, The Priest, and Little Priest, with The Cardinal to far right.

7.1   Switch back right, and descend through shagbark hickory and hemlock.

7.8   At dirt-road junction, reach Fish Hatchery Road (3,454 feet) and end of section. To continue on A.T., cross road, and ascend (see Section 17).

Road to left leads downhill 1.1 miles to Montebello State Fish Hatchery, with water available and a Trailhead parking lot. Va. 56 is 0.3 mile farther, at a point 0.4 mile southeast of Montebello.

Salt Log Gap (USFS 63) to
Long Mountain Wayside (U.S. 60)
Section Nineteen
8.5 miles

Brief Description of Section

The Trail in this section traverses Tar Jacket Ridge (3,840 feet), Cold Mountain (4,022 feet), and Bald Knob (4,059 feet), the latter two in the Mt. Pleasant National Scenic Area. The open areas along Tar Jacket Ridge and the summits of Cold Mountain, once pastures, are similar to the grassy balds in the southern Appalachians and have striking panoramic views. Although Bald Knob, the highest peak in the section, was once cleared pasture land, it is now densely wooded with no views. Three steep elevation changes in the 4.6-mile traverse of the Cold Mountain summit, Cow Camp Gap, and Bald Knob total more than 3,100 feet. Almost 2,000 feet of that change occurs between Bald Knob and U.S. 60.

About 2 miles of the section cross high, open land, which can be hazardous in electrical storms. Alternate routes are available. The remainder of the section passes through forests composed mostly of immature deciduous species. The open land along the section was once cleared, warm-weather pasture, where herds of cattle and hogs thrived on its vegetation. This land is now overtaken by a tough, scrubby type of privet shrub, coral berry, which provides wildlife cover and natural erosion control but could close the open meadows. Combined burning and mowing is being used as a joint program of ATC, NBATC, and USFS in an effort to keep Tar Jacket and Cold Mountain open. Bloodroot, Dutchman's breeches, cut-leaf toothwort, and other spring flowers bloom in the wooded part of Tar Jacket Ridge, and early fall flowers, such as stiff gentian, leather flower, and viper's bugloss, bloom later in the more open area. Similar spring ephemerals flower on the northern slope of Cold Mountain, and, about the first of June, many small phacelia may line the Trail down the southern slope. The rocky top of Cold Mountain is home to an unusual, but inconspicuous, plant, silvery

nailwort, which blooms a bit later. On Bald Knob, look for columbine, fly poison, Turk's cap lily, and jack-in-the-pulpit.

On Tar Jacket Ridge and Cold Mountain are the remains of a
network of 12 miles of stone fences built almost two hundred years
ago. Four-tenths of a mile south of Hog Camp Gap, the Trail
ascends for about one hundred feet along part of a seven-mile rock
fence around a 1,000-acre plot of land.

Water is available at Hog Camp Gap (on signed blue-blazed
trail), Cow Camp Gap Shelter, and a spring 0.5 mile east of the A.T.
on USFS 507, 0.9 mile from southern end of section. Wiggins Spring,
0.5 mile west of Hog Camp Gap on USFS 48, is an alternate water
source.

Mt. Pleasant

Two 4,000-foot mountains are included in the 7,580-acre Mt.
Pleasant National Scenic Area. Mt. Pleasant was identified as early
as a 1751 Fry and Jefferson map. Each year, hundreds of hikers
enjoy the views of Tobacco Row Mountain, Fletcher Mountain,
Bald Knob, Cold Mountain, Tar Jacket Ridge, and the Piedmont
from the rocky outcrops on both ends of Mt. Pleasant's summit as
they hike the Henry Lanum Trail. Of moderate difficulty, this loop
trail honors a former Trail supervisor for the Natural Bridge Appalachian Trail Club.

One encounters scarlet oak, much brachen fern, and mountain
laurel, with some interesting high-elevation plants blooming here
in June—yellow clintonia, pale corydalis, and michaux saxifrage—
as well as an impressive array of rhododendron. Later, the red
berries of mountain ash add color to the views.

Park in Hog Camp Gap (U.S. 60, Va. 634, Va. 755, USFS 48), and
walk east on USFS 48 briefly before bearing right on blue-blazed
USFS 51. After 0.4 mile, reach signboard and beginning of the 5.2-
mile Henry Lanum Trail. Hike in either direction, left to Pompey or
right to Mt. Pleasant. At the saddle, take the 0.5-mile spur trail south
for Mt. Pleasant's famous views, noting the short side trail left to the
spring (unprotected). Total hike involves 7.0 miles. Consider combining the Mt. Pleasant and Old Hotel (below) trails for a one- or
two-night, leisurely backpacking trip.

Old Hotel Trail

This attractive, blue-blazed trail, which connects Hog Camp Gap with Cow Camp Gap, is named for a wood-framed building no longer there. A Union soldier is buried along this trail (see "Some Local History"). In the last century, it was a summer retreat for the Richeson family and then shelter for seasonal herders, but it was never a hotel as such.

Combined with the A.T. over Cold Mountain, the Old Hotel Trail makes a superb circuit hike. Some stone walls of a 12-mile network of antebellum "hog walls" are encountered, as are fine views of Mt. Pleasant, with its southern rocky outcrops, the head-waters of the North Fork of the Buffalo River, and a beautiful oak grove, the open, grassy floor of which invites a campsite. Amid various pines, red maple, shagbark hickory, and yellow birch, Little Cove Creek is crossed, where one can contemplate the virgin forest downstream and a ravine called "Shades of Death." Lunch could be at the Cow Camp Gap Shelter. The views from the extended open areas on Cold Mountain can be excellent on a cold, clear day.

After parking in Hog Camp Gap (U.S. 60, Va. 634, Va. 755, USFS 48), the weather may control whether one starts south on the A.T. over Cold Mountain first or heads west on USFS 48 for 0.3 mile to begin the Old Hotel Trail, to right through the gate. From there, it is 2.8 miles to Cow Camp Gap Shelter and 0.6 mile farther to junction with A.T. in Cow Camp Gap, where one turns right over Cold Mountain for 2.5 miles to Hog Camp Gap, for a total of 6.2 miles.

Consider a combination of the Old Hotel and Mt. Pleasant Trails for a one- or two-night, leisurely backpacking trip.

Some Local History

The original road at the southern end of the section (now U.S. 60 where the A.T. crosses) was the Jordan Road, a stagecoach and toll road surveyed by Samuel Francis Jordan in 1835 and built within a few years after.

The building of the 12 miles of stone walls in the Tar Jacket and Cold Mountain area is attributed to two different men with con-trasting workmen. It is generally agreed that the land was cleared and the walls built in the early 1800s. Whether the walls were built by slaves of the Richeson family or by three Irishmen supervised by Zacharias Drummond's son, John, as stated by family descendants, may never be determined. The walls became known as "hog walls," because over the years hogs were driven up to the mountains to be fattened on chestnuts and acorns before butchering. Cows also were driven here from the Amherst area and grazed through the summer—hence, Hog Camp and Cow Camp. Local hikers remember cows on Cold Mountain as late as the 1970s

The term "Salt Log" comes from notches cut in a fallen log where handfuls of salt were placed for livestock—the forerunner of the modern salt block.

While herders in this century used the "Old Hotel" for quarters, it was believed originally built by Zacharias Drummond between 1820 and 1830 as "The old Mantion House." Drummond had bought the land (east) below Cold Mountain from George Higginbotham, and, in 1857, a later Higginbotham bought it back. The Old Hotel, never a real hotel, was known locally as the Higginbotham house. A wounded Union soldier, cared for by the family, died and was buried on the property.

During the Civil War, the Jordan Road was used on June 12, 1864, when Union General Hunter ordered "twenty of your best men, well-mounted," from Lexington to locate his two thousand cavalry who had crossed east at Tye River. The same day, two hundred mounted men from the 1st West Virginia Cavalry and the 14th Pennsylvania Cavalry also rode east from Lexington over the Jordan Road to cut railroad communications and to circle Lynchburg. Still later that day, Hunter's two thousand cavalry rode west to Lexington, crossing by what is now Long Mountain Wayside. A Union soldier wrote: "It was one of the worst roads the regiment had ever traveled—rocks, ravines, steep pitches up and down, and sidling places where it was difficult to keep the wagons from tipping over. More than a hundred horses gave out."

Several mountains here have undergone name changes. "Bald Friar" on the 1751 Fry and Jefferson map and others has become "The Friar." Amherst County deed books and will books involving Zacharias Drummond use "Cold Mountain" in the 1850s and 1870s. "Cold Mountain" appears on all maps from 1825 to 1894, when the first USGS map appeared with "Cole Mountain." Still, the Natural

Bridge National Forest maps went back to using "Cold Mountain" from 1924 to 1930. Forest Service and Appalachian Trail publications have reverted from "Cole" to the original "Cold Mountain" usage. Tar Jacket Ridge was "Buck Mountain" until 1927. Cecil DeMott, an early NBATC president, speculated that brush on this ridge was so dense that, when one walked through it, was likely to "t'ar yer jacket," hence the new name. The current "Fletcher Mountain" had been "Fork Mountain" from the 19th century until the mid-1970s when the name was changed.

The history of logging railroad tracks in the mountains of the area is mentioned in "Some Local History," Section 18. The Leftwich Timber Co. had its farthest inroad into the mountains at Hog Camp Gap, where a line came up the South Fork of the Piney River. Here, a railroad switchback led a track over to the side of Mt. Pleasant, now a part of the Henry Lanum Trail.

In October 1978, a Navy fighter jet flying westward on maneuvers crashed into the north ridge of Bald Knob, killing two aviators. A few scraps of wreckage might be seen near the Trail. Rescuers were struck by two things: Just a little higher and the plane would have cleared the ridge; and, in the midst of burned devastation, a helmet and a chart book were lying together beside the A.T., unscathed, "as if gently placed there."

Points of Interest

Tar Jacket Ridge: excellent views from open summit areas on north and south ends of ridge.

Cold Mountain: panoramic view from grassy summit similar to the southern Appalachian balds. Almost a mile of open walking.

Pre-Civil War stone fences: twelve miles of "hog walls" on Tar Jacket Ridge and Cold Mountain. See "Some Local History."

Mt. Pleasant National Scenic Area: a 7,850-acre area embracing Mt. Pleasant, Pompey Mountain, Little Mt. Pleasant, Cold Mountain, and parts of Chestnut Ridge and Cardinal Ridge. The Henry Lanum Trail affords access to superb views at both ends of Mt. Pleasant summit. See description above.

Hog Camp Gap: now an active center for day-hiking in the area, with access to the Mt. Pleasant National Scenic Area and the Old Hotel Trail, as well as the A.T. over Tar Jacket and Cold Mountain.

Camping available near Hog Camp Spring. Parking areas on USFS 48 and at Henry Lanum Trailhead.

The Sleeping Giant: As seen from the east at Amherst, Va., these mountains have been called "The Sleeping Giant" by local residents. Bald Knob on the left forms the knees and legs, Cold Mountain forms the trunk, and Mt. Pleasant on the right forms the head.

Lace Falls (pronounced "Lacy") or Statons Creek Falls: at north end of section, beautiful cascades on Statons Creek 4.7 miles west of A.T. in Salt Log Gap, *via* Va. 634 and 633. Falls are right next to Va. 633 but are best viewed down the steep path into the stream gorge. Caution: Avoid the dangerous wet rocks.

Davis Mill Creek Falls: at south end of section, another beautiful set of falls, about two miles from Long Mountain Wayside, with a vertical drop equal to Lace Falls. Lesser known, yet close to a road, they require a bit of a scramble to reach. They are located in the upper left corner of USGS Forks of Buffalo quadrangle. Turn right off U.S. 60 onto Va. 634. In 0.9 mile, the falls are steeply downhill to left on Forest Service land. Easier but longer access is at Oronoco *via* Va. 605, briefly, turning right in 150 yards on dirt road (USFS 1246). Proceed to Davis Mill Creek, and walk upstream.

Shades of Death: a local name for the trailless Little Cove Creek ravine below Cow Camp Gap Shelter; "so deep in there the sun never shines." Besides rattlesnakes, the ravine is known for old growth timber, with red oak and yellow poplar five feet in diameter. A difficult bushwhack down to USFS 51.

Circuit Hikes

More than twenty circuit-hike possibilities are available in this section, including the two excellent ones discussed earlier—Mt. Pleasant and the Old Hotel Trail. The others involve different configurations of the A.T., USFS 48, USFS 520, USFS 507 and, for greater distances, also the Mt. Pleasant and/or Old Hotel Trail loops.

1 . Loop C, Tar Jacket: Park at either Salt Log Gap or at Hog Camp Gap, and walk the A.T. across Tar Jacket, following USFS 48 for 3.2 miles back to the start. Wonderful views are available from the open areas at both ends of Tar Jacket Ridge, and USFS 48 is quite attractive in this section, especially in the lower Hog Camp area. Total mileage: 5.4 miles.

2. *Loop D, Cold Mountain:* From Hog Camp Gap, hike over Cold Mountain on the A.T. After wonderful views, turn right (west) at Cow Camp Gap on blue-blazed trail (0.7 mile), then right on USFS 520 (0.4 mile), and right on USFS 48 for 1.1 miles back to Hog Camp Gap. Total: 4.3 miles.

3. *Loop E, Bald Knob, short version:* When USFS 520 gates are open, drive to junction of USFS 520 and USFS 507, hike north on A.T. over Bald Knob, then, at Cow Camp Gap, turn left (west) on blue-blazed trail (0.7 mile) back to USFS 520, where you walk left 4.0 miles to your car. A fine walk, but with limited views and lots of elevation changes. Total: 7.6 miles.

4. *Loop F:* A 2-mile loop starting at Long Mountain Wayside on U.S. 60 and ascending A.T. north to USFS 507 for 0.9 mile, then turning back left on USFS 520 for 1.1 miles to U.S. 60. A woods walk, it is useful primarily in extending other loops.

By studying maps, the USFS quadrangles for Montebello and Forks of Buffalo, the A.T. Trail data, and the loop directions above, one can design other circuit hikes ranging from 2 to 27 miles in length.

Road Approaches

The northern end of the section at Salt Log Gap (limited parking) is reached from U.S. 60 *via* Va. 634 and its extension, USFS 63, a total of 7.1 miles. The U.S. 60 intersection is 8.1 miles east of Buena Vista and U.S. 501, 4 miles east of Blue Ridge Parkway milepost 45.6, and 18.2 miles east of the Amherst traffic circle, off U.S. 29.

The northern end also can be approached from Piney River on Va. 151, *via* Va. 778 to Lowesville, or from U.S. 60 *via* Va. 778 to Lowesville. Then, follow Va. 666, turn left on Va. 827, and left on Va. 745, which becomes USFS 63—a scenic approach not recommended in winter.

About 1.0 mile northwest of the southern end of this section on U.S. 60, Va. 634 leads 1.7 miles to Va. 755 ("Wiggins Spring Road"), which leads right to USFS 48, Hog Camp Gap, and the A.T. USFS 520 leads from Long Mountain Wayside, at the southern end of section, 5.5 miles to USFS 48, 1.1 miles west of Hog Camp Gap.

Access to Cow Camp Gap is possible by blue-blazed trail (0.7 mile), beginning on USFS 520 0.4 mile from USFS 48 and 5.1 miles from Long Mountain Wayside.

The southern end of the section is at Long Mountain Wayside on U.S. 60 (ample parking), 1.0 mile east of the U.S. 60/Va. 634 intersection and 17.2 miles west of the Amherst traffic circle, off U.S. 29.

Maps

For route orientation, refer to ATC Pedlar District Map or PATC Map 13. For more area detail, refer to USGS topographic quadrangles for Montebello, Forks of Buffalo, and Buena Vista.

Shelters and Campsites

This section has one shelter:
Cow Camp Gap Shelter: built in 1986 by ATC's Konnarock crew and Natural Bridge Appalachian Trail Club, with help from USFS; maintained by NBATC and USFS; on a 0.6-mile side trail 4.3 miles from northern end of section; accommodates eight; water from two unprotected springs. Campsites nearby.
Next shelter: north 10.2 miles (Seeley-Woodworth); south 5.6 miles (Brown Mountain Creek).

Camping is possible in meadow in Hog Camp Gap, on signed blue-blazed trail to Hog Camp Spring, or near a spring 0.5 mile east of A.T., on USFS 507, 0.9 mile from southern end of section.

Regulations

This section lies within the George Washington National Forest, where camping is permitted unless posted otherwise. Attend fires at all times. *Note:* All water is untested.

Supplies, Services, and Public Accommodations

One mile west of the A.T., on U.S. 60 at Va. 634, is Hamm's store, with limited groceries. Buena Vista (ZIP Code 24416, groceries, restaurants, motels, coin laundry, and other services) is 9.3 miles west of the southern end.

In an emergency, contact the Buena Vista Rescue Squad (same number as police department), (540) 261-8615, or the Amherst County sheriff's office, (804) 946-9300.

Trail Description, North to South

Miles	Data

0.0   From USFS 63 (Va. 634) in Salt Log Gap (Lowmans Gap, 3,257 feet), follow Trail south, and, in 250 feet, cross USFS 48, and gradually climb ten switchbacks 590 feet up northern slope of Tar Jacket Ridge.

> *An apple tree in the gap drops lots of apples on the Trail in the fall; they attract yellow jackets. USFS 48 leads left 3.2 miles along east side of Tar Jacket Ridge to Hog Camp Gap, roughly paralleling 2.2 miles of the A. T., an alternative route in an electrical storm. For circuit hike here, see section introduction.*

0.7   Three hundred forty yards after finishing six switchbacks, bear left with old trail straight ahead. Join main crest.

1.0   Switch back right, passing old trails to your right and left, and, in 85 yards, switch back left.

1.2   Again, switch back to right, and, in 60 yards, switch back to left.

1.3   In bend of Trail, reach high point of Trail on Tar Jacket Ridge (3,847 feet).

> *Panoramic views right to left of Cold Mountain, Mt. Pleasant, Pompey Mountain, The Friar, The Cardinal, Little Priest, Spy Rock, Main Top, and Elk Pond Mountain.*

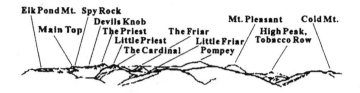

1.4   Pass through old stone wall.

1.6   Reach second crest of Tar Jacket Ridge, with expansive
      views near prominent rocks.

      *Left to right are Pompey Mountain, Mt. Pleasant, Cold
      Mountain, Bluff Mountain (at 228° SW), Rocky Mountain,
      and Elk Pond Mountain. Sometimes, McAfee Knob (at 241°
      SW) can be seen, 100 hiking miles away.*

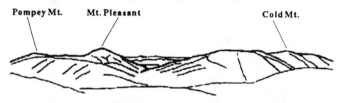

2.2   Fifty yards after a signed side trail to the left (leading 500
      yards to reliable, unprotected spring), pass barrier fence,
      and reach USFS 48 and ample Trailhead parking in Hog
      Camp Gap (3,485 feet). The A.T. crosses road and fence,
      bears left of blocked gate, and begins 537-foot ascent of
      Cold Mountain. Enter Mt. Pleasant National Scenic Area.

      *Camping possibilities here and nearer the spring. Without
      grazing, dense coral berry here must be cut back. A logging
      railroad had a switchback spur here in the 1920s and '30s.
      USFS 48 leads right (becoming Va. 755) 2.7 miles to Va. 634,
      then one can go left 1.7 miles to U.S. 60, 1.0 mile north of A.T.
      crossing. USFS 48 leads left 3.2 miles to Salt Log Gap,
      diverging left at fork en route. For circuit hikes here, see
      section introduction. As an alternate route in an electrical
      storm, consider descending right (west) 1.1 miles to USFS
      520, turning left 0.4 mile to blue-blazed trail, on which you
      ascend left 0.7 mile to Cow Camp Gap.*

2.5   Cross dirt road, and continue ahead up steps.

2.6   Bear left at end of rock wall, and, in 110 yards, pass
       overhanging rock on right (possible emergency shelter
       except during electrical storms).
       Watch for yellow lady's-slipper (an orchid) ahead.
2.8   Passing through shagbark hickory grove, ascend three
       steps, and turn right onto old road. Pass old trail to left in
       10 yards, and, in 60 yards, excellent view on right.
       *Left to right, view is of Rocky Mountain, Tar Jacket Ridge,
       Main Top, Spy Rock, Three Ridges, The Priest, The Cardinal,
       Little Priest, and The Friar.*

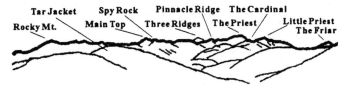

3.0   After 450 yards, leave old grassy road at post before knoll.
       *Pass views south of Tobacco Road and Fleming Mountain and
       west of Shenandoah Valley.*
3.3   Rejoin old grassy road, and, in 100 yards, bear right off
       road.
3.4   Reach cleared north summit of Cold Mountain. Watch for
       blazes on rocks.
3.5   After road enters from left, in 60 yards, bear left off road,
       ascend steeply to left, and reach rocks at summit of Cold
       Mountain (4,022 feet). Begin 594-foot descent to Cow
       Camp Gap.
       *Also called Cole Mountain. Grazing common here for more
       than a century. A resort was once planned for the top. In early
       1980s, a repeater station was removed from the summit. Great
       Indian plantain can be found here. Outstanding views to
       north, left to right, of Rocky Mountain, Tar Jacket Ridge (in
       foreground), Elk Pond Mountain, Main Top, Spy Rock, Three
       Ridges (in background), The Priest, The Cardinal, Little
       Priest, The Friar, Pompey Mountain, and Mt. Pleasant; to
       south, Bald Knob, with Apple Orchard Mountain to left, 42
       hiking miles away, and McAfee Knob to right (at 242° SW),
       98 hiking miles away.*

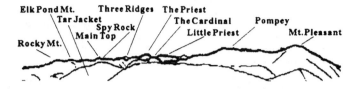

3.6   Fifty-five yards after reentering woods, pass gate in barbed-wire fence.

        On July 11,1975, Chris Denney, 26, was killed by lightning in the flat section ahead as he descended from Cold Mountain summit. Rescuers noted a history of lightning damage to a dozen trees nearby.

3.8   Pass through stone wall, and, in 35 yards, reach first of three overlooks at rocky outcroppings.

        Views west of Big House Mountain across Shenandoah Valley, nearby Bald Knob on left, Rocky Mountain (towers) on right. Ahead, views to east of Shades of Death and Chestnut Ridge.

4.7   Cross overgrown woods road in Cow Camp Gap (3,428 feet), and begin 631-foot ascent of Bald Knob.

        To left, blue-blazed Old Hotel Trail leads east 0.6 mile to **Cow Camp Gap Shelter** *and privy, with* **campsite** *and two unprotected springs. To right, blue-blazed trail leads 0.7 mile to USFS 520. Look for Great Indian plantain in the gap. For circuit hikes here, see section introduction.*

5.2   Just before switchback left, pass traces of aircraft wreckage on left and 50 yards below Trail. See "Some Local History."

5.3   Side trail to view, 20 feet to left.

        Cold Mountain, Pompey Mountain, Mt. Pleasant, and the Piedmont can be seen, left to right.

5.7   Reach wooded summit of Bald Knob (4,059 feet) where Trail crosses granite rock (no view). Start gradual descent of 1,984 feet southwest to U.S. 60, topping several small humps.

6.7   After distinct sag in ridge, cross final, short, grassy rise in ridge.

7.6   Cross USFS 507,15 yards east of dirt-road junction with USFS 520, leaving Mt. Pleasant National Scenic Area.

> *To left, road leads 0.5 mile to unprotected spring on Fletcher Mountain, 0.1 mile beyond ridge and* **campsite**. *For circuit hikes here, see section introduction.*

8.0   After steep descent, with gravel road in sight ahead, turn left off old woods road.

8.1   Cross old road.

8.3   Beyond last switchback, cross second old road.

8.5   Turn right at Long Mountain Wayside (2,065 feet), and, in 300 feet, reach end of section at U.S. 60. Trail continues diagonally to right across road (see Section 20).

> *To right, U.S. 60 leads 1.0 mile to phone and limited groceries, and 9.3 miles to Buena Vista. Amherst is 17.2 miles left.*

Trail Description, South to North

Miles   **Data**

0.0   From western entrance of Long Mountain Wayside (2,065 feet) on U.S. 60, enter woods on path to right of woods road, and ascend. Begin 1,984-foot ascent of Bald Knob.

> *For circuit hikes here, see section introduction.*

0.2   Cross old road, and begin switchbacks.

0.4   Cross second old road.

0.5   Turn right onto old road, and ascend steeply.

0.9   Cross USFS 507,15 yards east of dirt-road junction with USFS 520, and head uphill to right. Enter Mt. Pleasant National Scenic Area.

> *To right, road leads 0.5 mile to unprotected spring on Fletcher Mountain, 0.1 mile beyond ridge and* **campsite**. *For circuit hikes here, see section introduction.*

1.8   Reach short, grassy high point on ridge, and descend slightly through distinct sag. Several small humps follow.

2.8   Reach wooded summit of Bald Knob (4,059 feet) where Trail crosses granite rock (no view). Begin 631-foot descent to Cow Camp Gap, at first gently, for 380 yards, then more steeply.

3.2   Pass side trail to view 20 feet on right. Cold Mountain, Pompey Mountain, Mt. Pleasant, and the Piedmont can be seen, left to right.

3.3   Just after switchback right, pass traces of aircraft wreckage on left and 50 yards below Trail. See "Some Local History."

3.8   Cross overgrown woods road in Cow Camp Gap (3,428 feet), and begin 594-foot ascent. In 50 yards, bear right off ridgeline, with views of Shades of Death and Chestnut Ridge.

Blue-blazed Old Hotel Trail on right leads 0.6 mile east to **Cow Camp Gap Shelter**, *with privy and* **campsites**, *which has two unprotected springs and a privy. Look for Great Indian plantain in the gap. As an alternate route in an electrical storm, consider turning left (west) on blue-blazed trail for 0.7 mile, then right 0.4 mile on USFS 520, then right 1.1 miles on USFS 48 to Hog Camp Gap. For circuit hikes here, see section introduction.*

4.1   Reach first of three overlooks at rocky outcroppings. *Views west of Big House Mountain across Shenandoah Valley and nearby Bald Knob on left. Rocky Mountain (towers) to right.*

4.7   Pass by prominent rock formation on right, and, in 100 yards, cross over stone wall.

On July 11, 1975, Chris Denney, 26, was killed by lightning in the flat section ahead as he was descending from Cold Mountain summit. Rescuers noted a history of lightning damage to a dozen trees nearby.

4.9   Pass gate in barbed-wire fence, leave woods, and ascend along grassy crest (blazes on rocks).

5.0   Reach rocks at summit of Cold Mountain (4,022 feet). Begin 537-foot descent to Hog Camp Gap.

Also called Cole Mountain, a common grazing area for more than a century. A resort was once planned for the top. In early 1980s, a repeater station was removed from the summit. Great Indian plantain can be found here. Outstanding views to north, left to right, of Rocky Mountain, Tar Jacket Ridge (in foreground), Elk Pond, Main Top, Spy Rock, Three Ridges (in background), The Priest, The Cardinal, Little Priest, The Friar, Pompey Mountain, and Mt. Pleasant; to south, Bald Knob with Apple Orchard Mountain to left, 42 hiking miles away, and McAfee Knob to right (at 242° SW), 98 hiking miles away.

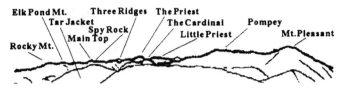

5.1   Taking left fork of road, reach northern summit of Cold Mountain.
5.2   Old grassy road joins from right, and, in 100 yards, A.T. bears left off road.
5.5   Rejoin old grassy road, and descend on road for 450 yards.
5.7   Sixty yards after excellent view on left and 10 yards after old trail enters on right, turn sharp left off old road, and descend through shagbark hickory grove.
        Left to right, view is of Rocky Mountain, Tar Jacket Ridge, Main Top, Spy Rock, Three Ridges, The Priest, The Cardinal, Little Priest, and The Friar. Watch for yellow lady's-slipper (an orchid) ahead.

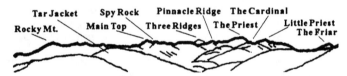

5.9   Pass overhanging rock (possible emergency shelter except during electrical storms), and, in 110 yards, bear right at rock wall.
6.0   Descend steps, and cross dirt road.
6.3   Cross fence, and reach USFS 48 and Trailhead parking in Hog Camp Gap (3,485 feet). Exit Mt. Pleasant National Scenic Area. Ahead, A.T. passes through barrier fence, and, in 50 yards, passes side trail to right that descends 500 yards to reliable, unprotected spring.
        Camping possibilities here and nearer the spring. Without grazing, dense coral berry here must be cut back. A logging railroad had a switchback spur here in the 1920s and '30s. See "Some Local History." USFS 48 leads left (becoming Va. 755) 2.7 miles to Va. 634, then left 1.7·miles to U.S. 60, one mile north of A.T. crossing. USFS 48 leads right 3.2 miles across

east side of Tar Jacket Ridge to Salt Log Gap, diverging left en route at fork and roughly paralleling 2.2 miles of the A.T., an alternative route in an electrical storm. For circuit hikes here, see section introduction.

6.9   Reach first crest of Tar Jacket Ridge, with expansive views near prominent rocks.

Left to right are Pompey Mountain, Mt. Pleasant, Cold Mountain, Bluff Mountain (at 228° SW), Rocky Mountain, and Elk Pond Mountain. Sometimes, McAfee Knob (at 241° SW) can be seen, 100 hiking miles away.

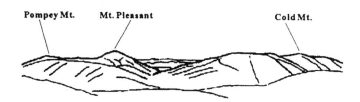

Pompey Mt.   Mt. Pleasant   Cold Mt.

7.1   Pass through old stone wall.
7.2   Reach high point of Trail on Tar Jacket Ridge (3,847 feet), in bend of Trail. Begin 590-foot descent on ten switchbacks to Salt Log Gap.

Panoramic views, left to right, of Elk Pond Mountain, Main Top Mountain, Spy Rock, The Priest, Little Priest, The Cardinal, The Friar, Pompey Mountain, Mt. Pleasant, and Cold Mountain.

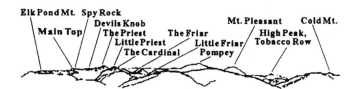

Elk Pond Mt. Spy Rock
            Devils Knob   Mt. Pleasant   Cold Mt.
   Main Top/ /The Priest   The Friar   High Peak,
            /Little Priest Little Friar/ Tobacco Row
             The Cardinal/ Pompey

7.3   Switch back to right, and, in 60 yards, switch back left.
7.5   Again, switch back right, passing old trail to your right and left, and, in 85 yards, switch back left.

7.8   Bear right, with old trail to left, and, after 340 yards, begin
       series of six switchbacks.

8.5   Two hundred fifty feet after crossing woods road (USFS
       48), reach end of section at USFS 63 (Va. 634) in Salt Log
       Gap (Lowmans Gap, 3,247 feet). To continue on Trail,
       cross road, and ascend (see Section 18).

       *An apple tree in the gap drops lots of apples on the Trail in the
       fall, attracting yellow jackets. USFS 48 leads right 3.2 miles
       along east side of Tar Jacket Ridge to Hog Camp Gap, roughly
       paralleling 2.2 miles of the A.T. Left on USFS 63, it is 7.1
       miles to U.S. 60 (1.0 miles north of A.T. crossing) via Va. 634.
       For circuit hikes here, see section introduction.*

Long Mountain Wayside (U.S. 60) to Blue Ridge Parkway (Punchbowl Mountain Crossing)
Section Twenty
10.2 miles

Brief Description of Section

The Trail in this section is partly graded and partly routed onto old woods roads through conifer and hardwood forest, with a few open areas. Water is abundant.

Southbound hikers descend Long Mountain and traverse Brown Mountain Creek Valley, known for its old rock walls, foundations, chimneys, and decaying timbers. The Trail follows attractive Brown Mountain Creek for almost two miles. Wildflowers and blooming shrubs are profuse in season, including rhododendron, showy orchis, marsh marigold, bee balm, yellow lady's-slipper, Oswego tea (a red-flowering mint), and ferns. Areas of large, beautiful trees are passed. The Trail skirts the eastern shore of Pedlar Lake (a public water supply), then turns abruptly westward over the Pedlar River footbridge. Several vantage points along the way provide views of the lake itself and of Shady, Hico, Coleman, and Rice mountains, with Bluff Mountain dominating.

The Trail leaves the Pedlar River (960 feet of elevation) footbridge and ascends Rice Mountain, climbing 1,248 feet in 1.8 miles. Near the beginning of the climb, a USFS sign indicates a 4.5-acre virgin-forest exhibit.

Rice Mountain has several knobs, the highest being 2,228 feet. The Trail descends from the mountain through laurel and rhododendron to Robinson Gap Road before gently ascending to the Blue Ridge Parkway.

The main northbound climb is 1,145 feet in about six miles, from the Pedlar River to Long Mountain Wayside.

Some Local History

Prior to 1740, the Saponi Indians, who lived in the nearby lowlands, came to Long Mountain and dug greenstone to make axes, tomahawks, and scrapes.

At Long Mountain Wayside (U.S. 60 where the A.T. crosses), the original road was the old Jordan Road, a stagecoach and toll road surveyed by Samuel Francis Jordan in 1835 and built within a few years thereafter.

During the Civil War, the Jordan Road was particularly busy one June Sunday in 1864 (see "Some Local History," Section 19).

Brown Mountain Creek Valley was cleared and farmed by slave labor from around 1800 to the end of the Civil War. In 1868, a former slave purchased the land in the narrow valley and built a series of cabins, the remains of which are evident. He rented the cabins to tenants, all former slaves, who sharecropped the land. The A.T. passes a remnant of a tobacco barn, half a dozen cabin foundations (one with a double chimney), an old walled spring, and many rock walls. As the tenants were about to leave the valley in 1918, one remembers looking up as a lad and seeing his first airplane fly over, a biplane.

In 1904, the valley was changed with the building of Pedlar Dam. (See entry below.)

Of several old homesteads passed by the A.T., one just below Punchbowl Crossing was especially active during Prohibition. Whiskey was made and sold there, with people walking over the mountain from Buena Vista to purchase it. Evidence of the still, with glass jars, can still be found down the bank in a ravine to the right of the cabin remains.

Scare Rock

A legend about a rock just below the A.T. bridge-crossing of Brown Mountain Creek has been passed down through the black community in Brown Mountain Creek Valley. It tells of Jess Richeson, who one day beat one of his slaves "almost to death." After he beat the slave, he got on his horse and headed home, down Brown Mountain Creek. As he went by a rock, something jumped off that rock and grabbed him around the waist. It didn't knock him off, and he didn't see what it was, but he felt it holding him tightly. The horse bolted. When Richeson reached home, he told what had happened. That night, both he and his horse died. After that, they called the rock "Scare Rock."

Pedlar Lake

As one hikes above attractive Pedlar Lake on the A.T., it's hard to imagine the small community of Waya that once stood at the lake's northern end. It's not hard to imagine, however, why the capture of the mountain streams here seemed so desirable.

Construction of Pedlar Dam began on July 11, 1904, and the first water flowed through the 22-mile California-redwood pipeline to Lynchburg in 1907. For years, one crew of men did nothing but walk the pipeline to adjust the tension on hoops, preventing leaks. The original concrete-and-stone dam, 50 feet high with a stair-step spillway, was raised to 60 feet in the 1930s and 75 feet in 1965 and widened from 415 feet to 435 feet. Today, the dam holds 138-acre, 82-million gallon Pedlar Lake, which furnishes up to 14 million gallons of water daily to Lynchburg.

The lake is a frequent stopover for migrating waterfowl. Among the species spotted have been bald eagles, blue heron, osprey, swans, loons, Canada geese, hooded and red-breasted mergansers, mallards, buffleheads, and blue-winged teal. Besides beaver and otter, coyotes have been seen nearby.

Visitors are welcome, but fires, camping, bathing, and swimming are prohibited. Several times, hikers in difficulty have been helped by Don Johnson, the caretaker, (804) 922-7222 (daytime).

Points of Interest

Davis Mill Stream Falls: near northern end of the section, a beautiful set of falls, about two miles from Long Mountain Wayside, with a vertical drop equal to Lace Falls. Lesser known, yet close to a road, they require a bit of a scramble to reach. They are located in the upper left corner of USGS Forks of Buffalo quadrangle. Turn right off U.S. 60 onto Va. 634. In 0.9 mile, the falls are steeply downhill to the left on Forest Service land. Easier but longer access is at Oronoco *via* Va. 605 briefly, turning right in 150 yards on a dirt road (USFS 1246). Proceed to Davis Mill Creek, and walk upstream.

Brown Mountain Creek Valley: remains of old settlements and nearly two miles of a beautiful stream walk.

Pedlar Lake: reservoir for the city of Lynchburg. The Trail passes above this attractive lake, with its waterfowl and background of mountains. See entry above.

Swapping Camp Creek: Early settlers swapped goods, horses, and liquor, as well as lies, here.

Little Irish Creek: lively mountain stream with campsites.

Virgin-forest exhibit: 4.5-acre remnant of the magnificent forest that once covered eastern North America, especially white pine and Canadian hemlock.

Scare Rock: A rock with a legend lurks near the A.T. See entry above.

Circuit Hikes

Two circuit hikes are possible for those who don't mind gravel roads and an occasional passing car.

1. *Pedlar Lake:* A walk around Pedlar Lake is always pleasant. Bring binoculars for bird-watching. From the dam parking area, walk 0.2 mile back out access road, and turn right on USFS 39. After 2.2 miles, turn right on USFS 38, cross bridge, and ascend 1.2 miles to the A.T. Turn right (south) on the A.T. for 2.3 miles to the dam and parking area, for a total of 4.7 miles. Take U.S. 60 to Long Mountain Wayside, then take USFS 28 (south), and go left on USFS 39 to dam access road to parking area. Notify caretaker, (804-922-7222, 8 a.m. to 5 p.m.). No overnight parking.

2. *Brown Mountain Creek:* A walk that allows one to experience the history and beauty of the Brown Mountain Creek Valley without having to retrace one's steps. This utilizes USFS 38, which has some nice views on Long Mountain. Park at Long Mountain Wayside on U.S. 60, head south on A.T., down Brown Mountain Creek, for 3.8 miles. Turn left on USFS 38, and ascend 3.4 miles to U.S. 60. Total, 7.2 miles.

Road Approaches

The northern end of the section with ample parking is on U.S. 60, 17.2 miles west of the Amherst traffic circle off U.S. 29, 5 miles east of the parkway, and 9.3 miles east of Buena Vista (U.S. 501). USFS 38 begins at U.S. 60, 300 feet east of the A.T., and leads 3.5 miles along Long Mountain until it crosses the Trail 3.8 miles from the northern end. It then connects with USFS 39 about a mile south of the Trail intersection. USFS 38 and 39 are known jointly as Pedlar Lake Road. USFS 39 extends for 7.5 miles from U.S. 60, 2.5 miles west of the northern end of the section, to the A.T. near Pedlar Lake. In another six miles, it connects with Va. 607. USFS 311 (Little Irish Creek Road) follows the creek for 3 miles and roughly parallels the Trail to USFS 39, about 0.3 mile north of the A.T. crossing near Pedlar Lake.

Mostly unpaved Va. 607 (Robinson Gap Road) intersects the A.T. 0.3 mile from the southern end of the section, 6.6 miles southeast of Buena Vista and 9.0 miles northwest of Pleasant View (*via* Va. 640).

The southern end of the section, also with ample parking, is at milepost 51.7 of the Blue Ridge Parkway, 6.1 miles south of U.S. 60 and 9.9 miles north of Va. 130. You must notify a ranger if you wish to park a vehicle overnight.

Maps

For route orientation, refer to ATC Pedlar District Map or PATC Map 13. For area detail, see USGS Buena Vista topographic quadrangle.

Shelters and Campsites

This section has one shelter:

Brown Mountain Creek Shelter: built in 1961 by USFS; maintained jointly by USFS and the Natural Bridge Appalachian Trail Club; 1.8 miles from the northern end of the section; accommodates six; ample water (unprotected). Shelter often full; tent space nearby.

Next shelter: north 5.6 miles (Cow Camp Gap, on a 0.6-mile side trail); south 8.8 miles (Punchbowl, on a 0.2-mile side trail).

Attractive campsites can be found along Brown Mountain Creek opposite the shelter and 0.3 and 0.9 mile downstream.

A campsite is on Little Irish Creek 6.2 miles from the northern end of the section, about 0.1 mile west of USFS 39.

Regulations

The Trail crosses through the Pedlar Lake property on an 0.8-mile easement granted by the city of Lynchburg. Campfires, camping, swimming, and bathing are prohibited in this area. Elsewhere, the Trail is located in the George Washington National Forest, where camping and campfires are permitted, unless otherwise noted. *Note:* All water is untested. Blue Ridge Parkway rangers must be notified if vehicles are parked overnight at the southern end of the section.

Supplies, Services, and Public Accommodations

Hamm's Country Store, with limited groceries, is one mile west of the northern end of the section, at the intersection of Va. 634 and U.S. 60. On U.S. 60, 9.3 miles west, is Buena Vista (ZIP Code 24416), with groceries, restaurants, motels, and a coin laundry, and other services. Amherst (ZIP Code 24521) is 17.2 miles east on U.S. 60, with groceries, restaurants, motels, and coin laundry. The nearest bus stop is in Lexington, 9.9 miles west on U.S. 60. Buses also stop at Amherst, but none go to the A.T. Trailhead. Buena Vista is 7 miles northwest of the A.T. on Va. 607, 0.3 mile from the southern end of the section. Otter Creek Restaurant and Campground, 9.4 miles south from A.T. at milepost 60.8 on the parkway, is open from May to November. Wildwood Campground (commercial, 804-299-5228) is 1.4 miles south of the Blue Ridge Parkway on Va. 130.

In emergencies, contact the Amherst County sheriff's office in Amherst, (804) 946-9300.

Trail Description, North to South

Miles   **Data**

0.0   From Long Mountain Wayside (2,065 feet) on U.S. 60 near
       crest of mountain, cross highway diagonally to right, and
       descend through open area, passing beneath telephone
       cable. Begin gradual descent of 1,145 feet to Pedlar Dam.
       For circuit hike here, see section introduction.

0.1   Descend steps, and cross old road.

0.9   Crossing small branch, in 25 yards join old road and
       follow Brown Mountain Creek for next 1.8 miles, joining
       and leaving several old roads.
       During next 1.4 miles, pass old rock walls, foundations,
       chimneys, flood walls, property walls, road walls, rock piles
       from field clearing, and a deep, walled spring.

1.2   Cross side branch, and, in 90 yards, pass double chimney
       still standing across stream to right.

1.6   Sixty yards after ruins of house on left, pass old walled
       spring (Joseph Richeson Spring) 15 yards to left—unpro-
       tected water source.

1.8   Reach side trail to **Brown Mountain Creek Shelter** and
       privy, 45 yards uphill to left (two unprotected springs
       near shelter). Just beyond, cross foot log over Brown
       Mountain Creek, pass **campsites** on right, and follow
       right bank of creek.

1.9   Cross small side branch. In 75 yards, a rock flood wall
       appears on left bank of creek.

2.1   Pass campsite on left by stream.

2.2   A more prominent, 230-yard flood wall begins on far
       bank.

2.7   On left, pass **campsite** by stream and swimming hole.

2.8   Leaving old road, in 35 yards, cross footbridge over Brown
       Mountain Creek, and ascend.
       An excellent swimming hole is on the left at the bridge. As one
       ascends beyond the bridge, one can see Scare Rock across the
       creek along the old road. See entry in section introduction.

3.2   Cross old logging road.

3.4   Reach stone-framed spring (unprotected) 30 feet to left,
       and, in 90 yards, cross small branch.

In 0.1 mile, a yellow poplar tree, five feet in diameter and one of the largest in the Pedlar District, is 500 feet right (west) of Trail.

3.8   After joining old road and turning sharp left, in 20 yards, descend steps, and cross gravel Pedlar Lake Road (USFS 38). Descend from road.
For circuit hikes here, see section introduction.

4.0   Cross foot log over Swapping Camp Creek.

5.4   Trail skirts Piney Mountain 200 feet above Pedlar Lake, crossing nine gullies, several with seasonal water. Reach view to right before crossing small ridge in 190 yards.
View of Pedlar Lake and dam, Rice Mountain, and Bluff Mountain summit. Swimming, bathing in lake, and camping along the shore are prohibited. Atop Piney Mountain to left, a plaque to Chris Denney, killed by lightning on Cold Mountain, is on "The Magic Rocks," his favorite retreat, where his ashes were scattered.

5.8   Pass Forest Service boundary post at edge of Trail.

5.9   Descending steps, cross footbridge over Pedlar River at base of Pedlar Dam (elevation 960 feet). The A.T. crosses field diagonally left, and, in 250 feet, passes through fence onto dirt-and-gravel road, beginning 1,248-foot ascent of Rice Mountain, with its double crest of two high points each.

6.1   Join paved road.
Water faucet (caretaker's well water) available up paved road at end of dam by boat ramp. For circuit hike here, see section introduction.

6.2   Pass through gate. In 60 yards, paved road ends. Turn right onto gravel USFS 39 for 120 feet, then turn left from road. Cross footbridge over Little Irish Creek at large **campsite**, and follow creek upstream a short distance.

6.3   Turn sharp left, ascend 35 yards through barrier fence, and then switch back right.

6.5   Pass sign for 4.5-acre exhibit of virgin forest of white pine and Canadian hemlock on right. In 140 yards, just beyond gully, ascend left from old road, which continues ahead.

6.9   Cross dirt road, ascending steps on both sides.

7.3   Pass unprotected spring on right.

8.0   Pass wooded high point of Rice Mountain (2,228 feet), then descend through sag, and pass second rise.

Rice Mountain has seven high points of varying prominence.

8.5   In gap between the two high crests of Rice Mountain, cross overgrown old road.

Robinson Gap Road (Va. 607) near Enchanted Creek is 0.5 mile left. Little Irish Creek Road (USFS 311) is right 0.6 mile.

8.9   Pass crest of second-highest knob of Rice Mountain, then descend through sag, and cross second rise.

9.3   After distinct sag, cross first of two additional matching knolls.

9.8   Crossing another sag, reach final crest in the series of knobs.

9.9   Pass through barrier fence, and reach Robinson Gap Road (Va. 607), at intersection with Little Irish Creek Road (USFS 311). The A.T. crosses diagonally right.

Pedlar Lake is 4 miles downhill to immediate right on Little Irish Creek Road and USFS 39. Va. 607 to far right leads 6.6 miles to Buena Vista. Road to left leads 9 miles to Pleasant View (via Va. 640).

10.1   Pass side trail on left—which goes downhill 150 feet to reliable, unprotected, piped spring near large rocks just beyond culvert—then enter open area along parkway embankment.

10.2   Passing old homestead foundation 150 feet downhill to left, reach Trailhead parking area (elevation 2,170 feet) at parkway milepost 51.7, the end of the section. Trail continues diagonally right across parkway to bank on west side (see Section 21).

In ravine beyond cabin is evidence of an old whiskey still. See "Some Local History." Left is Va. 130 in 10 miles and U.S. 501 (near Big Island) in 12.2 miles. U.S. 60 is 6.1 miles to right. May through October, phone available at Otter Creek Campground 9.4 miles left.

Trail Description, South to North

Miles   **Data**

0.0   From parking area at milepost 51.7 of parkway (2,170 feet), Trail descends through trees, passing old homestead foundation 150 feet downhill to right, then bears left across parkway embankment.

In ravine beyond cabin is evidence of an old whisky still. See "Some Local History." Right is Va. 130 in 10 miles and U.S. 501 (near Big Island) in 12.2 miles. U.S. 60 is 6.1 miles to left. May through October, phone available at Otter Creek Campground, 9.4 miles right.

0.1   Pass side trail downhill, right, which leads to reliable, unprotected, piped spring near large rocks just beyond culvert.

0.3   Cross Robinson Gap Road (Va. 607) diagonally, at intersection with Little Irish Creek Road (USFS 311). Pass through barrier fence, and ascend on wide trail through laurel and rhododendron.

Buena Vista is 6.6 miles left on Va. 607. Pedlar Lake is 4 miles downhill to far left on USFS 311 and USFS 39. Road to right leads nine miles to Pleasant View (via Va. 640).

0.4   Cross first crest in a series of seven high points of varying prominence on Rice Mountain.

0.7   After crossing sag, bear right where old road heads left uphill.

0.9   After the first of two matching knolls, reach the second of this pair of knolls.

1.3   Ascend over rise, and, passing through sag, reach crest of second-highest knob of Rice Mountain.

1.7   Cross overgrown old woods road in major sag between two high crests of Rice Mountain.

Little Irish Creek Road (USFS 311) is 0.6 mile to the left and Robinson Gap Road (Va. 607) is 0.5 mile to the right near Enchanted Creek.

2.2   Skirt rise on right, and pass wooded top of Rice Mountain (2,208 feet). Begin descent, northeast, 1,248 feet to Pedlar Dam.

2.9   Pass unprotected spring on left.

3.3   Cross dirt road, descending steps on both sides.

3.6   One hundred forty yards after meeting old road on left, with Little Irish Creek below, pass sign on left for 4.5-acre virgin-forest exhibit of white pine and Canadian hemlock.

3.8   Switch back left downhill, and, in 35 yards, turn right.

3.9   Cross footbridge over Little Irish Creek. At far end, beyond large **campsite**, turn right onto gravel USFS 39. In another 120 feet, turn left onto paved service road to dam, and pass through gate.

4.1   Bear right from paved road onto gravel road along over-grown field.

> *Water faucet (caretaker's well water) available up paved road at end of dam by boat ramp. For circuit hike here, see section introduction.*

4.3   Cross footbridge (elevation 960 feet) over Pedlar River at base of Pedlar Dam. Ascend steep steps, then switchbacks, into woods, and begin gradual ascent of 1,145 feet to U.S. 60.

4.5   Pass Forest Service boundary post at edge of Trail.

4.7   Cross small ridge, and pass view to left. Trail skirts Piney Mountain about 200 feet above Pedlar Lake and crosses nine gullies, several with seasonal water.

> *View is of Pedlar Lake and dam, Rice Mountain, and Bluff Mountain. Swimming, bathing in lake, and camping along the shore are prohibited. Atop Piney Mountain to right, a plaque to Chris Denney, killed by lightning on Cold Mountain, is on "the Magic Rocks," his favorite retreat, where his ashes were scattered.*

6.3   Cross foot log over Swapping Camp Creek, and ascend.

6.4   Cross gravel Pedlar Lake Road (USFS 38), ascend steps, and, in 40 yards, bear left off old road.

> *In 0.2 mile, a yellow poplar tree five feet in diameter and one of the largest in the Pedlar District, is 50 feet left (west) of Trail. For circuit hikes here, see section introduction.*

6.8   Ninety yards after crossing small branch, reach stone framed spring (unprotected) 30 feet to right.

7.0   Cross old logging road, bear right, and descend slightly.

> *Descend to the bridge, and see Scar Rock across the creek along the old road. See entry in section introduction.*

7.4   Cross footbridge over Brown Mountain Creek, and, climbing bank, join old road in 35 yards. Trail follows creek upstream next 1.8 miles, joining and leaving several old roads.

> *An excellent swimming hole is on the right at the bridge.*

7.5   On right, pass **campsite** by stream and swimming hole.

7.9   Old stone flood wall is visible on other side of creek.

> *Other stonework ruins visible during the next 1.4 miles include foundations, chimneys, a deep walled spring, property walls, road walls, and rock piles from field clearing.*

8.1   Pass campsite on right by stream.

8.3   Cross small side branch.

8.4   Just after crossing foot log over creek, side trail leads right 45 yards uphill to **Brown Mountain Creek Shelter** and privy and two unprotected springs.

8.6   Pass old walled spring (Joseph Richeson Spring) 15 yards to right—unprotected water source.

9.0   Pass double chimney across stream to left, and, in 90 yards, cross side branch.

9.3   Rock ruins end here. Turn right, leaving old road and creek, and, in 25 yards, cross small branch. Trail ascends steeply by switchbacks.

10.1   Cross old road, and ascend steps.

10.2   After crossing under telephone cable in open area, reach end of section at U.S. 60 near crest of Long Mountain (2,105 feet). Trail continues diagonally right across highway to Long Mountain Wayside (see Section 19).

To left, U.S. 60 leads 1.0 mile to phone and limited groceries and 9.3 miles to Buena Vista. Right, Amherst is 17.2 miles. For circuit hike here, see section introduction.

Blue Ridge Parkway
(Punchbowl Mountain Crossing)
to James River (U.S. 501)
Section Twenty–one
10.9 miles

Brief Description of Section

The Trail in this section follows the sharply defined crest of the main Blue Ridge. It passes over the summits of Punchbowl Mountain (2,848 feet), Bluff Mountain (3,372 feet), Big Rocky Row (2,992 feet), and Little Rocky Row (2,448 feet), with excellent views from all but Punchbowl. The Amherst–Rockbridge county line is followed whenever the Trail is on the ridgeline. It then comes to the James River, where the Trail has its lowest point (659 feet), between Springer Mountain, Ga., and Harpers Ferry, W.Va.

Fullers Rocks, located near the summit of Little Rocky Row, provides the most spectacular view in this section of the James River, flowing through the Blue Ridge Gorge, and on between the Piedmont hills past the city of Lynchburg, where it turns northeast and disappears from view. About 1,800 feet above the valley bottom, this outlook also has a good view of the James River Face Wilderness and its bluffs on the southern side of the river.

The route passes over a number of sags, gaps, summits, and ridges. The hiking in this section is strenuous for the northbound hiker, who must climb 1,000 feet in one mile over a series of switchbacks to the summit of Little Rocky Row. The southbound hiker faces an easier walk. After the first two miles up Bluff Mountain, the Trail primarily descends.

The Trail follows old woods roads near both ends of the section. At the southern end, it reaches the James River just before the James River Foot Bridge. The remainder of the section is graded trail, with a number of switchbacks on steeper slopes, most notably those on the southeast side of Little Rocky Row.

Among the many wildflowers on Bluff Mountain, several orchids—pink lady's-slipper, whorled pogonia, and Southern rein orchid—have been found. Another, nodding ladies' tresses, has been seen near the Punchbowl Shelter. The rest of this section has its share of wildflowers, too, especially in the Johns Hollow area. In spring, look for trailing arbutus, birdfoot violet, bleeding heart, obolaria, and wild geranium, with redbud and shadbush above. Later, blazing star, cardinal flower, and false foxglove add color.

Rocky Row Trail

This 2.8-mile trail leads along a rocky backbone from U.S. 501, at a point 3.2 miles west of the A.T. and 2.3 miles from Glasgow (limited parking), to the A.T. and the top of Little Rocky Row. There are fine views both east toward Big Island and the James River Gorge and west toward Glasgow.

Saltlog Gap Trail

This attractive 3.8-mile trail, with nice views south, combines gracious old tread with roads of the abandoned mine in Slaty Gap. From end gate of USFS 36 (Va. 812), Hercules (Amlite) Road, take right fork (0.3 mile), reaching Slaty Gap in 1.3 miles. Switch back left (post) at 1.6 miles and at next switchback (2.7 miles), notice unusual quartzite field to left. A hike of 3.8 miles brings you to the A.T. at Saltlog Gap. See "Circuit Hikes."

Saddle Gap Trail

Part of the original 1930 A.T., this trail leads 2.5 miles from Hercules (Amlite) Road, USFS 36 (Va. 812), to the A.T. at Saddle Gap. On USFS 36 (Va. 812), the Trailhead is 1.7 miles north of the A.T. crossing and 2.7 miles from U.S. 501. Look for a large berm on left, in road curve 300 yards before quarry gate. Limited parking near gate. A fine circuit hike is possible here; see "Circuit Hikes."

Some Local History

The James River Gorge, a geologic anticline composed of Pre-cambrian and Paleozoic rock formations, is rich with history, due to its being a natural passageway through the mountains. Indians who traveled through the gorge had different names for the mountains north of the James River (Taweasus) and south of it (Occonachie). Buffalo, here in large numbers until the mid-1700s, used the gorge to move between the Piedmont and the Great Valley.

The first clash between Indians (Iroquois) and settlers in the area, on December 18, 1742, was near the confluence of the Fluvanna (now the James) and the North (now the Maury) rivers. The site can be seen from the Trail when descending south from Big Rocky Row. Some on both sides were killed, and the Iroquois fled along the chain of mountains to the Potomac. Later, a mediator ruled the settlers the aggressors, but, with payment of 100 pounds sterling, the Iroquois eventually relinquished their claim to these hunting grounds.

Pastor Robert Rose (see "Some Local History," Section 18) rode through the gorge c. 1750 with John Peter Sallings. Soon, Rose's double dugout canoe design was being used for commercial travel on the river. Then, Anthony Rucker's flat-bottomed batteaux navigated the James River, with one man to steer and two to pole. From the 1790s on, a rope ferry operated not far upriver from the Snowden (U.S. 501) Bridge.

A seven-mile Blue Ridge Canal, with towpath, was completed through the gorge on the Amherst side in 1828. John Jordan hired 100 men to build the Balcony Falls section. A towpath bridge was washed out in 1836 and never replaced.

Between 1829 and 1831, Col. Claudius Crozet engineered the Blue Ridge Turnpike, or the Natural Bridge Stage Road, "high above the river" where U.S. 501 is now.

The 49-mile segment of the James River and Kanawha Canal between Lynchburg and Buchanan was opened in November 1851. From Lynchburg to the James River Gorge, the canal was on the south side of the river. Packet boats and batteaux, pulled by horses and mules, moved commerce in both directions.

Aboard the packet boat Marshall, the body of Stonewall Jackson was brought through the gorge by canal, back to Lexington on May 14, 1863. As the Union Army took Staunton, the Virginia Military Institute (VMI) corps of cadets moved by road and canal through the gorge with horses and artillery from Lynchburg to Lexington on the evening of June 9,1864. Two days later, 250 cadets, forced to retreat from Lexington, fell back 2 miles from the mouth of the

North (Maury) River, taking "a position at a strong pass in the mountains to await the enemy." This area can be seen today upstream from the Trail.

The canal also was used for social travel. In May 1878, a group of gentlemen and ladies took "The Lady of the Lake" from Lynchburg to spend the day at the Natural Bridge.

Railroad competition and floods took their toll. The towpath became a railroad bed in 1881, first for the Richmond and Allegheny Railroad, later the C&O, now CSX.

In 1880, the Virginia Slate Mining Co. opened a quarry in what became Slate Quarry Hollow. Before that, slate could be picked up or pried out of the ground. The quarry, known as "Blue Hole" for decades, was expanded in the last thirty years to the Hercules, then Amlite, mine one sees from Rocky Row on the A.T. A legendary 19th-century bear hunter, "Bear" Tolley, was born in that hollow in 1811.

Other name changes are interesting. Bluff Mountain was known in the 19th century as "Thunder Hill." From Bluff Mountain, one can see Target Hill, where Stonewall Jackson did field-testing on the Parrott rifle in the late 1850s. Many now call it Hunter Hill, because Union General Hunter placed cannon there to fire on VMI in June 1864.

There are eleven maps with Belle Coe (not Belle Cove) Branch. After a century of being Piney or Big Piney Mountain, the mountain suddenly became Peavine Mountain in 1924. Silas Knob acquired the name of a surveyor who got lost there. Strangely, some early 20th-century maps show Fullers Rocks located on the west side of Big Rocky Row, yet shortly thereafter the name was used to designate the rocks on Little Rocky Row, as it does today.

The earliest Natural Bridge A.T. Club hike, and part of the original 1930 A.T., wound through this section. Much of the original route is still used along Rocky Row and over Bluff Mountain. North of Bluff Mountain, the original route was lost to the Blue Ridge Parkway. South of Saddle Gap, the original Trail descended to Rocky Row Run, where it followed a dirt road to the James River and U.S. 501.

Mention was made in Section 20 of the homestead at Punchbowl Crossing that produced moonshine. NBATC members ran into a moonshine operation in the 1930s, near Rocky Row. "The operator appeared not at all perturbed and asked them to sample his product. One member did a fair job of slaking his thirst and, when hiking was resumed, felt like he had wings on his feet and a most exhilarating feeling of buoyancy," said the leader.

In 1935, a different industry came to the area of the 1742 Iroquois-settler fight in Glasgow. Today, Lees Carpet, a division of Burlington Industries, has a thirty-four-acre building, the largest carpet manufacturing facility under one roof in the world, visible from the A.T. at two places just south of Big Rocky Row.

From the 1920s until 1976, a fire tower graced the summit of Bluff Mountain—first a wooden (log) structure, then a steel structure with a live-in cab. The area had been hit by two bad fires earlier. In 1894, a large fire swept over the whole Rocky Row area and over Bluff Mountain. Then, in 1918, a big fire destroyed everything on the north side of the James River to the Pedlar River. A 2,300-acre fire in 1963 moved from the river in the James River Gorge up to the summit of Rocky Row, where it stopped near the A.T. and moved around the west side to Battle Run.

Little Ottie

For years, hikers on the A.T. have been touched by the poignancy of a small monument a few yards from the summit of Bluff Mountain.

> *This is the exact spot Little Ottie Cline Powell's*
> *Body was found April 5, 1891,*
> *After Straying from Tower Hill School House Nov. 9,*
> *A distance of 7 miles.*
> *Age 4 years, 11 months.*

The events actually happened one year later than indicated. On a Monday afternoon in November 1891, five days shy of his fifth birthday, little Ottie did not return to Tower Hill School with the other boys as they returned with wood for the stove. A dragged stick in the path suggested he had turned the wrong way. The weather was cold. The search party grew to hundreds of people over many weeks. His father, a country preacher, ran a newspaper notice that described his son: "blue eyes, fair complexion, and light hair. He is intelligent."

Five months later, on April 3, 1892, four young men were using "the old Bear Trail" to cross from Amherst County to Rockbridge County, when their dog began barking on the top of Bluff Mountain. Little Ottie's remains had been found, his hat still on his head. His schoolhouse was 3.7 miles as the crow flies, and 150 degrees, or 8 degrees east of south-southeast, from where his body was found.

Points of Interest

Bluff Mountain (3,372 feet): an area landmark topped by prominent Norway spruce trees, visible for miles. A memorial plaque to "Little Ottie," lost in the 1850s, is at the summit (see entry above). Without the fire tower of 50 years, the Forest Service keeps vegetation cleared and vistas open for better fire detection.

Big Rocky Row (2,992 feet): spectacular rock cliffs, best viewed from the southern side of James River. Viewpoint just north of summit overlooks Peavine Mountain and Rocky Row Run area.

Fullers Rocks, Little Rocky Row: a popular destination for day hikes. Excellent view of James River Gorge and mountains from Big Rocky Row to Thunder Hill.

James River Face Wilderness/James River Gorge: On southern side of James River, the rugged terrain and steep bluffs of this 8,903-acre wilderness area can best be seen from the A.T. on Little Rocky Row. The James River is the largest waterway within Virginia, flowing 450 miles from east of the Allegheny Mountains to the Chesapeake Bay. It is estimated to be more than 160 million years old. Most rivers cut through the surrounding rocks, but the James River did not. Rocks on either side were uplifted.

Hercules (Amlite) Mine: This abandoned mine has graded trails leading to Blue Hole Quarry or Slaty Gap and Saltlog Gap. Fine views from the top.

Three Sisters Knobs: west of Big Rocky Row, an 8,150-acre roadless area now managed by the Forest Service as a remote highlands.

Circuit Hikes

1. *Bluff Mountain:* Wonderful views and access, twice, to Punchbowl Shelter and pond mark this circuit. Park at the A.T. crossing of Blue Ridge Parkway, milepost 51.7, ten miles north of

Va. 130 (ample parking). Walk 0.4 mile north on parkway to first gated road on left (unnumbered). Take that road for 0.2 mile, turning left on USFS 164. From here, almost to Bluff Mountain, one is walking on original 1930 A.T. In 0.1 mile at slight rise, bear left on USFS 164 where USFS 1154 continues straight ahead. In 0.2 mile, a side trip to Punchbowl Shelter (0.1 mile) is possible. On USFS 164, it is 2.1 miles to the A.T., near the memorial to Little Ottie Cline Powell and the summit of Bluff Mountain, with excellent views. Continuing on the A.T. (north) for 1.6 miles over Punchbowl Mountain brings you to a junction and a possible side trip of 0.2 mile to Punchbowl Shelter; 0.4 mile farther on the A.T. is the parkway starting point, after a total of 4.8 miles.

2. *Fullers Rocks:* The popular day-hike to the views from the ledges at Fullers Rocks can be enhanced by making it a loop hike that includes lots of elevation change and a segment of original 1930 A.T. Begin where the A.T. crosses Hercules (Amlite) Road, USFS 36 (Va. 812), 1.0 mile north from U.S. 501/Va. 130 (limited parking). Take the A.T. left (north), past the side trail to Johns Hollow Shelter, for 2.6 miles to junction with blue-blazed Rocky Row Trail. Bear right on A.T. Fullers Rocks—ledges with superb views—are on right in 0.1 mile. Continue on A.T. north for 2.5 miles, over Big Rocky Row, with another excellent view 0.1 mile beyond summit, to Saddle Gap. Here, turn right on Saddle Gap Trail for 2.5 miles of original 1930 A.T. At USFS 36, turn right for 1.7 miles to A.T. crossing and vehicle. Total, 9.4 miles.

3. *Sheppe Pond:* Take the Snowden USGS 7½-minute quadrangle with you on this short, but interesting loop to a hidden pond seen by few. The pond harbors a Coastal Plain disjunct, American storax, and several circumboreal sedges. Park at the A.T. crossing of Hercules (Amlite) Road, USFS 36 (Va. 812), 1.0 mile north from U.S. 501/Va. 130 (limited parking). Hike north (left) on the A.T. 0.6 mile to side trail for Johns Hollow Shelter, then about 0.2 mile farther on A.T. to an abandoned woods road. Here, turn right on unmaintained old road, which improves as it approaches USFS 36. After 0.7 mile, look for sign for trail left 0.1 mile to Sheppe Pond. After visiting the pond, continue on the old road 0.6 mile to USFS 36, where you turn right for 0.1 mile to the A.T. crossing and your vehicle. Total, 2.4 miles.

   4. Saddle Gap: This attractive loop includes 3.6 miles of original 1930 A.T. Begin at end of Hercules (Amlite) Road, USFS 36 (Va. 812), and follow Saltlog Gap Trail up to the A.T. From here to the end was part of the NBATC's first club hike in 1930. Turn left (south) for 1.1 miles to Saddle Gap (north end has rocky "horn" of saddle). Then descend left on Saddle Gap Trail to the road, turning left to quickly reach car. Total, 7.7 miles.

   5. Rocky Row Run: A simple, short loop hike that involves a walk on the A.T. along pleasant Rocky Row Run, beginning at the James River parking lot. Then on reaching USFS 36 (Va. 812), Hercules (Amlite) Road, turn left and return *via* the road (little traffic). Total, 2.0 miles.

   6. Combinations: Longer combinations of hikes 2, 3, 4, and 5 are possible.

Road Approaches

   The northern end of the section is on the Blue Ridge Parkway at milepost 51.7 (ample parking), 6.1 miles south of U.S. 60 and 12.2 miles north of U.S. 501.

   USFS 36 (Va. 812) begins 0.8 mile west of Snowden Bridge on U.S. 501/Va. 130 at the A.T. Trailhead and, in 0.9 mile, comes to the A.T. crossing 1.1 miles from the southern end of the section. This allows a shorter approach *via* the A.T. to Fullers Rocks on Little Rocky Row, and access to Saddle Gap and Saltlog Gap trails.

   The southern end is on U.S. 501/Va. 130, 4.0 miles west of Blue Ridge Parkway milepost 63.9, on the northern side of the James River; 5.6 miles west of Big Island; 5.8 miles east of Glasgow *via* Va. 130; and 13 miles east of Natural Bridge (on U.S. 11, near I-81). Ample parking. U.S. 501 and Va. 130 converge for 6.5 miles west of the Snowden Bridge.

Maps

   For route orientation, refer to ATC Pedlar District Map or PATC Map 13. For area detail, refer to the following USGS topographic quadrangles: Buena Vista, Snowden, and Glasgow.

Shelters and Campsites

This section has two shelters:

Punchbowl Shelter: built by USFS in 1961 and maintained jointly by USFS and Natural Bridge Appalachian Trail Club; 0.4 mile from northern end of section, on 0.2-mile side trail; accommodates six; water from unprotected spring in front of shelter, below the pond. This shelter is often full; tent space is nearby.

Next shelter: north 8.8 miles (Brown Mountain Creek); south 8.8 miles (Johns Hollow).

Johns Hollow Shelter: built by USFS in 1961 and maintained jointly by USFS and Natural Bridge Appalachian Trail Club; 2.3 miles from southern end of section, on a 0.1-mile side trail; accommodates six; ample water. Overflow tent space is nearby.

Next shelter: north 8.8 miles (Punchbowl); south 3.9 miles (Matts Creek).

This section has a number of possible campsites, and all have water (unprotected), except as indicated: Punchbowl Pond, summit of Bluff Mountain (no water), Saltlog Gap (water 0.5 mile west), Johns Hollow, and Rocky Row Run.

Regulations

Except for 0.1 mile within the Blue Ridge Parkway boundary at the northern end, the entire section lies within the Pedlar District of the George Washington National Forest. Camping is permitted in the national forest. Attend fires at all times. Campfires and camping are permitted on Blue Ridge Parkway land only at designated sites. *Note:* All water is untested. Blue Ridge Parkway rangers must be notified if vehicles are parked overnight at the northern end of the section.

Supplies, Services, and Public Accommodations

The A.T. crosses Va. 607 0.3 mile north of the northern end of the section. From this crossing, it is 6.6 miles north to Buena Vista (ZIP Code 24416, groceries, restaurants, motels, coin laundry, and other services).

From the southern end of the section, it is 5.9 miles west to Glasgow (ZIP Code 24555, groceries, coin laundry, restaurant, and motel) and 5.6 miles east to Big Island (ZIP Code 24526, groceries).

Otter Creek Campground and Recreation Area (camping fee, restaurant) is located on the Blue Ridge Parkway at milepost 60.8, 0.8 mile north of U.S. 130. Wildwood Campground (commercial, 804-299-5228) is 1.4 miles south of Blue Ridge Parkway on Va. 130.

In an emergency, contact the Amherst County sheriff's office, (804) 946-9300.

Trail Description, North to South

Miles   **Data**

0.0   Cross diagonally right from parking area on parkway at milepost 51.7 (2,170 feet), ascend bank on western side, and enter woods. Begin 700-foot ascent of Punchbowl Mountain.
      For circuit hike here, see section introduction.

0.1   Turn sharp left, with old trail to right.

0.4   Turn sharp left at junction with old road, straight ahead.
      *Side trail leads right 0.2 mile to **Punchbowl Shelter** and privy, with pond, **campsites**, and apple orchard nearby. Spring (unprotected) in front of shelter, about 50 feet downstream from pond outlet.*

0.6   Bear left, as old road enters right.
      Pass scattered stands of red spruce, planted by the Forest Service years ago, in next mile.

0.9   Cross wooded summit of Punchbowl Mountain (2,868 feet).
      The A.T. joins the Amherst–Rockbridge county line from Punchbowl Mountain to Little Rocky Row, whenever the Trail is on the ridgeline.

1.1   Cross old road in sag, and begin 600-foot ascent of Bluff Mountain.

1.5   Bear left, joining old road, and begin ascending seven switchbacks.

2.0   Reach summit of Bluff Mountain (3,372 feet), at site of former fire tower. *Caution:* Just beyond memorial to Ottie Cline Powell on left, take sharp left off road; begin 777-foot descent to Saltlog Gap.

Many l9th-century maps called this mountain "Thunder Hill." In recent years, the mature Norway spruce here have been dying. Views to northwest of Buena Vista, Lexington, Shenandoah Valley with Allegheny Mountains beyond and to southeast of High Peak on Tobacco Row Mountain. During very dry seasons, expect Forest Service personnel with binoculars and a radio to be on top. For circuit hike here, see section introduction.

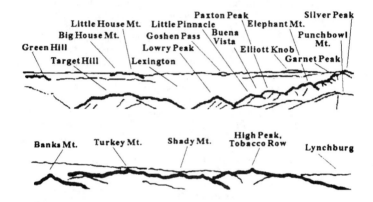

2.2   Switch back left. Old trail on right.
      From here to Saddle Gap the Trail follows original 1930 A.T. route.
2.8   Passing view of Little Apple Mountain to east and Silas Knob, Rocky Row, and Apple Orchard Mountain ahead to southwest, cross buried pipeline in small, cleared sag.
3.0   Cross small knoll with glimpses of Bluff Mountain behind, and, in 200 yards, bear left through tight saddle.
3.3   At large rock, switch back right.
3.5   Reach Saltlog Gap (2,573 feet).
      Not to be confused with Salt Log Gap between Rocky Mountain and Tar Jacket Ridge, 22.2 miles north. Water from Belle Cove Branch is normally available 0.5 mile to the west. To left, blue-blazed Saltlog Gap Trail leads 3.8 miles to USFS 36 (Va. 812), Hercules (Amlite) Road terminus. The term "salt log" comes from notches cut in a fallen log where handfuls of salt

> *were placed for livestock—the forerunner of the modern salt block. Ahead, look for spleenwort, a fern.*

3.7   Pass rock overhang on left.

4.6   Skirt natural amphitheater on the west side of Silas Knob and pass view to west of Maury River Valley and Allegheny Mountains, southwest of Three Sisters Knobs, and north of Hellgate Ridge. Reach Saddle Gap (2,590 feet).

> *Blue-blazed trail in gap leads left 2.5 miles to Hercules (Amlite) Road, USFS 36 (Va 812), and 27 miles farther, right, to U.S. 501. The rocks on the north end of gap have been called the "horn of the saddle." Silas Knob supposedly was named for an early surveyor briefly lost on the knob. The Three Sisters roadless area of 8,150 acres is being managed by the Forest Service as a remote highlands. For circuit hike here, see section introduction.*

5.2   Reach level area in minor sag, with views east.

6.0   Side path leads left 40 feet to excellent view (2,906 feet).

> *Left to right are the slate quarry, Peavine Mountain (Big Piney, until 1920s), High Peak of Tobacco Row Mountain, the James River, Terrapin Mountain, High Cock Knob, and Apple Orchard Mountain. The first slate quarry in operation here opened in 1880.*

6.1   Cross summit of Big Rocky Row (2,992 feet), and begin steep, rocky descent of 641 feet.

6.2   Pass upper rock field on right, with views west of Glasgow and Burlington Industries plant.

> *This rock field was labeled "Fullers Rocks" on maps of the Natural Bridge National Forest and the George Washington National Forest from 1927 to 1936. Currently, "Fullers Rocks" are identified as rocky ledges 0.9 mile south on A.T. In 100*

yards, there is a good view, 10 feet to left, as Trail switches back to the right.

6.6   Pass side trail, which leads right 40 feet to large flat rock with view west to Glasgow and Burlington Industries plant.

In May, note the carpet of moss pink or creeping phlox here and ahead.

6.7   Reach sharp sag, then begin ascent of Little Rocky Row.

7.1   Pass path leading left 30 feet to Fullers Rocks (2,472 feet), with view. In 35 yards, the Trail passes a second viewpoint, and, in another 35 yards, the Trail passes an excellent viewpoint 20 feet on the left.

North, east, and south are Peavine Mountain, High Peak on Tobacco Row, the James River as it winds through its gorge, and the James River Face Wilderness, with steep, forested bluffs, on south side of river. One is now standing on a dike of Unicoi quartzite, visible as a band of rock from Bluff Mountain to Little Rocky Row, that is part of the Blue Ridge Fault Scarp in the Loudoun-Weverton formation, extending some 200 miles.

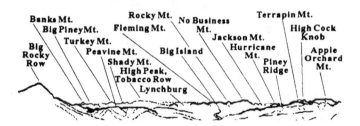

7.2   Reach trail junction (2,431 feet). A.T. turns left and begins 1,630-foot descent to Hercules (Amlite) Road, USFS 36 (Va. 812). Begin series of twenty-one switchbacks, with outstanding views of James River Gorge.

Blue-blazed Rocky Row Trail leads straight ahead 2.8 miles to U.S. 501. Follow U.S. 501, then Va. 130, to right about 3 miles to reach Glasgow. At the view beyond the junction, contemplate the fires of 1894, 1918, and 1963 here. The last one took 2,300 acres, from the river uphill to within yards of your viewpoint. See "Some Local History."

8.1 After sixteenth switchback, cross old road.

8.5 After switchbacks end, enter old road for 125 yards, then bear left away from road.

8.7 One hundred twenty yards after old road enters right, pass posts, and cross old logging road in slight sag.

8.8 Go down bank, and cross woods road.

9.2 Blue-blazed side trail leads left 400 feet to **Johns Hollow Shelter** and privy, between creek and unprotected spring.
     Many campsites behind shelter. Use stream for water, not the spring. One map calls this hollow the John S. Tyler Hollow.

9.4 Seventy-five feet after old trail joins from left, cross Johns Creek.

9.6 Cross minor crest.

9.8 Cross USFS 36 (Va. 812), Hercules (Amlite) Road.
     Road leads right 0.9 mile to U.S. 501/Va. 130 via Va. 812. For circuit hikes here, see section introduction.

9.9 Reach Rocky Row Run (760 feet) and turn sharp right on old woods road. Pleasant, level stream walk ahead.
     Good campsite 35 yards to left, with several campsites along the stream ahead. For 0.6 mile, the Trail is almost entirely on original 1930 A.T. route. Road used to haul slate from Slate Quarry Hollow.

10.1 Cross Johns Creek on old culvert, with swimming hole below in Rocky Row Run.
     Another good swimming hole is 0.4 mile ahead.

10.3 Pass under powerlines about 150 feet overhead.

10.6 Descend left, as original 1930 A.T. rises right.

10.7 Cross upper Rocky Row Run bridge.

10.8 Avoiding side trail ahead to boat ramp parking area, cross lower Rocky Row Run bridge.

10.9 Crossing terminus of USFS 36 (Va. 812), Hercules (Amlite) Road, leave the Pedlar District of the George Washington National Forest, and reach U.S. 501/Va. 130 and end of section. Ample parking nearby. To continue on Trail, cross U.S. 501/Va. 130 and approach James River Foot Bridge (see Section 22).
     Big Island is 5.6 miles east on U.S. 501, one mile beyond the Blue Ridge Parkway. Glasgow is 5.8 miles west on Va. 130. For services, history, or for circuit hikes here, see section introduction.

Trail Description, South to North

Miles   **Data**

0.0   From terminus of USFS 36 (Va. 812), Hercules (Amlite)
       Road, on U.S. 501/Va. 130, walk 45 yards north on USFS
       36 and enter Trail to right.
          Enter Pedlar District, George Washington National Forest.
          For services, history, or for circuit hikes here, see section
          introduction.

0.1   Cross lower Rocky Row Run Bridge. Avoiding access trail
       leading right to boat ramp parking area, turn sharp left.

0.2   Cross upper Rocky Row Run bridge.

0.3   Ascending, join old woods road entering from left.
          For next 0.6 mile, the Trail is almost entirely on original 1930
          A.T. route. Several **campsites** *can be found along the creek*
          ahead, with a good swimming hole in 0.1 mile.

0.6   Pass under powerlines about 150 feet overhead.

0.8   Cross Johns Creek on old culvert, with swimming hole
       below in Rocky Row Run.

1.0   Turn sharp left and ascend, leaving old woods road and
       original 1930 A.T.
          Good **campsite** *35 yards straight ahead.*

1.1   Cross USFS 36 (Va. 812), Hercules (Amlite) Road. Begin
       1,630-foot climb to Fullers Rocks.
          Road goes 0.9 mile left to U.S. 501/Va. 130. For circuit hikes
          here, see section introduction.

1.3   Cross minor crest.

1.5   Cross Johns Creek, and, in 75 feet, veer left, avoiding old
       trail to right.

1.7   Blue-blazed side trail leads 400 feet right to **Johns Hollow
       Shelter** and privy, between creek and unprotected spring.
          Many **campsites** *beyond shelter. Use stream for water, not*
          the spring. One map calls this hollow the John S. Tyler
          Hollow.

2.1   Cross woods road, and ascend bank.

2.2   Cross old logging road in slight sag. In 120 yards, old road
       leaves left.

2.3   Reenter old road, bear right, and, in 125 yards, as old road
       branches left, begin final 1,000-foot climb on twenty-one
       switchbacks to Fullers Rocks.

2.8   Cross old road.
3.7   Reach trail junction (2,431 feet) and crest of Little Rocky
      Row. A.T. turns right.

> *At the view before the junction, contemplate the fires of 1894,
> 1918, and 1963 here. The last one took 2,300 acres, from the
> river uphill to within yards of your viewpoint. See "Some
> Local History." To left, blue-blazed Rocky Row Trail leads 2.8
> miles to U.S. 501. Follow U.S. 501, then Va. 130, to right 2.3
> miles to reach Glasgow. The A.T. joins the Amherst–
> Rockbridge county line from Little Rocky Row to Punchbowl
> Mountain, whenever the Trail is on the ridgeline.*

3.8   Pass excellent view 20 feet on right at Fullers Rocks (2,472
      feet). In 35 yards, there is a second viewpoint, and, in
      another 35 yards, a path leads right to the last view from
      the Fullers Rocks area.

> *North, east, and south are Peavine Mountain, High Peak on
> Tobacco Row, the James River as it winds through its gorge,
> and James River Face Wilderness, with steep, forested bluffs,
> on south side of river. In May, note the carpet of moss pink or
> creeping phlox here and ahead. One is now standing on a dike
> of Unicoi quartzite, visible as a band of rock from Bluff
> Mountain to Little Rocky Row, that is part of the Blue Ridge
> Fault Scarp in the Loudoun-Weverton formation, extending
> some 200 miles.*

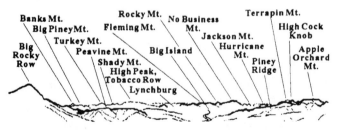

4.3   After small dip, reach major sag, and begin 641-foot ascent
      of Big Rocky Row.
4.4   Pass side trail leading left 40 feet to large, flat rock, with
      view west to Glasgow and Burlington Industries plant
      (see "Some Local History").
4.7   One hundred yards after good view 10 feet to right (south-
      east), as Trail switch backs left, pass upper rock field on

left, with views west of Glasgow and Burlington Industries plant.

> *These rocks were labeled "Fullers Rocks" on maps of the Natural Bridge National Forest and the George Washington National Forest from 1927 to 1936. Currently, "Fullers Rocks" are identified as rocky ledges 0.9 mile south on A.T.*

4.8   Reach summit of Big Rocky Row (2,992 feet).

4.9   Side path 40 feet right to excellent view (2,906 feet).

> *Left to right are the slate quarry, Peavine Mountain (Big Piney until 1920s), High Peak of Tobacco Row Mountain, the James River, Terrapin Mountain, High Cock Knob, and Apple Orchard Mountain. The first slate quarry in operation here opened in 1880.*

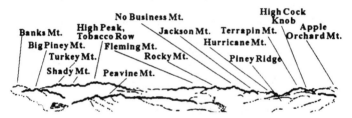

5.6   After 0.5-mile descent, Trail levels in minor sag with views east.

6.3   Reach Saddle Gap (2,590 feet).

> *Blue-blazed trail leads right 2.5 miles to Hercules (Amlite) Road, USFS 36 (Va. 812), and 2.7 miles farther right to U.S. 501. The rocks on the north end of gap have been called the "horn of the saddle." Ahead, the Trail is original 1930 A.T. route and skirts the natural amphitheater on the west side of Silas Knob, with views of Hellgate Ridge to north, Three Sisters knobs to southwest, and of Maury River Valley and Allegheny Mountains. Silas Knob supposedly was named for an early surveyor briefly lost on the knob. Ahead, look for spleenwort, a fern. The Three Sisters roadless area of 8,150 acres is being managed by the Forest Service as a remote highlands. For circuit hike here, see section introduction.*

7.2   Pass rock overhang on right.

7.4   Reach Saltlog Gap (2,573 feet). The A.T. begins ascent northeast 777 feet to Bluff Mountain.

Not to be confused with Salt Log Gap between Rocky Mountain and Tar Jacket Ridge, 22.2 miles north. Water from Belle Cove Branch is normally available 0.5 mile to the west. To right, blue-blazed Saltlog Gap Trail leads 3.8 miles to USFS 36 (Va. 812), Hercules (Amlite) Road terminus. The term "salt log" comes from notches cut in a fallen log where handfuls of salt were placed for livestock, the forerunner of the modern salt block.

7.6   Switch back left at large rock.

7.9   Two hundred yards after bearing right through small saddle, top small knoll with glimpses of Bluff Mountain summit ahead.

8.1   Cross pipeline in small, cleared sag, and ascend, passing views of Little Apple Mountain to right and Silas Knob to rear.

8.7   Switch back right, as old trail continues ahead.

8.9   Just beyond memorial on right to Ottie Cline Powell, reach summit of Bluff Mountain (3,372 feet) at site of former fire tower. Begin 600-foot descent by seven switchbacks.

Many 19th-century maps called this mountain "Thunder Hill." In recent years, the mature Norway spruce here have been dying. Views to northwest of Buena Vista, Lexington, and Shenandoah Valley, with Allegheny Mountains beyond, and to the southeast of High Peak on Tobacco Row Mountain. During very dry seasons, expect Forest Service personnel with binoculars and a radio to be on top. For circuit hike here, see section introduction.

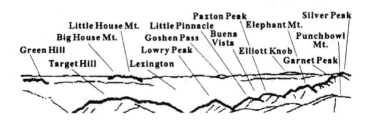

9.4   Trail veers right downhill as old road continues ahead.
       *A few red spruce, planted by the Forest Service years ago, can
       be seen in the next mile.*
9.8   Cross old road in sag.
10.0   Cross wooded summit of Punchbowl Mountain (2,868
       feet), and begin 700-foot descent to Blue Ridge Parkway.
10.3   Bear right, away from old road.
10.5   Reach old road and junction. A.T. turns right and de-
       scends.
       *Side trail leads straight ahead 0.2 mile to **Punchbowl Shelter**
       and privy, with pond, **campsites**, and apple orchard nearby.
       Spring (unprotected) in front of shelter, about 50 feet down-
       stream from pond outlet.*
10.8   Turn sharp right where old trail continues straight, and
       continue descent.
10.9   Reach Blue Ridge Parkway, milepost 51.7 (2,170 feet), and
       end of section. To continue on Trail, cross parkway diago-
       nally to right, and proceed north from parking area (see
       Section 20).
       *Right is Va. 130 in 10 miles, and U.S. 501 (near Big Island)
       in 12.2 miles. U.S. 60 is 6.1 miles to left. May through
       October, phone available at Otter Creek Campground, 9.4
       miles right. For circuit hike here, see section introduction.*

Glenwood District of Jefferson National Forest
James River (U.S. 501) to U.S. 220

This part of the Appalachian Trail follows the central Blue Ridge from the James River to the Great Valley of Virginia, just north of Roanoke. Although the route periodically crosses Blue Ridge Parkway land, most of it lies within the Glenwood District of the Jefferson National Forest.

Depressed near the James River, the Blue Ridge increases in elevation toward the south. Just south of the James, the A.T. route rises steeply to High Cock Knob and, from there to Floyd Mountain, follows the main crest of the Blue Ridge. On Apple Orchard Mountain, the southbound Trail reaches its highest elevation (4,225 feet) since Mt. Moosilauke in New Hampshire, more than 1,000 miles north. At Floyd Mountain, just south of Apple Orchard Mountain, the Trail leaves the main Blue Ridge, swings north into the Jennings Creek watershed, and traverses several long ridges, with winter views of the main crest. The route regains the main Blue Ridge at Bearwallow Gap and follows the crest, often very close to the parkway, until it descends to U.S. 11 and then U.S. 220 in the Valley of Virginia.

The Trail in this area passes through forests with occasional open views. The country is wild, and, after years of protection from fire, rhododendron and laurel surround the Trail. The parkway provides frequent access to the Trail but does not intrude on the impression of remoteness, except between Bearwallow Gap and Black Horse Gap, where the narrow crest of the Blue Ridge forces the Trail and parkway to remain close together.

As in the Pedlar District of the George Washington National Forest, the parkway was built along much of the original Trail route. The Trail was relocated primarily onto national forest lands, where it was initially protected by a 1938 Appalachian Trailway agreement between the U.S. Forest Service and the National Park Service. Much of the relocation was done before 1941, but World War II interrupted the work. It was finally completed in 1951.

Today, two member clubs of the Appalachian Trail Conference maintain this part of the Trail, in cooperation with the USFS. The Natural Bridge Appalachian Trail Club maintains the Trail from the James River to Black Horse Gap; the Roanoke Appalachian Trail Club, from Black Horse Gap to the Great Valley of Virginia (and beyond).

Shelters are located at regular intervals along the Trail in the Glenwood District. The few commercial accommodations available are listed in the individual sections.

Jefferson National Forest

South of the James River, the national forest lands through which the Trail runs are part of the Jefferson National Forest. Part of this forest was established in 1918 as the Natural Bridge National Forest under the Weeks Act of 1911, which provided for the purchase of "forested, cut-over or denuded lands" in order to protect watersheds from flooding and water-quality degradation. The Weeks Act was adopted at a time when much of the Appalachian and Allegheny ridges had been haphazardly logged and burned many times. The main thrust of the law was to protect watersheds from being destroyed by flooding. Later, as these lands again became productive, "multiple use," including recreation, became the guiding congressional philosophy for management of the eastern national forests.

In 1935, the name of the national forest was changed briefly to the Mountain Lake National Forest. Then, in 1937, the major boundaries of the newly named Jefferson National Forest were officially established, with 671,082 federally owned acres in Virginia, 18,211 in West Virginia, and 961 in Kentucky. Today, the Jefferson National Forest is administered jointly with the George Washington National Forest from a central office in Roanoke, Virginia. The boundaries of the federally owned land are marked with red-paint splotches on trees and by small metal signs on wooden backs attached to metal posts.

Trail Route in Glenwood District

This part of the Trail begins (southbound) at the James River (659 feet) and climbs 2,414 feet to the summit of High Cock Knob (3,073 feet). Along the ascent, the Trail passes views of the James River and its gorge and of the cliffs of Big Rocky Row on the northern side of the river. The route enters the 9,156-acre James River Face Wilderness, one of the first wilderness areas to be designated in the eastern United States (1975), just south of the James River and leaves it after descending High Cock Knob.

South of Petites Gap Road, the Trail passes through the 2,450-acre Thunder Ridge Wilderness. About thirteen miles of Appalachian Trail pass within the boundaries of those two wilderness areas.

The Trail passes through Petites Gap, just west of the parkway, and climbs steeply to traverse wooded Thunder Ridge. After descending the ridge, the route passes by Thunder Ridge Overlook on the parkway, providing extensive views to the north and west, including the James River and the Allegheny Mountains. The Trail then crosses the parkway twice, passes under The Guillotine, a suspended overhead boulder, and rises to 4,225 feet on the summit of Apple Orchard Mountain, the highest point in the central Virginia Blue Ridge. Spectacular views are afforded of the Valley of Virginia, the Allegheny Mountains, the 4,000-foot peaks the A.T. crosses to the north in the Pedlar District of the George Washington National Forest, and the Peaks of Otter area to the south.

South of Apple Orchard Mountain, the Trail traverses the west side of the main Blue Ridge for some distance, passing a side trail to Apple Orchard Falls and skirting Black Rock, a diorite outcrop with fine views to the west. The route then veers west, descending steadily from the main Blue Ridge across Floyd Mountain (3,560 feet), Bryant Ridge, and Fork Mountain, into the Jennings Creek watershed. It crosses Jennings Creek (951 feet) and ascends across the ten knobs of Cove Mountain, back to the main Blue Ridge at the south end of Cove Mountain and Bearwallow Gap, passing interesting rock formations.

Between Bearwallow Gap and Black Horse Gap, a distance of 8.1 miles, the Trail closely parallels the parkway. Hikers are never far from the sound of parkway traffic, but the frequent parkway overlooks provide excellent views. The parkway also provides easy access to the Trail at different points in the section.

South of Black Horse Gap, the Trail swings away from the parkway for the final time. It traverses the west side of the main Blue Ridge for some distance and eventually climbs to Fullhardt Knob (2,676 feet). As it leaves the Blue Ridge, it descends to the Valley of Virginia, which it crosses going into the Allegheny Mountains. This part of the Trail ends just west of I-81 in the valley.

The Appalachian Trail does not cross Virginia's famous Peaks of Otter—Flat Top (4,004 feet), Sharp Top (3,870 feet), or Harkening Hill (3,372 feet)—but the Peaks of Otter Recreation Area lies within 5 miles of the A.T. at Bearwallow Gap and within 6 miles of the A.T. at Cornelius Creek Shelter. This recreation area offers a number of facilities, programs, and side trails of interest to hikers (see Section 24 and 25).

James River (U.S. 501) to
Petites Gap (USFS 35)
Section Twenty–two
9.9 miles

Brief Description of Section

This section presents a strenuous challenge for hikers, especially for those walking south, as the Trail climbs from the James River Gorge (659 feet) to the summit of High Cock Knob (3,073 feet). The final stretch from Marble Spring to the summit of the knob is particularly steep, with an elevation change of nearly 700 feet in one mile over rough, partly ungraded footpath.

Hikers can see from the A.T. in this section the James River Gorge (see "Points of Interest") and the rocky cliffs that form Little and Big Rocky Row on the northern side of the river. The James River is the largest waterway within Virginia, flowing 450 miles from the Allegheny Mountains to the Chesapeake Bay. Its gorge, a geologic anticline composed of Precambrian and Paleozoic rock formations, cuts through the Blue Ridge between the Maury River near Glasgow and the Blue Ridge Parkway crossing at Otter Creek.

This section features a variety of terrain, ranging from the bluffs overlooking the James River to the hollows formed by Matts Creek and Big Cove Branch.

The variety of plant life in this area is probably unmatched elsewhere on the central Virginia Blue Ridge. There are 964 species of plants known to grow on the watersheds between Snowden and Glasgow, a river distance of 4.5 miles. The forest is an oak-hickory pine complex mixed with a number of other species. Carolina hemlock, in a unique mixing with Canadian hemlock, grows at its northernmost known point, where Matts Creek enters the James River. Mountain laurel and rhododendron, along with other evergreen and deciduous understory species, flourish in sheltered areas. Wildflowers abound in spring and summer—gay wings, trailing arbutus, galax, wintergreen, vernal dwarf iris, columbine, starry campion, Solomon's plume, and Solomon's seal. The fall brings purple asters, blazing star, Maryland golden aster, and the bright fruit of the strawberry bush (hearts-a-bustin'). Ferns are a prominent part of the Trail's edge. In Petites Gap, look in April for bloodroot, yellow violet, and trillium, wild geranium with rosypink flowers, both true and false Solomon's seal, and bellworts with drooping yellow flowers.

The Trail traverses 8.5 miles of the James River Face Wilderness. The wilderness has fewer blazes than elsewhere, but all trail junctions are indicated by signs, and points of ambiguity have the familiar white double blazes. This 9,156-acre wilderness, designated by Congress in 1975, was one of the first to be established in the eastern United States.

The longest stretch without water is the 3.6 miles between Big Cove Branch and Marble Spring.

Balcony Falls Trail

Fine views of Glasgow and the James River Gorge, with its rapids, are offered as this trail climbs through hardwoods and pines in the James River Face Wilderness. The Balcony Falls Trail, 4.1 miles long, connects Va. 782 and USFS 3093 with the end of the Sulphur Spring Trail 1.4 miles from the A.T. Hikers pass the Locher tract, where, until the 1970s, a 1792 log cabin with gun holes bored in the logs stood. Now, only the chimney remains. A circuit hike is possible using this trail. To reach the Trailhead, from Va. 130 at Natural Bridge Station, turn south on Va. 759 for 0.9 mile before turning left on Va. 782. Beyond James River Recreation Area, continue straight on a gravel road that becomes USFS 3093 for 0.7 mile to a parking area and Trailhead. Horses are permitted on this trail.

Sulphur Spring Trail

Utilizing an old roadbed, this 6.6-mile trail immediately enters the James River Face Wilderness and climbs past Sulphur Spring (unprotected), up Sulphur Spring Hollow to the A.T. (2.9 miles). Shortly before reaching the A.T., climb the 18-foot-high rocks on the left for a fine view. Then, with easy grades, Sulphur Spring Trail passes the Piney Ridge Trail, allows fine views of James River

Gorge, then crosses the A.T. again, and ends where the Balcony Falls Trail descends to Locher Farm and Va. 782. Just before Hickory Stand, the trail crosses a promontory called Lovers Retreat in the 1800s. Several circuit hikes are possible using this trail. The Trailhead can be reached by descending 2.6 miles from the Blue Ridge Parkway, near milepost 71, on USFS 35 through Petites Gap. Another approach is *via* Va. 130 at Natural Bridge Station, south on Va. 759 for 3.2 miles, then left (east) 3.2 miles on Va. 781, becoming USFS 35. A trailhead with limited parking is on the left by a bridge. Horses are permitted on this trail.

Piney Ridge Trail

This wonderful ridgetop hike of 3.5 miles was original 1930 Appalachian Trail. Amid chestnut and chinquapin shoots, hemlock, mountain laurel, and pine woods, the trail ascends Piney Ridge between Snow Creek and Peters Creek watersheds. The James River Face Wilderness is entered in 1.8 miles. One enters the 19th-century Glenwood Estate 0.3 mile beyond. Sulphur Spring Trail is reached at the terminus, where the current A.T. is 125 feet to the left or 2.3 miles to the right. The Trailhead is reached by turning west off U.S. 501 onto gravel USFS 54 (unmarked) about two miles northwest of Blue Ridge Parkway James River Bridge or 0.9 mile southeast of the south end of Snowden Bridge (U.S. 501). After 0.6 mile, just beyond Big Island Hunt and Fish Club, bear right uphill to limited parking. Beyond, the trail begins at a gated road. A circuit hike is possible here. Horses are permitted on this trail.

Belfast Trail

The main feature of this often-strenuous, 2.8-mile trail is access to the Devils Marbleyard or Belfast Slide, long a popular day-hike. (See page 135.) The East Fork of Elk Creek and the Glenwood Horse Trail are crossed quickly. Then, the ruins of Camp Powhatan, a former Boy Scout summer camp, are passed before reaching the Devils Marbleyard, an 8-acre scenic outcrop of loose Antietam quartzite boulders, at 1.4 miles. The open boulder field provides fine views of Arnold Valley and the Thunder Ridge Wilderness. Belfast Creek is crossed several times, and a small waterfall is passed. The terminus of the Gunter Ridge Trail is passed at 2.4 miles, and the Appalachian Trail is reached in 0.4 mile, on the west shoulder of Hickory Stand. Several circuit hikes are possible here. From Va. 130 at Natural Bridge Station, turn south on Va. 759, and go 3.2 miles to Va. 781. Turn left on Va. 781 for 1.5 miles to reach the Trailhead. Roadside parking is limited, with additional space on the left beyond the Trailhead. Another approach is *via* USFS 35 for 4.2 miles from Petites Gap on Blue Ridge Parkway, near milepost 71.

Gunter Ridge Trail

An old woods road is followed for 1.2 miles before the actual trail begins. Views of Bluff Mountain and Arnold Valley then reward one after ascending 18 switchbacks. Along the way, one passes Little Hellgate Creek and woods of hemlock, pine, beech, hickory, and oak, as well as galax, blueberry, and mountain laurel. Gunter Ridge Trail ends after 4.6 miles, when it intersects the Belfast Trail 0.4 mile from the A.T. To reach the Trailhead, from Va. 130 at Natural Bridge Station, turn south on Va. 759, and go 1.5 miles, turning left on an unpaved road just past the bridge over Elk Creek. Park here or farther along on the old road. At a house, take the right fork and, at the barn, the right fork again. Blue blazes then begin; they must be followed carefully.

Some Local History

The James River Gorge is rich with history as a natural passageway through the mountains. Indians who travelled through the gorge had different names for the mountains north of the James River (Taweasus) and south of it (Occonachie). Buffalo, here in large numbers until the mid-1700s, used the gorge to move between the Piedmont and the Great Valley.

Pastor Robert Rose (see "Some Local History," Section 18) rode through the gorge circa 1750 with John Peter Sallings, and soon Rose's double-dugout canoe design was being used for commercial travel on the river. Later, Anthony Rucker's flat-bottomed batteaux navigated the James River, with one man to steer and two to pole.

In the 1790s, a rope ferry began operating not far above Snowden Bridge (probably just below the current A.T. crossing).

The James River drops 26 feet per 0.6 mile in the gorge. A 7-mile Blue Ridge Canal, with towpath, was completed through the gorge in 1828. A towpath bridge, washed out in 1836, was replaced by a rope ferry.

Between 1829 and 1831, Col. Claudius Crozet engineered the Blue Ridge Turnpike, or the Natural Bridge Stage Road, "high above the river" where U.S. 501 is now.

The 49-mile segment of the James River and Kanawha Canal between Lynchburg and Buchanan was opened in November 1851. From Lynchburg to the James River Gorge, the canal was on the south side of the river. Now, packet boats and batteaux, pulled by horses and mules, could move goods in both directions. According to an 1852 account by H. Clay Pate, workmen building canal at the west end of James River Gorge blasted open a cave, inadvertently finding a skeleton on an old chest containing gold then worth more than $700, with a cross nearby. Relatives of the deceased had searched for three generations for gold bars hidden during the Revolution.

The 29,000-acre Glenwood Estate, now the heart of the Glenwood District, was owned by the Anderson family throughout the 1800s. Between 1850 and 1875, much of the lower forest area was clear-cut to fuel pits needed to produce charcoal for the production of pig iron. The Glenwood Furnace, a cold-blast charcoal furnace in Arnold Valley 32 feet high and 8 feet across, was built in 1849 and last operated in 1876. In 1864, Glenwood Furnace employed 116 men and 32 women and children and used 53 animals. The A.T. hiker enters the former Glenwood Estate either on the south slope of Apple Orchard Mountain or just south of Matts Creek.

Around 1740, John Poteet settled west of Petites Gap at the foot of the mountain, buying his land from John Greenlee. The gap that bears his name, misspelled, had a road through it within several decades. Thomas Jefferson, whose Poplar Forest estate in Bedford County was just east of the Blue Ridge, is documented as having crossed the mountains at Petites Gap in 1815 and 1817, *en route* to Natural Bridge, which he owned.

For a while in the mid-1800s, legendary bear hunter "Bear" Tolley had a cabin below Petites Gap on the east side. He supposedly had two roosters that would go high on a big oak tree on the side of the nearby promontory, provoking the name, "High Cock Knob." That name was used on all maps from 1893 to 1940, when "Highcock" appeared.

In the 1880s, maps show that Hickory Stand was known as Hellgate Mountain and that the knob on the southeast shoulder of that mountain was called Lovers Retreat. An 1881 map labels the bluffs in the west part of James River Gorge the "Balcony," now part of James River Face Wilderness.

Fire was a recurring threat to this area, apparently due to the nearby railroad. Forest Service reports indicate extensive fire damage in the Glenwood District area prior to 1911, with 10,000 acres "in a precarious condition from repeated fires." Major fires occurred in 1889, 1909,1920, and 1942. In the late l920s, many ridges were bare, according to hikers.

In 1930, the original A.T. entered this section from the north by proceeding east on U.S. 501 (0.9 mile), then right on USFS 54 (0.6 mile). The A.T. then ascended Piney Ridge Trail and, swinging left, followed the current path of the A.T. beyond Marble Spring to where it took the former Sulphur Ridge Trail around High Cock Knob to Petites Gap.

Beginning in 1933, various primitive shelters were built and destroyed at Marble Spring. NBATC members then scouted sites for a better Forest Service shelter, which was constructed in 1961. However, with the new wilderness status for that location, Marble Spring Shelter was removed in 1980 and rebuilt on Cove Mountain, 22.8 miles south. (See Section 25.)

The Devils Marbleyard

Also called Belfast Slide, this 8-acre boulder field of fractured Antietam quartzite is probably the most popular destination for dayhikers in the entire James River Face Wilderness. On the Belfast Trail, 1.4 miles from USFS 35 and Va. 781 and 1.4 miles from the A.T., it offers excellent views from the huge rocks. (See page 132.)

Geologists speak of such rock piles as talus. In this case, as with the dikes of Antietam quartzite visible in the James River Gorge, unusual metamorphic rocks still contain fossils—here, wormholes. As the mountain above (called Hunting Mountain in the late 19th century) was thrust upward, a plate of sedimentary rocks, originally at the edge of a sea, buckled and cracked.

The legendary version of this strange spectacle is more interesting. As the story goes, in the early 17th century, an older missionary, accompanied by a young woman, came to the valley and converted to Christianity the Indians who had in the past worshipped the Great Spirit on a high ledge under a pinnacle. An intense drought ruined crops and dispersed game, and blame was placed on the missionary. As the two intruders were being sacrificed by burning, a terrible storm smashed the pinnacle and ledge, turning them into the boulder field.

Points of Interest

James River Face Wilderness/James River Gorge: The James River, estimated to be more than 160 million years old, is Virginia's largest waterway, flowing 450 miles from the Allegheny Mountains to the Chesapeake Bay. Most rivers cut through the surrounding rocks, but the James River did not. Rocks on either side were uplifted. The gorge contains 964 plant species in 4.5 miles. The 9,156-acre wilderness is marked by rugged terrain and steep bluffs, along which trails offer views into the gorge.

James River Foot Bridge: at 625 feet long, it is the longest foot-use-only bridge on the A.T., and was constructed in 2000 on piers left from an 1881 railroad bridge. It is dedicated to Bill Foot (see page 139).

Devils Marbleyard: Eight acres of fractured boulders of Antietam quartzite, 1.4 miles from the A.T. See separate entry.

Glenwood Iron Furnace: an example of the stone furnaces scattered throughout the Appalachians; built in 1849 and located near Gunter Ridge Trailhead, 5.0 miles from A.T. See "Some Local History."

Locker Farm site: 1792 log cabin with gun holes bored in the logs, at trailhead for Balcony Falls Trail. Only the chimney remains.

Cave Mountain Lake Recreation Area: USFS campground with swimming, hiking, and picnicking facilities (6 miles south of Natural Bridge Station *via* Va. 759 and Va. 781).

Hickory Stand: for more than a century, a focal point for hiking in first the Glenwood Estate and then the national forest. Five trails converge around the top, while none actually crosses it. The knoll of Hickory Stand's SE shoulder called Lovers Retreat in the 1880s.

Circuit Hikes

Here are six circuit hikes that explore the major features of the James River Face Wilderness. Most are challenging, either through length, occasional steepness, or elevation change. By combining elements of these loops, one can create at least six other circuits, ranging from 9.4 to 17 miles.

1. *Balcony Falls–Gunter Ridge:* Segments of six trails comprise this loop, with excellent views of the James River Gorge, its rapids, and Arnold Valley. From elevation of 760 feet, ascend Balcony Falls Trail (4.1 miles), turn right on Sulphur Spring Trail (1.4 miles), then right on A.T. along side of Hickory Stand (0.5 mile). At high point of hike (2,650 feet), turn right on Belfast Trail (0.4 mile), then right on Gunter Ridge Trail (about 3 miles). At the Glenwood Horse Trail, the Gunter Ridge Trail turns right, joining the horse trail for 1.3 miles to Hellgate Parking Area at USFS 815. Turn left on USFS 815 (0.4 mile), then right on Va. 782 (0.7 mile) to starting point, for total of about 11.8 miles. To reach Trailhead, see directions above under Balcony Falls Trail.

2. *Devils Marbleyard–Gunter Ridge:* This loop features the popular 8-acre boulder field, with fine views of Thunder Ridge Wilderness. From a start at 1,040 feet, climb the Belfast Trail past the former Camp Powhatan to the Devils Marbleyard (1.4 miles). Continue uphill for 1.0 mile to loop's high point (2,517 feet) at junction with Gunter Ridge Trail, which you descend left (about 3 miles) to Glenwood Horse Trail. Turn left on the horse trail for about 1.9 miles to Belfast Trail, where you turn right 0.2 mile to reach starting point, for a total of about 7.5 miles. To reach trailhead, see directions above under Belfast Trail.

3. *Devils Marbleyard–Hickory Stand:* Another loop takes you by Devils Marbleyard and then along the A.T. in a pleasant walk above Sulphur Spring Hollow. Beginning at 1,040 feet, take the Belfast Trail up 1.4 miles to Devils Marbleyard, with its views of Thunder Ridge Wilderness, and then another 1.4 miles, past the junction with Gunter Ridge Trail, to the high point of the loop (2,650 feet) at the A.T. Turn right on A.T. (1.8 miles) to junction with Sulphur Spring Trail, on which you turn right (2.9 miles) to USFS 35. Here, turn right, and descend 1.6 miles on USFS 35 to starting point, for a total of 9.1 miles. In the last segment, it is possible to bear right off USFS 35 in 1.2 miles onto the Glenwood Horse Trail to the Belfast

Trail, where you turn left to your starting point (adds about 0.6 mile). To reach trailhead, see directions above under Belfast Trail.

4. *Sulphur Spring–Marble Spring:* Here are nice views down the East Fork of Elk Creek watershed and a nostalgic visit to Marble Spring, where a series of shelters existed from 1933 to 1980. An optional segment over High Cock Knob would add 1.2 miles and a 500-foot elevation gain. From 1,451 feet, climb Sulphur Spring Trail (2.9 miles) to A.T., turning right (south) 0.9 mile past Marble Spring area, to old junction where A.T. makes sharp turn left at high point in loop, 2,570 feet. (If High Cock Knob option is taken, turn left here on A.T. to Petites Gap, then turn right on USFS 35 to junction with Glenwood Horse Trail, left, and former Sulphur Ridge Trail, right.) Circuit hike continues straight 1.2 miles on former Sulphur Ridge Trail to USFS 35. *Note:* From junction of Sulphur Spring Trail to USFS 35, *via* former Sulphur Ridge Trail (2.1 miles), is original 1930 A.T. Cross USFS 35, and descend Glenwood Horse Trail 1.7 miles to USFS 35. Here, walk road back right 1.0 mile to starting point, for total of 7.7 miles. To reach trailhead, see directions under Sulphur Spring Trail description.

5. *High Cock Knob:* This loop ascends 704 feet over High Cock Knob, descends with views north of Rocky Row and Bluff Mountain, then returns on a little-used segment of the original 1930 A.T. Hike north on A.T. from Petites Gap for 1.8 miles, being careful at two steep spots descending north from High Cock Knob. Turn sharp left on former Sulphur Ridge Trail at junction where current A.T. goes sharp right. From here back to your car is original 1930 A.T., which Myron Avery (see page 152) measured then in the same direction. After 1.2 miles, reach USFS 35. Turn left, and ascend road 0.6 mile to the A.T. crossing in Petites Gap, for a total of 3.6 miles. Trailhead is on USFS 35, 340 feet west of Blue Ridge Parkway, near milepost 71.

6. *Piney Ridge–Matts Creek:* After a fine ridgewalk on original 1930 A.T., this loop provides outstanding views of the James River Gorge. Beginning at 960 feet, ascend Piney Ridge Trail (3.5 miles) to the Sulphur Spring Trail. Here, there are two options for the next segment: (1) Turn left on Sulphur Spring Trail for 120 feet, then right on well-maintained A.T. (2.3 miles), past Belfast Trail junction on west shoulder of Hickory Stand (2,650 feet), to junction with Sulphur Spring Trail. (2) Turn right on less-maintained Sulphur

Spring Trail (2.3 miles), with a fine view (2,600 feet) of James River Gorge. At this northern junction of A.T. and Sulphur Spring Trail, join A.T. downhill (5.3 miles) past open views of James River Gorge, Big Cove Branch, and Matts Creek Shelter. In 0.1 mile, turn sharp right on blue-blazed Matts Creek Trail to U.S. 501. Turn right on U.S. 501 for 0.9 mile, then right on gravel USFS 54 (0.6 mile) to starting point, for total of 12.6 miles. To reach trailhead, see directions under Piney Ridge Trail description.

Road Approaches

The northern end of the section (ample parking) is on U.S. 501, on the north side of the James River, 4 miles northwest of the Blue Ridge Parkway. U.S. 501/Va. 130 (combined for 6.5 miles) leads 5.9 miles west to Glasgow, 9 miles west to Natural Bridge Station, and 13 miles west to Natural Bridge interchange on I-81; Va. 130 leads 2.6 miles east to Lynchburg; U.S. 501 leads east 5.1 miles to Big Island, and 15 miles farther to Lynchburg.

The A.T. at Marble Spring, 2.2 miles from southern end of section, can be approached by an unmarked 0.8-mile side trail from Blue Ridge Parkway, milepost 68.7. Parking is 0.6 mile uphill at James River Valley Parking Area. Parkway rangers must be notified of overnight parking.

The southern end of the section is on USFS 35 (a continuation of Va. 781), 340 feet west of milepost 71 of the parkway (limited parking). It is 9.6 miles from Natural Bridge Station and 12.1 miles from Natural Bridge on U.S. 11, *via* Va. 130, Va. 759, Va. 781, and USFS 35. USFS 35 ends at the parkway and may be closed in the winter at the parkway.

Maps

For route orientation, refer to ATC Glenwood–New Castle Districts Map. For area detail, refer to the following USGS topographic quadrangles: Snowden and Glasgow.

Shelters and Campsites

This section has one shelter:

Matts Creek Shelter: built by USFS in 1961 and maintained jointly by USFS and Natural Bridge Appalachian Trail Club; 2.6 miles from northern end of section; accommodates six; water from creek above shelter.

Next shelter: north 3.9 miles (Johns Hollow); south 12.4 miles (Thunder Hill).

Campsites with water may be found upstream at Matts Creek and at the Marble Spring saddle. A dry campsite is passed on Grassy Island Ridge, at the northeast end.

Regulations

Most of this section lies within the Jefferson National Forest, except in the vicinity of Petites Gap, which is on Blue Ridge Parkway land. Campfires and camping are not permitted on parkway land, except in designated areas. Camping is permitted throughout the national forest, unless specifically noted otherwise. Attend fires at all times. Motorized equipment is not permitted in the wilderness area. *Note:* All water is untested.

Supplies, Services, and Public Accommodations

From the northern end of the section, it is 5.9 miles west to Glasgow (ZIP Code 24555, groceries, coin laundry, restaurant, and motel) and 5.6 miles east to Big Island (ZIP Code 24526, groceries).

Otter Creek Campground and Recreation Area (camping fee, restaurant) is located on the Blue Ridge Parkway at milepost 60.8, 0.8 mile north of U.S. 130. Wildwood Campground (commercial, 804-299-5228) is 4.0 miles east of the A.T. on Va. 130.

The southern end of the section is a considerable distance from supplies or services. A store with limited groceries is 8 miles north of Petites Gap on Va. 759 in Arnold Valley. Fifteen miles south on the Blue Ridge Parkway are the Peaks of Otter Lodge, restaurant, and campground. Seven miles north on the parkway and one mile east on U.S. 501 is Big Island (ZIP Code 24526), with groceries.

James River Recreational Campground (commercial, (540)-291-2727) is on Va. 782, about one mile east of Va. 759.

In the event of an emergency on the eastern side of the Blue Ridge, contact the Bedford County sheriff's office, Bedford, by calling 911 or (540) 586-7827. On the western side, contact the Rockbridge County sheriff's office, Lexington, (540) 463-7328.

Trail Description, North to South

Miles   **Data**

0.0   From U.S. 501/Va. 130, at junction with USFS 36 (Va. 812), Hercules (Amlite) Road, cross under CSX railroad bridge in 100 yards.

> *Under bridge, lowest point (659 feet) between Springer Mountain (southern A.T. terminus) and Harpers Ferry, W.Va. Here, boats entered a lock for the James River and Kanawha Canal after crossing river by towpath bridge (later, rope ferry) in mid-19th century. See section introduction.*

0.2   Leaving Amherst County, cross 625-foot James River Foot Bridge. Now in Bedford County, leave 1881 train bed and turn right at rock cliffs.

> *Bridge dedicated in honor of the late Bill Foot, thru-hiker, Natural Bridge A.T. Club president, member of ATC Board of Managers, and the driving force behind the bridge's construction. Trail follows both Blue Ridge Turnpike (1835) and old canal for 230 yards. The packet boat Marshall, carrying body of Stonewall Jackson, passed predawn, May 14, 1863, going to Lexington.*

1.4   Entering James River Face Wilderness (next 8.5 miles), Trail passes high rock walls along river and reaches **campsites** where Matts Creek enters the James River. Ascend along Matts Creek.

2.1   Pass blue-blazed Matts Creek Trail, leading left 2.5 miles to U.S. 501 at Snowden Bridge.

> *In 1920, a 2,000-acre fire burned Matts Creek and Big Cove Branch drainages.*

2.2   Passing **Matts Creek Shelter** and privy, cross wooden bridge over creek, and begin 1,820-foot ascent to Hickory Stand.

Bridge dedicated to Henry Lanum, former Trail supervisor, NBATC. Area by creek has Carolina hemlocks at the northern extent of their range. Rocks here are of the Hampton Formation, a Cambrian shale deposit more than 500 million years old. A.T. here enters the 29,000-acre Glenwood Estate of late 1800s, which it leaves on south shoulder of Apple Orchard Mountain.

2.9   Join Grassy Island Ridge at old **campsite**.

Occasional views to right of James River Gorge for next 2 miles. Rock outcroppings along here are Unicoi quartzite, results of pressure from the African plate colliding with the North American plate. In the gorge below, note the outcroppings of Antietam quartzite, crossing the James River near the Maury River, remnants of the African continent.

3.5   Bear right off Grassy Island Ridge, and ascend, then contour north slope.

4.1   Descending slightly, cross Big Cove Branch (1,853 feet). Sharply ascend nine switchbacks.

Avoid shortcuts on switchbacks. In this ravine, you'll find Hampton shale, but on the switchbacks ahead, you cross into Erwin quartzite.

4.5   Pass open view to right of James River Gorge, Big Rocky Row, and Bluff Mountain. Ascend two more switchbacks.

4.9   Shortly after another fine view to right of James River Gorge, reach crest of ridge (2,588 feet), turn sharp left, and immediately reach junction with Sulphur Spring Trail.

Sulphur Spring Trail leads right 1.4 miles to Balcony Falls Trail, which leads 1.1 miles to fine views of James River Gorge and then 3.0 miles to USFS 3093 and Va. 782. Sulphur Spring Trail to left leads along rim of James River Gorge, with good views, and rejoins the A.T. (at mile 7.2) in 2.3 miles. From this junction to Petites Gap, A.T. follows or crosses Bedford–Botetourt county line whenever on ridgeline. For circuit hikes here, see section introduction.

5.4   Reach trail junction on crest of western spur (2,650 feet) of Hickory Stand. A.T. turns sharply left.

Belfast Trail leads right 0.4 mile to junction with Gunter Ridge Trail; Belfast Trail then leads left 1.0 mile to Devils Marbleyard (see "Points of Interest") and 1.4 miles farther to Va. 781. Gunter Ridge Trail diverges right at that junction and leads 0.5 mile to a 250-foot path on right to a view to northeast of Bluff Mountain. Gunter Ridge Trail continues

       4.7 miles farther, joining the Glenwood Horse Trail northeast to the Hellgate Parking Area on USFS 815 near the James River Recreation Area on Va. 782. For circuit hikes here, see section introduction.

5.9   After rocky descent, reach low point with saddle on left.
       Ahead, in 1930s when this Trail segment was established, terrain here was very open, with a bare knife ridge separating Matts Creek and Elk Creek. Knoll ahead on left called "Lovers Retreat" in 1880s.

6.3   After ascending, bear left around shoulder, then descend.

6.5   Bear right, with distinct old trail to left, and, in 150 yards, curve left around shoulder.
       Views of High Cock Knob and Thunder Ridge to right.

7.2   In a level clearing in a saddle, cross Sulphur Spring Trail (2,415 feet), then bear right.
       Sulphur Spring Trail leads sharp right 2.9 miles to USFS 35 (Va. 781). Sulphur Spring Trail leads left 125 feet to Piney Ridge Trail, which diverges right and leads 3.5 miles to USFS 54, which leads left 0.6 mile to U.S. 501, 2.2 miles south of northern end of section. Sulphur Spring Trail to left continues 2.3 miles and rejoins A.T. at mile 4.9 above. Ahead, bearing left, is a side trail 0.25 mile to a seasonal spring (unprotected). For next 0.9 mile, the Trail is original 1930 A.T. For circuit hikes here, see section introduction.

7.4   Pass open view of East Fork of Elk Creek Valley and Thunder Ridge to right.

7.7   Pass **campsite** and site of former Marble Spring Shelter in sag (2,300 feet), with path leading right 330 feet downhill to Marble Spring (unprotected). A.T. continues straight and begins 773-foot ascent of High Cock Knob.
       Side trail bears left 0.8 mile to Blue Ridge Parkway (milepost 68.7), with parking 0.6 mile uphill at the James River Valley Parking Area.

8.1   Turn sharp left off graded trail, and continue up northern slope of High Cock Knob. Trail gradually becomes steep and rough, with views behind of Rocky Row and Bluff Mountain in distance.
       On left, 50 yards beyond sharp turn, is reported to be the site of bear-hunter Archibald "Bear" Tolley's cabin until 1879. For circuit hikes here, see section introduction.

8.7   Reach rocky, wooded summit of High Cock Knob (3,073 feet), and begin 704-foot descent to Petites Gap.

9.1   Crossing sharp sag after short, steep ascent, reach lower knob. The sharp sag is known by local natives as Archie's Notch, for Archibald "Bear" Tolley, a bear-hunter.

9.4   Reach broad sag, followed by two small rises.

9.9   Reach James River Face Wilderness information station, Petites Gap Road (USFS 35; 2,369 feet), and limited Trailhead parking 340 feet west of Blue Ridge Parkway, near milepost 71. Trail continues across road (see Section 23).
       Gap named for John Poteet, c. 1740; see "Some Local History." Fine stand of white pine and hemlock. For early flowers, and for circuit hike here, see section introduction.

Trail Description, South to North

Miles   Data

0.0   From Petites Gap Road (USFS 35; 2,369 feet) and limited Trailhead parking 340 feet west of Blue Ridge Parkway near milepost 71, pass James River Face Wilderness information station, and ascend steadily on wide trail, beginning 704-foot climb of High Cock Knob.
       A.T. traverses 9,156-acre wilderness area for next 8.5 miles. Gap named for John Poteet, c. 1740; see "Some Local History." Fine stand of white pine and hemlock. A.T. follows or crosses Bedford–Botetourt County line whenever on ridgecrest. For early flowers, and for circuit hike here, see section introduction.

0.5   Reach sag after second rise, then ascend steadily on rough trail.

0.8   Reach false summit, and descend steeply. The sharp sag ahead is known by local natives as Archie's Notch, for Archibald "Bear" Tolley, a bear-hunter.

1.2   Reach rocky, wooded summit of High Cock Knob (3,073 feet). Begin 773-foot descent to Marble Spring, on rough trail initially, with views ahead of Rocky Row and Bluff Mountain.

1.8   Turn sharp right onto graded trail, and descend gradually.

For next 0.9 mile, the Trail is original 1930 A.T. On right, 50 yards before this sharp turn, is reported to be the site of "Bear" Tolley's cabin until 1879. For circuit hikes here, see section introduction.

2.2   Pass **campsite** and site of former Marble Spring Shelter in sag (2,300 feet); path leads left 330 feet downhill to Marble Spring (unprotected).

Side trail leads right 0.8 mile to Blue Ridge Parkway (milepost 68.7), with parking 0.6 mile uphill at James River Valley Parking Area.

2.5   Pass open view of East Fork of Elk Creek Valley and Thunder Ridge to left. Trail circles deep gorge ahead.

2.7   In a level clearing in a saddle, cross Sulphur Spring Trail (2,415 feet). Beyond, A.T. leads left, following ridge around Hickory Stand, with views of High Cock Knob and Thunder Ridge to left.

Sulphur Spring Trail leads left 2.9 miles to USFS 35 (Va. 781). Sulphur Spring Trail also leads right 125 feet to fork where Piney Ridge Trail diverges right and leads 3 miles to USFS 54, which leads 0.6 mile to U.S. 501, 2.2 miles south of northern end of section. Sulphur Spring Trail continues from fork 2.3 miles and rejoins A.T. at 5.0 below, following rim of James River Gorge, with good views. To immediate right is a side trail angling back 0.25 mile to a seasonal spring (unprotected). For circuit hikes here, see section introduction.

3.4   After curving right around shoulder, in 150 yards, turn sharp left, avoiding old trail straight ahead.

When this Trail segment was established in the 1930s, terrain here was very open, with bare knife-edge ridge separating Matts Creek and Elk Creek.

3.6   Bear right around shoulder, and descend.

Knoll ahead on right called "Lovers Retreat" in 1880s.

4.0   Reach low point with saddle on right, and begin rocky ascent.

4.5   Reach trail junction on crest of western spur (2,650 feet) of Hickory Stand, where A.T. turns sharp right.

Belfast Trail continues ahead 0.4 mile to junction with Gunter Ridge Trail; Belfast Trail then leads left 1.0 mile to Devils Marbleyard (see "Points of Interest") and 1.4 miles farther to Va. 781. Gunter Ridge Trail diverges right at that junction and leads 0.5 mile to a 250-foot path on right to a view to northeast of Bluff Mountain. Gunter Ridge Trail continues

4.7 miles farther, joining the Glenwood Horse Trail northeast to the Hellgate Parking Area on USFS 815, near James River Recreation Area on Va. 782. Hickory Stand was called Hellgate Mountain in 1880s. For circuit hikes here, see section introduction.

5.0   Reach crest of ridge (2,588 feet) at junction with Sulphur Spring Trail. A.T. continues right, beginning 1,820-foot descent to Matts Creek, and soon passes fine view to left of James River Gorge. Descend two switchbacks.

Sulphur Spring Trail leads left 1.4 miles to Balcony Falls Trail, which leads 1.1 miles to fine views of James River Gorge and then 3.0 miles to USFS 3093 and Va. 782. Sulphur Spring Trail to right leads 2.3 miles back to A.T. at mile 2.7 above. Here, A.T. leaves Bedford-Botetourt county line, which it has followed or crossed whenever on ridgeline since south shoulder of Apple Orchard Mountain. Ahead, note in the gorge below the outcroppings of Antietam quartzite, crossing the James River near the Maury River, remnants of the African continent. For circuit hikes here, see section introduction.

5.4   Pass another open view to left of James River Gorge, Big Rocky Row, and Bluff Mountain, and begin steep descent by nine switchbacks.

During switchbacks (avoid shortcuts), you see Erwin quartzite, but, at Big Cove Branch, you'll see Hampton shale.

5.8   Cross Big Cove Branch (1,853 feet), then skirt northern side of ridge, with views left of James River.

In 1920, a 2,000-acre fire burned Big Cove Branch and Matts Creek drainages.

6.4   Join Grassy Island Ridge.

Rock outcrops along here are Unicoi quartzite, results of pressure from the African plate colliding with the North American plate.

7.0   At old **campsite**, descend right off Grassy Island Ridge.

A.T. leaves 29,000-acre Glenwood Estate of late 1800s, which it entered on south shoulder of Apple Orchard Mountain.

7.7   Cross wooden bridge, and reach **Matts Creek Shelter** and privy.

Bridge dedicated to Henry Lanum, former Trail supervisor, Natural Bridge Appalachian Trail Club. Area by creek has Carolina hemlocks at northern end of their range. Rocks here *are of the Hampton Formation, a Cambrian shale deposit more than 500 million years old.*

7.8   Pass blue-blazed Matts Creek Trail, leading right 2.5 miles to U.S. 501 at Snowden Bridge.

8.5   Reach **campsites** where Matts Creek enters the James River. Exit James River Face Wilderness, passing rock cliffs along river.

For 230 yards before bridge, Trail follows both Blue Ridge Turnpike (1835) and old canal. The packet boat Marshall, carrying body of Stonewall Jackson, passed predawn, May 14, 1863, going to Lexington.

9.7   Turning left onto 1881 train bed, and leaving Bedford County, cross 625-foot James River Foot Bridge.

Bridge dedicated in honor of Bill Foot, thru-hiker, Natural Bridge A.T. Club president, member of ATC Board of Managers, and the driving force behind the bridge's construction. Cross under CSX railroad bridge, lowest point (659 feet) between Springer Mountain (southern A.T. terminus) and Harpers Ferry, W.Va. Here, boats entered a lock for the James River and Kanawha Canal after crossing river by towpath bridge (later, rope ferry) in mid-19th century.

9.9   Reach U.S. 501/Va. 130 and end of section. To continue on Trail, cross U.S. 501/Va. 130 and go 35 yards up USFS 36 (Va. 812), Hercules (Amlite) Road, and turn right onto trail (see Section 21).

Big Island is 5.6 miles east on U.S. 501 and Glasgow is 5.8 miles west on Va. 130.

Petites Gap (USFS 35) to
Parkers Gap Road (USFS 812)
Section Twenty–three
7.3 miles

Brief Description of Section

In this section, the Trail crosses the summit of Apple Orchard Mountain (4,225 feet), the highest point on the central Virginia Blue Ridge. The peak was named for the similarity of its weather-beaten northern red oaks to the trees of an old, neglected apple orchard. The Trail that originally passed over the summit was relocated to make way for the Bedford Air Force Station. The station has since been phased out, and, although the summit is dominated by a facility for monitoring air traffic, the A.T. has been returned to the top of Apple Orchard Mountain, with its superb views both north and south. On a clear day, the Natural Bridge of Virginia is visible to the north-northwest, eight miles away. On the north side of Apple Orchard Mountain, the Trail passes through an interesting rock formation called The Guillotine, where the hiker must walk under a suspended boulder.

The Trail in this section also traverses the summits of Thunder Ridge (3,683 feet) and Thunder Hill (3,970 feet). No views are available from these summits, but the route has a number of outlooks. The Blue Ridge Parkway's Thunder Ridge Overlook, near milepost 74.7, provides unobstructed views north and west across the Valley of Virginia and toward the Allegheny Mountains. In winter and spring, the Trail provides many other vistas. Much of this section traverses the 2,450-acre Thunder Ridge Wilderness, designated in 1984.

For the southbound hiker, the 1,314-foot, 2.0-mile climb from Petites Gap (2,369 feet) through the Thunder Ridge Wilderness to Thunder Ridge is the most strenuous part of the section. For the northbound hiker, the major climb is the 790-foot ascent from Parkers Gap Road to Apple Orchard Mountain in 1.4 miles. Extreme caution is suggested in crossing Apple Orchard Mountain during electrical storms or in icy conditions at The Guillotine. During wet weather, the Trail immediately south of Petites Gap and the 0.3 mile south of Thunder Hill Shelter become soggy.

From Petites Gap to the Peaks of Otter, the hiker is on the Pedlar Formation, consisting of hard, granitelike, igneous rock, hypersthene granodiorite, that is a batholith more than fifty miles long. The whole group of peaks—Thunder Ridge, Thunder Hill, Apple Orchard, Onion, Rich, Headforemost, Flat Top, Sharp Top, and Harkening Hill—represent one vast mass of rock, which was at one time intruded, while molten, into overlying rocks, which were later removed by erosion, leaving the hypersthene granodiorite exposed. This rock forms a very fertile soil upon weathering, which accounts for all the luxuriant plant growth of these mountains. The finest forests, largest individual trees, and best laurel and rhododendron thickets of this area are to be found here. While rare stands of Carolina hemlocks are at the Thunder Ridge Overlook and Petites Gap, most of the forest cover in this section is mature hardwood with evergreen understory. Directly below Thunder Ridge, to the northwest, is a seldom-visited jumble of rocks and twisted trees, reputed to be a refuge for black bears.

This area is famous for its spring flowers—acres of large-flowered trillium, being crowded by mayapple, as well as a showing of bloodroot, showy orchis, large-flowered bellwort, mountain lily-of-the-valley, blue cohosh, and rattlesnake plantain (an orchid). Later, jewelweed takes over. The Thunder Hill stretch may provide yellow lady's-slipper, spiderwort in a variety of shades, tasselrue, fly poison, white clintonia, and more. Yellow clintonia, blue bead lily, twisted stalk, and spicy rose azalea bloom on Apple Orchard Mountain in May; later, there are stiff gentian, Turk's cap, and monkshood. There is a profuse display of rhododendron and laurel in the whole section in June. Some natives use the name "ivy," to mean rhododendron, while others use it to mean mountain laurel.

Except for a few stretches of old logging road, the section is graded trail. Water (unprotected) is available at trailside springs 0.9 mile (left) from the northern end of the section; at 1.4 miles (left) at Harrison Ground; at 4.7 miles (Thunder Hill Shelter); and at 4.9 miles at Apple Orchard Spring, a wet-weather spring 400 feet south of the upper Blue Ridge Parkway crossing at milepost 76.3. Off the Trail, water is available near the upper Blue Ridge Parkway crossing by walking 0.2 mile south on the parkway to a barred gate across from the road to the Apple Orchard FAA installation and going 300 feet down to the left on the timber road to a concrete structure on left with a spring. Three hundred feet farther is a second structure with a spring on the right. Water is also available from Harrison Ground Falls, with a steep, rocky descent less than 0.2 mile due west from the A.T. crossing of USFS 35 at Petites Gap.

Hunting Creek Trail

When the rhododendron or mountain laurel are in bloom, this is a very lovely approach trail to the A.T. In early summer, the rhododendron thickets, plus the mossy rocks along the short stream walk amid the hemlocks, make this two-mile trail an attractive segment in one of several loop hikes. On the A.T., the upper end is 0.5 mile south of the Thunder Ridge Overlook parking area and 0.1 mile south of the lower Blue Ridge Parkway crossing. For the lower trailhead at a switchback of Va. 602 (USFS 45), approach by either Va. 122, turning west on Va. 602, or by leaving the Blue Ridge Parkway on USFS 951 at the James River Valley Parking Area, milepost 69.3, then turning right on Va. 602.

Some Local History

Around 1740, John Poteet settled west of Petites Gap at the foot of the mountain, buying his land from John Greenlee. The gap which bears his name, misspelled, had a road through it within several decades of his arrival. In 1746, Poteet sold his land to Charles Sinckler, and the valley west of Petites Gap was known for years as Sinckler's Valley .

Arnold Valley, spread out to the west below Thunder Ridge Overlook, was named for Stephen Arnold, who established a homestead there in 1749.

Apple Orchard Mountain has been known by that name for at least 160 years, save for a period of about thirty years when it appears to have also been called Lee Mountain, after General Robert E. Lee. (See separate entry.)

Onion Mountain, also named for more than 160 years, has been called Ingin, Big Onion, Big Engen, and Big Indian. At one time, wild onions or ramps appear to have been abundant here.

The 29,000-acre Glenwood Estate, now the heart of the Glenwood District of the Jefferson National Forest, was owned by the Anderson family throughout the 1800s. Between 1850 and 1875, much of the lower forest area was clear-cut to fuel pits needed to produce charcoal for the production of pig iron. The Glenwood Furnace, a cold-blast charcoal furnace in Arnold Valley 32 feet high and 8 feet across, was built in 1849 and last operated in 1876. In 1864, Glenwood Furnace employed 148 people and 53 animals. The A.T. enters the former Glenwood Estate either on the south slope of Apple Orchard Mountain or just south of Matts Creek, depending on the hiker's direction of travel.

A legendary bear hunter, "Bear" Tolley, is believed to have had a cabin on the flat north shoulder of High Cock Knob until 1879 (see Section 22). The A.T. passes the location. After tramping these mountains for decades in pursuit of bears, he moved to Purgatory Mountain, visible from the top of Apple Orchard Mountain.

In the late 1800s, a hermit named George Harris lived on the side of Thunder Ridge high above Petites Gap; since then, the area often has been called Harrison Ground. See separate entry.

Around 1880, a tremendous fire on the Bedford side of the Blue Ridge ranged from Stony Creek, between Flat Top and Headforemost mountains, all the way north to the James River, more than seventeen miles.

On maps of the 1800s, Parkers Gap is shown as the site of several residences of Parker families. Calahil Parker, a Confederate sharpshooter, lived just below the gap on the North Creek side. Over a single glass of wine at supper each night, he always offered the same toast: "And likewise to General Lee, who tended strictly to his own business and let everybody else's be." Parkers Gap Trail, along which were telephone lines to the fire tower on Apple Orchard, became Parkers Gap Road in the 1930s, opening car access to Sunset Field and Camp Kewanzee from Arnold Valley.

On July 18, 1928, at 11:00 p.m., the German balloon, "Muenster," in an international race involving twelve balloons, crashed on Thunder Hill, after flying 415 miles from Detroit. The balloonists said that "they ascended to a height of 15,000 feet during a terrific windstorm and were immediately dashed down on the side of the mountains."

Their major injuries occurred in descending from the tangled wreck in the trees at night.

Much of the northern portion of this section follows the original 1930 Appalachian Trail. Two early metal diamond markers can still be found Trailside. The building of the Blue Ridge Parkway in the 1940s and the establishment of the Air Force radar station on Apple Orchard Mountain in the 1950s forced adjustments in the location of the southern portion.

Apple Orchard

This mountain, highest in the central Virginia Blue Ridge, has long been the visual focus for area mountain lovers, certainly for the seven decades that a tower in one form or another has been on top. Joseph Martin, in his gazetteer of 1836, noted that "the old hunters say that the most northern one, which is called the Apple Orchard, is the highest of all; its name is derived from the appearance of the trees on its top, which resembles an old, deserted orchard." The twisted and dwarfed northern red oaks have been distorted due to ice damage, more than just wind, and were recently cited as "an exemplary old-growth northern hardwood forest, classified as permesotrophic forest."

From the mid–1920s until 1942, a fire tower and a tiny one-room shack were on Apple Orchard. Then, a modern steel tower with a live-in cab was built. Bill Dawson, lookout in the summers of 1928 to 1930, remembered Myron Avery coming by in 1930 with a measuring wheel to establish the A.T.

Early in the 20th century, Patterson's Apple Orchard Camp became Gus Welch's Camp Kewanzee, serving young people for more than forty years high on a shoulder of the mountain. The original structure there was "The Bathhouse,"built of chestnut logs in 1829. The camp became a hiking center for the region and was host to a 1930 Potomac Appalachian Trail Club camp that helped further A.T. fever in this area.

Without roads, the mountain had a wild, remote feeling. One lookout said that wildcats screeching near the tower would "make your hair stand up on your head." A group day-hiking to the tower in 1939 recorded fifty-seven varieties of birds.

The A.T. crossed Apple Orchard for more than twenty years, until the 649th Radar Squadron, Strategic Air Command, established a radar station on top from 1954 to 1975. Gradually, more than thirty structures serving 225 men were constructed in a 15-acre area. After 1975, as the FAA continued radar for domestic flights, buildings languished, and a minimum-security prison was considered for the top of Apple Orchard. Then, U.S. Representative James Olin of Virginia worked to effect a successful cleanup of the mountain.

With the cooperation of the Forest Service and the efforts of an ATC seasonal crew and the Natural Bridge Appalachian Trail Club, the Appalachian Trail was restored to the summit of Apple Orchard in the 1990s. In the interest of the environment and safety, and to preserve the beauty of the setting, camping and fires are prohibited on or near the summit.

Harrison Ground

High on the slopes of Thunder Ridge, on the first level area (1.4 miles) as one climbs south above Petites Gap, the A.T. passes a small spring. In the 1860s, a bachelor built a cabin near the spring, secluding himself, one theory states, to evade conscription during the Civil War. His name is thought to have been George Harris, who was "in trouble in Lynchburg." A 1939 book states, "Legend has it that he was a murderer who fled from justice." Harris lived out his life there, and, according to a man who knew Harris, it was "Bear" Tolley who found Harris "laying across the bed stiffly, froze to death. His chickens were froze, too."

"Harris" probably became "Harrison." In the early 1930s, Ruskin Freer and other NBATC members passed a cabin there, but no trace appears to be left. During World War II, a logging road was built right to the area where the cabin had been. Older hunters remember their fathers telling of only a cabin foundation remaining thereafter. Hunters today refer to the dense rhododendron above the spring and on the summit of Thunder Ridge as Harrison Ground thickets.

From this spring and cove, a small stream—underground at times—descends and develops into some narrow, picturesque cascades close to Petites Gap. In wet seasons, the falls, now known as Harrison Ground Falls, can be heard from the A.T. crossing of USFS 35 in Petites Gap. Those small cascades can be found in the second ravine about 300 yards due west of the Trail crossing, after a very rocky descent.

Points of Interest

Apple Orchard Mountain: highest point on A.T. between Mt. Moosilauke in New Hampshire and Chestnut Knob, almost 200 miles to the south. Sweeping views. See separate entry.

Arnold Valley: historic, scenic, and recreational area to north of the Trail. Site of Glenwood Furnace (see "Some Local History"). The view of the west wall of the Blue Ridge from the valley is impressive.

Thunder Ridge Overlook: breathtaking view of Arnold Valley, James River, Valley of Virginia, and Allegheny Mountains.

Thunder Ridge Wilderness: 3.8 miles of Appalachian Trail pass through this 2,450-acre wilderness, designated in 1984.

The Guillotine: a narrow cleft of rock where the A.T. passes underneath a suspended boulder. Impressive example of Trail rock-work construction in the 110 rock steps nearby.

Harrison Ground: location of spring and former site of hermit's cabin above Petites Gap on Thunder Ridge. See separate entry.

Circuit Hikes

Six circuit hikes are possible in this section. All are pleasant, with some fine views, but none are less than eight miles long. Use of USGS 7½-minute quadrangles for Snowden and Arnold Valley would be helpful.

1. Apple Orchard Mountain: This loop crosses Apple Orchard for an expansive view, utilizing some original 1930 A.T. treadway in the ascent. It passes The Guillotine and then descends pleasant old woods roads on White Oak Ridge and the Glenwood Horse Trail for even more views. Park at Sunset Field on the Blue Ridge Parkway, milepost 78.4 (ample parking), and descend Parkers Gap Road (USFS 812) for 0.3 mile to A.T. Turn right (north) on A.T., and go 2.3 miles over Apple Orchard to the upper Blue Ridge Parkway crossing. Turn right on parkway for 0.2 mile to gate on left, across from road leading to FAA installation on Apple Orchard. Turn left on barred woods road, and, in 2.2 miles, reach USFS 45 (Glenwood Horse Trail) at rock cairn and Reed Creek. Turn right on Glenwood Horse Trail for 5.0 miles to end of road. Bear left on horse trail for 0.2 mile, then join old road uphill for 0.1 mile to Glenwood Horse Trail (wooden post at former Camp Kewanzee clearing). Here, angle right, following overgrown road 0.5 mile to parkway and starting point, for a total of 10.8 miles.

   2. *White Oak Ridge:* For this hike, one can either park at Thunder Ridge Overlook (view and ample parking) and then descend White Oak Ridge (view at old clear-cut) and end the hike by ascending Hunting Creek Trail, or start at a lower elevation, climbing to the A.T. and then ending by descending White Oak Ridge. The former adds 1.0 mile to total. The latter is described here. To reach Trailhead, (limited parking), follow directions for Hunting Creek Trail. Ascend Hunting Creek Trail 2.0 miles to A.T., turn left on A.T. for 1.2 miles, past Thunder Hill Shelter, to upper Blue Ridge Parkway crossing. Turn left on parkway 0.2 mile to gate on left, across from road to FAA installation on Apple Orchard. Descend left on barred road, and, in 2.2 miles, reach USFS 45 (Glenwood Horse Trail) at rock cairn and Reed Creek. Turn left on Glenwood Horse Trail for 2.6 miles, past Camping Gap (Reeds Gap), to sharp switchback in road (starting point). Total, 8.2 miles.

   3. *Apple Orchard/White Oak:* This hike is a combination of hikes 1 and 2. Park at Sunset Field, parkway milepost 78.4 (ample parking), and descend Parkers Gap Road (USFS 812) for 0.3 mile to A.T. Turn right (north) on A.T., and go over Apple Orchard, past The Guillotine, the upper Blue Ridge Parkway crossing, and Thunder Hill Shelter for 3.5 miles to Hunting Creek Trail. Descend Hunting Creek Trail for 2.0 miles to USFS 45 (Glenwood Horse Trail), where you turn right. Go 7.6 miles to the end of the road, then bear left on horse trail for 0.2 mile, then join old road uphill for 0.1 mile to Glenwood Horse Trail (wooden post at former Camp Kewanzee clearing). Here, angle right, following overgrown road 0.5 mile to parkway and starting point, for a total of 14.2 miles.

   4. *Thunder Ridge:* Here one can begin the loop at Petites Gap (ample parking) or at the Glenwood Horse Trail parking area on USFS 45. With the former, one climbs 770 feet at the end of the hike, while the latter has all the climbing in the first half of the hike, as described here. To reach Trailhead, from Va. 122, take Va. 602

(USFS 45) for 3.5 miles to parking area for the Glenwood Horse Trail. Begin by walking back down USFS 45 0.6 mile, then bear left off road onto the Glenwood Horse Trail for 2.8 miles, up Battery Creek to Petites Gap, and to the A.T., 340 feet beyond the parkway. Turn left on A.T for 3.8 miles, on original 1930 A.T. over Thunder Ridge, past Thunder Ridge Overlook and the lower Blue Ridge Parkway crossing to Hunting Creek Trail. Here, turn left for 2.0 miles to USFS 45 (Glenwood Horse Trail), and turn left on road for 1.0 mile to parking lot and starting point. Total, 10.2 miles.

5. *White Oak/Thunder Ridge:* Combining elements of hikes 2 and 4 produces a hike of 14.4 miles. One can begin at Thunder Ridge Overlook, Petites Gap, or the Glenwood Horse Trail Parking Area on USFS 45, all with ample parking. The advantage to the latter is that one starts low, climbs high, and descends during the last half of the hike. To reach parking area from Va. 122, take Va. 602 (USFS 45) for 3.5 miles. Follow directions for hike 4 to junction of A.T. and Hunting Creek Trail. Staying on A.T. south, follow directions for last half of hike 2, adding 1.0 mile farther on USFS 45 from Hunting Creek Trail (switch back in road) to parking area and starting point.

6. *Combination:* This huge leg-stretcher combines parts of hikes 2 and 4 or hikes 5 and 1, for a total of 20.4 miles. The idea is to walk the A.T. between Petites Gap and Parkers Gap Road over Apple Orchard, utilize Parkers Gap Road and the 0.5-mile access road to former Camp Kewanzee, then use the Glenwood Horse Trail between there and Petites Gap. One could start at Sunset Field, Petites Gap, or the Glenwood Horse Trail parking area on USFS 45, but, again, the latter is recommended, as is hiking in a counterclockwise direction toward Petites Gap first.

Road Approaches

The Trail crosses or comes near the Blue Ridge Parkway at five points in the section, making it easily accessible: at the northern end of the section in Petites Gap (340 feet west of milepost 71, on USFS 35, limited parking), at Thunder Ridge Overlook (milepost 74.7 on short side trail, ample parking), at the lower Blue Ridge Parkway crossing (milepost 74.9), at the upper Blue Ridge Parkway crossing (milepost 76.3), and at the southern end of the section near Sunset Field (0.3 mile north of milepost 78.4 on USFS 812). The parkway has ample parking 0.4 mile north of the lower crossing and limited parking 0.2 mile south of the upper crossing. Trail mileages corresponding to these points, from the northern end of the section, are 0.0, 3.3, 3.7, 5.0, and 7.3, respectively. Several short hikes are possible by using these access points.

From the northern end of the section on USFS 35, it is 12.5 miles north through Arnold Valley to Natural Bridge *via* Va. 781, Va. 759, and Va. 130. Using the parkway, it is 7.1 miles east from Petites Gap to U.S. 501.

The southern end of the section is on USFS 812 (Parkers Gap Road), 0.3 mile north of the parkway at Sunset Field, which has ample parking. Note parkway regulations regarding overnight parking. USFS 812 is not recommended as a road approach as it winds nearly 10 miles from Va. 781 in Arnold Valley through mountainous terrain to the Trail. The parkway is the best approach to the southern end of the section. Sunset Field is 14.5 miles south of U.S. 501 and 7.6 miles north of the point where Va. 43 enters the parkway from Bedford, Virginia. Also, see sections 25 or 26 for parkway approaches from Buchanan *via* Va. 43.

Maps

For route orientation, refer to ATC Glenwood–New Castle Districts Map. For area detail, refer to the following USGS topographic quadrangles: Glasgow, Snowden, and Arnold Valley.

Shelters and Campsites

This section has one shelter:

Thunder Hill Shelter: built by USFS in 1962 and maintained jointly by USFS and Natural Bridge Appalachian Trail Club; 4.7 miles from northern end of section; accommodates six; attractive walled spring (unprotected), an unreliable source after long dry season. See Trail data for alternate water source.

Next shelter: north 12.4 miles (Matts Creek); south 5.3 miles (Cornelius Creek).

Camping is possible in the area of Harrison Ground Spring (unprotected), 1.4 miles from northern end of the section. See "Harrison Ground." Good campsites (dry) are located on and around the summit of Thunder Ridge, 2.1 miles from the northern end of the section, where the nearest unprotected spring lies 0.7 mile north, 500 vertical feet downhill, on the A.T. Camping is prohibited on or near summit of Apple Orchard Mountain for environmental and safety reasons.

Regulations

Camping and campfires are prohibited within the Blue Ridge Parkway boundary, except at designated camping or picnic areas. In this section, the Petites Gap area east of the Trail, the Thunder Ridge Overlook area to about 0.4 mile south of the Hunting Creek Trail junction, and the upper Blue Ridge Parkway crossing area, about 1.3 miles of Trail in total, lie within the parkway boundary. The rest of the section passes through Jefferson National Forest, where camping is permitted unless noted otherwise. Please see restriction regarding Apple Orchard Mountain. *Note:* All water is untested.

Supplies, Services, and Public Accommodations

A store with limited groceries is 8 miles north of Petites Gap on Va. 759 in Arnold Valley. Peaks of Otter Lodge (reservations required), located at milepost 85.6 on the parkway, 7.2 miles south of the southern end of the section, provides the nearest lodging and restaurant (see also Section 18). Some 0.4 mile farther, the Peaks of Otter Camp Store has limited groceries and supplies (May through October).

Peaks of Otter Campground, 7.6 miles south of the southern end of the section at parkway milepost 86, has campsites with fireplaces (fee charged May through October). The USFS Cave Mountain Lake Campground (open May to November; bathhouse and swimming), 10 miles north of the southern end of the section on USFS 812 (more easily reached from northern end, *via* USFS 35 and Va. 781), also provides campsites with fireplaces. USFS Hopper Creek Group Campground on Va. 759, about 10 miles north of the northern end of the section *via* USFS 35 and Va. 781, offers campsites and fireplaces; reservations required.

In emergencies, contact the appropriate agency east or west of the crest ridgeline or on Blue Ridge Parkway land. East of the ridgeline county line, contact the Bedford County sheriff's office, Bedford, by calling 911 or (540) 586-7827. On the west side, from Petites Gap to 0.4 mile south of lower parkway crossing, contact the Rockbridge County sheriff's office, Lexington, (540) 463-7328. On the west side from 0.4 mile south of lower parkway crossing to Parkers Gap Road, contact the Botetourt County sheriff's office, Fincastle, by calling 911 or (540) 473-8320. Along the Blue Ridge Parkway, call (800) PARKWATCH.

Trail Description, North to South

Miles   **Data**

0.0   From Petites Gap Road (USFS 35; 2,369 feet) and limited
        Trailhead parking, 340 feet west of parkway near milepost
        71, begin 1,314-foot ascent of Thunder Ridge.
            Trail for next 3.0 miles is basically original 1930 A.T. Log-
            ging road was added in 1940s over much of original route. For
            circuit hikes here, see section introduction. Water is available
            at Harrison Ground Falls, 0.2 mile due west in second ravine
            after very rocky descent.
0.2   Pass sign for Thunder Ridge Wilderness.
0.4   Turn sharp left, leaving old road.
0.6   Descending, join old road.
0.9   Pass small, intermittent spring (unprotected) on left in
        moss-covered rocks.
            If dry, flow may be available 150 yards downhill. Note short
            loop of original 1930 A.T. a few feet above Trail.
1.1   At ridgecrest with views of Elk Creek and Arnold Valley,
        switch back left.
            Ahead, views of High Cock Knob to left.
1.4   Turn left, with old road going straight ahead, ascending
        steeply with occasional log steps. In 65 yards, pass Harrison
        Ground Spring (unprotected), 100 feet to left.
            Area here, to the summit of Thunder Ridge, is called Harrison
            Ground. See section introduction.
1.8   As old road turns right, A.T. bears left steeply.
2.1   After dry **campsite** to right, reach flat, wooded summit of
        Thunder Ridge (3,683 feet), with single large rock to right.
            Trail joins Bedford–Rockbridge county line which it follows

closely until 0.4 mile south of lower Blue Ridge Parkway crossing. Early in the 1900s, this summit was known as Blue Grass Knob and also as the north end of Thunder Hill.

2.2   Pass path to right leading to rocks with winter view of Arnold Valley and Devils Marbleyard.

Note rusted A.T. diamond marker from original 1930 Trail on tree here. Another one is 0.5 mile ahead on left.

2.7   Reach low point in sag.

3.0   Reach high point, passing top of knoll, and, in 140 yards, leave Thunder Ridge Wilderness. Small sign to left.

3.2   Cross gated gravel road.

Parkway is 85 feet to left.

3.3   Thunder Ridge loop trail leads left 140 feet to parking area. Bear right, and reach elevated stone overlook on right (3,501 feet), with extensive views north and west, including James River and Allegheny Mountains.

Several Carolina hemlocks, rare this far north, can be found here. Parkway milepost 74.7 is 0.2 mile beyond parking lot; U.S. 501 10.8 miles to left (north) along parkway.

3.4   Loop trail leads left to Thunder Ridge Overlook parking area.

3.7   Reach lower Blue Ridge Parkway crossing, at milepost 74.9.

3.8   Reach junction with blue-blazed Hunting Creek Trail (3,601 feet). A.T. ascends again, passing through rhododendron and sparse woods.

Hunting Creek Trail leads 2.0 miles downhill to Hunting Creek and USFS 45. In 0.3 mile, ridgeline becomes Bedford–Botetourt county line, which A.T. follows closely to the south shoulder of Apple Orchard Mountain. For circuit hikes here, see section introduction.

4.2   Ascending steeply, join old road, and bear left.

4.5   Pass high point in Trail on Thunder Hill.

4.7   Reach **Thunder Hill Shelter** and privy and walled-in spring (unprotected) 70 feet ahead, to right of Trail.

Spring unreliable in very dry weather; see alternate water source at parkway ahead.

4.9   Cross woods road. In 140 feet, to left under rock, is Apple Orchard Spring (unprotected), unreliable in very dry weather.

See alternate water source at parkway ahead.

5.0   Reach upper Blue Ridge Parkway crossing, at milepost
        76.3. Eighty yards beyond crossing, bear left, and gently
        ascend where old trail continues straight ahead.

> *For alternate water source, go left 0.2 mile along parkway to
> barred gate on left, across from road to FAA installation;
> descend 300 feet on old road to a concrete structure on left with
> spring. A second spring is another 300 feet downhill on right.
> Both springs are unprotected. To right on parkway, it is 12.4
> miles to U.S. 501. For circuit hikes here, see section introduc-
> tion.*

5.3   Leave woods, and ascend right edge of open, grassy field.
        Reenter woods in 100 yards.

5.6   Bear left, pass through The Guillotine, a large boulder
        suspended directly over Trail in a narrow rock cleft, and
        ascend rock steps.

> *Nearby, right and left, are two overhanging rocks (possible
> emergency shelter except during electrical storms). Begin
> series of 110 rock steps.*

5.7   Switch back right, beginning series of three switchbacks.

5.9   Bearing right onto old, grassy road near Thunder Ridge
        Wilderness sign, in 100 yards, reach top of Apple Orchard
        Mountain (4,225 feet), with FAA air-traffic radar dome.
        One hundred yards farther, reenter woods, and begin 790-
        foot descent to Parkers Gap Road, often on original A.T.

> *Apple Orchard is the A.T.'s highest elevation between New
> Hampshire's Mt. Moosilauke (4,802 feet, more than 1,000
> miles north) and Virginia's Chestnut Knob (4,409 feet, al-
> most 200 miles south). The radar dome can be seen from
> McAfee Knob, 55 hiking miles south, and from Cold Moun-
> tain, about 42 hiking miles north. Camping and fires are
> prohibited on or near the summit. Superb views from summit
> rocks of (left to right from radar dome) Little Onion Moun-
> tain, Suck Mountain, Onion Mountain, Headforemost Moun-
> tain, Flat Top, Harkening Hill, Purgatory Mountain, Back
> Creek Mountain, Pine Ridge, Thomas Mountain, Wilson
> Mountain, Natural Bridge, Big House Mountain, Little House
> Mountain, Goshen Pass, Elliott Knob (48 miles away), Thun-
> der Hill, Big Rocky Row, Punchbowl Mountain, Bluff Moun-
> tain, Rocky Mountain, Main Top, Bald Knob, Thunder Ridge,
> The Cardinal, Pompey Mountain, and Mt. Pleasant. See
> separate entry in section introduction.*

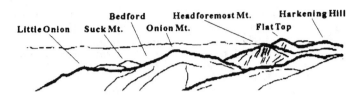

6.1   Bear right, with Coffee Table Rock (4,180 feet) to left.
6.2   Sharp switchback left, with old trail ascending to right.
6.6   One hundred yards after old trail enters from right, cross flat area.
6.8   Switch back sharply left, beginning series of six switchbacks over next 0.4 mile.
7.3   Descend steps, and reach Parkers Gap Road, USFS 812 (3,430 feet), with limited parking and end of section. Trail continues across road (see Section 24).

   Sunset Field, parkway milepost 78.4, is 0.3 mile left with ample parking. For circuit hikes here, see section introduction.

Trail Description, South to North

Miles   **Data**

0.0   From Parkers Gap Road, USFS 812 (3,430 feet), and limited parking, 0.3 mile north of Sunset Field at parkway milepost 78.4, climb wooden steps, and begin 790-foot ascent of Apple Orchard Mountain, often on original 1930 A.T.
   For circuit hikes here, see section introduction.

0.2   Switch back sharply left, beginning series of six switch-
       backs over next 0.4 mile.

> *Along main ridgeline, A.T. begins to follow Bedford–Botetourt county line closely, until 0.4 mile south of lower Blue Ridge Parkway crossing.*

0.7   Cross flat area, and, in 100 yards, bear right, with old trail
       continuing straight ahead.

1.1   Sharp switchback right, with old trail straight ahead.

1.2   Bear left. Coffee Table Rock (4,180 feet) is straight ahead.

1.4   Leaving woods, in 100 yards, reach top of Apple Orchard
       (4,225 feet), with FAA air-traffic radar dome. One hun-
       dred yards down slope, enter grassy road near Thunder
       Ridge Wilderness sign, and turn left immediately into
       woods.

> *Apple Orchard is the A.T.'s highest elevation between Virginia's Chestnut Knob (4,409 feet almost 200 miles south) and New Hampshire's Mt. Moosilauke (4,802 feet, more than 1,000 miles north). The radar dome can be seen from McAfee Knob, 55 hiking miles south, and from Cold Mountain, about 42 hiking miles north. Camping and fires are prohibited on or near the summit. Superb views from summit rocks of (left to right from radar dome) Little Onion Mountain, Suck Mountain, Onion Mountain, Headforemost Mountain, Flat Top, Harkening Hill, Purgatory Mountain, Back Creek Mountain, Pine Ridge, Thomas Mountain, Wilson Mountain, Natural Bridge, Big House Mountain, Little House Mountain, Goshen Pass, Elliott Knob (48 miles away), Thunder Hill, Big Rocky Row, Punchbowl Mountain, Bluff Mountain, Rocky Mountain, Main Top, Bald Knob, Thunder Ridge, The Cardinal, Pompey Mountain, and Mt. Pleasant. See section introduction.*

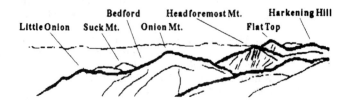

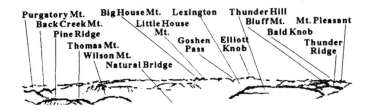

1.5   Switch back left, beginning series of three switchbacks. Begin series of 110 rock steps.

1.7   After rock steps, pass through The Guillotine, a large boulder suspended directly over Trail in a narrow rock cleft. Ascend, and bear right.
      Two overhanging rocks (possible emergency shelters except during lightning storms) are nearby, right and left.

1.9   Leave woods, and cross left edge of open, grassy field. Reenter woods in 100 yards.

2.3   Bearing right, with old trail on left, in 80 yards reach upper Blue Ridge Parkway crossing at milepost 76.3.
      Within 0.3 mile ahead are two water sources, both unreliable in very dry weather. For alternate water source, go right on parkway 0.2 mile to a barred gate, left, across from road to FAA installation; descend 300 feet on timber road to a concrete structure on left with spring. A second spring is another 300 feet downhill to right. Both springs are unprotected. To left on parkway, it is 12.4 miles to U.S. 501. Level ridge between Thunder Hill and Apple Orchard was called Camping Ridge in the 1920s. For circuit hikes here, see section introduction.

2.4   One hundred forty feet beyond Apple Orchard Spring (unprotected), to right under rock, cross woods road.
      Spring is unreliable in dry weather.

2.6   Reach **Thunder Hill Shelter** and privy and walled-in spring (unprotected) 70 feet before shelter, to left of Trail.
      Spring is unreliable in very dry weather.

2.8   Pass high point in Trail on Thunder Hill.
      In 1928, a German balloon in an international race crashed on Thunder Hill.

3.1   Turn right off old road, and descend. In 0.1 mile, ridgeline
      becomes the Bedford–Rockbridge county line, which the
      A.T. follows closely until the top of Thunder Ridge.

3.5   Reach junction with blue-blazed Hunting Creek Trail
      (3,601 feet).
          *Hunting Creek Trail leads right 2.0 miles downhill to Hunt-
          ing Creek and USFS 45. For circuit hikes here, see section
          introduction.*

3.6   Reach lower Blue Ridge Parkway crossing at milepost
      74.9.

3.9   Loop trail leads right to Thunder Ridge Overlook parking
      area.

4.0   Reach elevated stone overlook on left (3,501 feet), with
      extensive views north and west, including James River
      and Allegheny Mountains.
          *Thunder Ridge Loop Trail, which enters from right, leads 140
          feet to parking area. Several Carolina hemlocks, rare this far
          north, can be found here. A 2,450-acre section of Jefferson
          National Forest between Blue Ridge Parkway and Arnold
          Valley comprises Thunder Ridge Wilderness. Parkway mile-
          post 74.7 is 0.2 mile beyond parking lot, with Va. 501 10.8
          miles to left (north).*

4.1   Cross gated gravel road.
          *Parkway is 85 feet to right. Trail for next 3.0 miles is basically
          original 1930 A.T. Logging road added in 1940s over much of
          original route.*

4.3   Reenter Thunder Ridge Wilderness. Small sign on right.

4.4   Reach high point, passing top of knoll.
          *Ahead on right is tree with rusted A.T. diamond marker from
          original Trail.*

4.6   Reach low point in sag, then ascend Thunder Ridge.

5.1   Pass path on left leading to rocks with winter view of
      Arnold Valley and Devils Marbleyard.
          Another rusted 1930 diamond marker on tree here.

5.2   Reach flat, wooded summit of Thunder Ridge (3,683 feet),
      with single large rock to left, and begin 1,314-foot descent
      to Petites Gap.
          Trail left leads to dry **campsite**. *Early in the 1900s, this
          summit was known as Blue Grass Knob, and also as the north
          end of Thunder Hill. Area here to the spring called Harrison
          Ground. See section introduction.*

5.9   Pass Harrison Ground Spring (unprotected), 100 feet to right, and, in 65 yards, join another old road, and bear right, with views of High Cock Knob ahead.

6.2   At ridgecrest with views of Elk Creek and Arnold Valley, switch back sharply right.

6.4   Pass intermittent spring (unprotected) on right in moss-covered rocks.

If dry, flow may be available 150 yards downhill.

6.7   Bear right uphill off old road.

6.9   Rejoining old road, turn sharp right.

7.2   Leave Thunder Ridge Wilderness.

7.3   Reach Petites Gap Road (USFS 35; 2,369 feet) and limited Trailhead parking, 340 feet west of parkway milepost 71, and end of section. Trail continues across road (see Section 22).

Water is available at Harrison Ground Falls, 0.2 mile due west in second ravine after very rocky descent. For circuit hikes here, see section introduction.

Parkers Gap Road (USFS 812) to Jennings Creek Road (Va. 614)
Section Twenty–four
11.4 miles

Brief Description of Section

The Trail in this section leads over high land that divides the headwaters of North and Middle creeks, both of which are tributaries of Jennings Creek. More expansive views of the Blue Ridge are visible after the leaves fall in autumn. While some limited views east of Apple Orchard Mountain and south of Peaks of Otter are possible elsewhere along this section of the Trail, Black Rock provides an outstanding vista.

The northern three miles of the section make a U-shaped traverse on the northern side of the main Blue Ridge, at about 3,200 feet in elevation. Generally paralleling the Blue Ridge Parkway, the route passes over several spur ridges in a mature forest. It skirts the edge of the "Mash," a jungle-like area of dense laurel, rhododendron, and large hemlocks (ideal wildlife cover). At edge of the Trail, yellow and pink lady's-slippers, galax, Canada mayflower, starflower, and purple-fringed orchid may be found in the spring. The Trail then passes Black Rock, an outcrop of diorite with views to the north and west. In the vicinity of Black Rock and the headwaters of Cornelius Creek is a very rich cove of hardwood forest with large, virgin sugar maples and hemlocks and an understory of ericaceous shrubs, including the Catawba rhododendron, azaleas, and fetter bush, which exhibit a brilliant display during May.

In the middle part of the section, the Trail traverses the crest of Floyd Mountain (3,560 feet), the highest point in the section, and Bryant Ridge. A number of fallen chestnut trees on Floyd Mountain and Bryant Ridge are evidence of the widespread oak-hickory-chestnut forests common to the eastern United States before the chestnut blight in the early part of the 20th century. A variety of plants, such as columbine, starry campion, jewelweed (including an unusual white form), Deptford pink, tall bellflower, bergamot, false foxglove, and many others, bloom in late summer and early fall in this part of the section.

The Trail leaves the main Blue Ridge at Floyd Mountain and swings north, then west, descending steadily to Hamps Branch, before ascending Fork Mountain (2,042 feet) and descending to Jennings Creek (951 feet). Northbound hikers face a total climb of more than 3,500 feet in 7.6 miles from Va. 614 to the summit of Floyd Mountain. The Fork Mountain area contains many wildflowers, including turkey beard, violet wood sorrel, hepatica, partridge berry, gay wings, and pink lady's-slipper.

Water (unprotected) is available at two branches of Cornelius Creek, 2.4 and 2.7 miles from the northern end of the section; at Cornelius Creek Shelter; at a spring on a 0.2-mile side trail on Floyd Mountain, 4.4 miles from the northern end; at Hamps Branch (Bryant Ridge Shelter), and at creeklets before Fork Mountain. Any water from Jennings Creek definitely should be boiled or treated before using. The best water source is a well with a pump at the USFS Middle Creek picnic area, 0.3 mile from the Trail at the southern end of the section. This water is tested periodically to assess its safety.

Apple Orchard Falls National Recreation Trail

This outstanding 3.6-mile trail leads past the popular 150-foot Apple Orchard Falls on the headwaters of North Creek, for a 2,000-foot descent to USFS 59 (North Creek Road). Hemlock forests, rock outcroppings with moss and lichen, rhododendron, cascades, and pools all contribute to the wild, remote, wilderness atmosphere of the walk. A large overhanging rock 0.1 mile above the falls could provide emergency shelter except during lightning storms.

One can begin at Sunset Field, Blue Ridge Parkway milepost 78.4 (ample parking), descend 1.4 miles and 1,000 feet to Apple Orchard Falls, and then return, for a total of 2.8 miles and 2,000 feet. By using a two-car shuttle, utilizing USFS 812 from Sunset Field, turning left on USFS 768 and again left on USFS 59 to its terminus and the lower Trailhead, one can enjoy a totally downhill hike past the falls and along the stream. A first-rate circuit hike is also possible here.

The lower Trailhead is on 4.5 miles from Va. 614 on USFS 59. To reach USFS 59 from I-81, take Exit 168 and follow Va. 614 for 3 miles;

from Powell Gap on the Blue Ridge Parkway, milepost 89.1, take Va. 618, then Va. 614, for 7.4 miles.

Cornelius Creek National Recreation Trail

This 2.9-mile trail along attractive old logging roads has been raised to national recreation trail status. From the upper terminus with the A.T., the trail follows a creeklet that is one of the headwaters of North Creek, before crossing Backbone Ridge. Along Cornelius Creek, one passes pools with native trout, cascades, some shining club moss, and beautiful hemlocks, as well as the site of a 1910 logging-train crash (see "Some Local History"). After an elevation change of 1,760 feet, the trail reaches a junction with USFS 59 and the Apple Orchard Falls National Recreation Trail, where all three reach their terminus. An excellent circuit hike or a good two-car shuttle hike is possible here.

The higher end begins on the A.T., 1.2 miles south of Parkers Gap Road, and the lower Trailhead, with ample parking, is 4.5 miles from Va. 614 on USFS 59. to reach USFS 59 from I-81, take Exit 168 and follow Va. 614 for 3 miles; from Powell Gap on the Blue Ridge Parkway, milepost 89.1, take Va. 618, then Va. 614, for 7.4 miles.

Some Local History

On early 19th-century maps, Jennings Creek was first named Orrix Creek, then Youen's Creek.

An early legend claims a woman and her child were killed by a mountain lion while starting to cross Jennings Creek where the A.T. now crosses. The place came to be known as Panther Ford. Among local residents, the Trailhead bridge-crossing of Jennings Creek is still known as Panther Ford Bridge.

In the 1850s, an overseer named Wallace Lawless had a reputation for meanness, and eventually, near Jennings Creek, two young slaves turned their axes on him. After killing him, they took off running, quickly followed by men on horseback, tracking with dogs. Near the present A Wonderful Life Campground, a ravine descends from Fork Mountain. The two ran up the ravine, trying to get over Fork Mountain, but were caught as they crossed the ridge.

There, just below the summit, on the east ridge the A.T. now traverses, a rope was thrown over a limb, and the two were hanged.

On maps of the 1800s, Parkers Gap is shown as the site of several residences of Parker families. Parkers Gap Trail, along which were telephone lines to the fire tower on Apple Orchard, became Parkers Gap Road in the 1930s, opening car access to Sunset Field and Camp Kewanzee from Arnold Valley.

Folks planted crops wherever a flat spot could be found. Natives of the Middle Creek area knew of a spot from an earlier time called "Old Man's Garden," the northernmost flat spot on Backbone Ridge, which the A.T. crosses higher to the south. Even in the woods, a heavy-leafed, dark tobacco, for chewing and pipe-smoking, was planted for curing over an open fire in a shed.

A freed slave, a bachelor named George Bannister, grew tobacco at Bannister's Flat, about 2.5 miles upstream from Panther Ford. He had just returned from Buchanan with $300 in gold coins from selling his tobacco when Jennings Creek began to rise rapidly from "The Freshet of 1877." He took refuge in his tobacco shed, which was quickly swept away. His body washed up, without the gold coins, at Panther Ford, and he was buried in the flat area by the current A.T. Trailhead. In 1936, Stuart Carter arranged for his remains to be moved to Indian Rock Methodist Church.

The entire Middle Creek–Jennings Creek area had soil that was perfect for the growth of a flavorful tomato with a hint of acidity. From 1890 to 1920, 19 different tomato canneries were in operation, until a blight, fusarium wilt, began around 1920 and destroyed the industry.

The Arcadia Lumber Company had a short existence of less than a decade. It went bankrupt due to a single, expensive logging railroad wreck on lower Cornelius Creek. "Old man Hendricks" was thrilled with the new gear-driven Shay engine that had cost $125,000, on credit. Instead of the normal three carloads of logs, he decided to take ten carloads as he headed down Cornelius Creek. Speed picked up, and he tried throwing the Shay in reverse, ripping out gears. He and the crew jumped, just before the uninsured engine landed in Cornelius Creek, a quarter-mile above North Creek. Fitzhugh Worley was just ending lunch with the crew that was digging more railroad bed along Hamps Branch, precisely where Bryant Ridge Shelter and its latrine are now, when the foreman rushed up, "No, boys, it's all over. Don't dig no more." The engine sat in Cornelius Creek from 1910 to 1940, when it was recovered for scrap iron.

In the 1930s, Bryant Ridge and Fork Mountain were all open fields on top with good views, quite unlike today. This was a major factor in locating the A.T. there when the Blue Ridge Parkway displaced part of the original 1930 A.T.

Among the early hikers on the A.T. who stopped by Jesse Gilliam's place on Middle Creek was Dr. Robert Oppenheimer, the physicist who oversaw the development of the first U.S. atomic bomb. In 1946, he stepped off the Trail to ask for some water. Ida Gilliam packed him a lunch with some biscuits. Two weeks later, a box of chocolates arrived from Dr. Oppenheimer, who passed by again in 1948 with a group of Boy Scouts.

Black Rock

As long as people have hiked in the Apple Orchard area, Black Rock has been a popular destination, particularly with the blooming in June of the dense rhododendron thickets nearby. In the early years of the Natural Bridge Appalachian Trail Club, an annual hike was planned to see the purple display. Even earlier, hikes from Apple Orchard Camp were a regular attraction. A wooden ladder, carefully secured, allowed access to the top of the rocks. The view includes Headforemost Mountain, Flat Top, Floyd Mountain, and several ridges leading to the Allegheny Mountains in the distance.

One can reach Black Rock either from Sunset Field, Blue Ridge Parkway milepost 78.4, or from Cornelius Creek Shelter and Floyd Field, parkway milepost 80.4, utilizing the A.T., the Apple Orchard National Recreation Trail, and the Cornelius Creek Shelter Trail. On the A.T., Black Rock is 1.9 miles from Sunset Field and 1.1 miles from Floyd Field.

Peaks of Otter Recreation Area

Near milepost 86 of the Blue Ridge Parkway, the National Park Service has set aside the 4,000-acre Peaks of Otter Recreation Area for the public's enjoyment. A.T. hikers may want to take advantage of the facilities, programs, and side trips to interesting points in the area. The twin peaks, Sharp Top (3,875 feet) and Flat Top (4,002 feet), and a third peak, Harkening (or Hurricane) Hill, rise prominently above the valley at the headwaters of Otter River. Flat Top and Sharp Top are the sites of the northernmost large stands—more than 3,000—of Carolina hemlock forest. The programs, facilities, and activities of interest in the area are:

Peaks of Otter Lodge: motel with restaurant, coffee shop, and gift shop; open year-round (reservations required by mail or telephone: Peaks of Otter Lodge, Bedford, VA 24523, 703-586-1081).

Visitor Center and Ranger Station: nature exhibit, gas, and camp store (open May through October). Nature-study lectures and hikes. Phone available year round. Restrooms are seasonal.

Peaks of Otter Campground: open May through October (fee, water, fireplaces, and restrooms).

Flat Top Mountain: 4.4-mile trail over summit (1,500-foot climb and descent).

Sharp Top Mountain National Recreation Trail: 3.2-mile (round trip) trail to summit (1,300-foot climb and return). A historic attraction; Thomas Jefferson, who owned property in Bedford County east of the Peaks, climbed and measured Sharp Top in September 1815. A stone block from the top was used in 1851 in the construction of the Washington Monument.

Harkening Hill: 3.3-mile loop trail to summit (850-foot climb).

Johnson Farm: typical farm of 1920–39 period, on spur trail from Harkening Hill Trail.

Elk Run Loop Trail: 0.7-mile circuit hike behind visitor center.

Polly Woods Ordinary: restored early-19th-century log inn.

Falling Water Cascades National Recreation Trail: 250-foot-high, 0.3-mile-long cascade on 1.5-mile loop trail. Trail leaves parkway at milepost 83.1 (Wilkerson Gap).

Big Spring picnic area (free): across Va. 43 from campground.

Abbott Lake between lodge and campground: Fishing allowed with permit, no swimming or boating.

The Appalachian Trail originally crossed the basin immediately west of Flat Top and Sharp Top (Peaks of Otter) but is now six miles away on the parkway and Cornelius Creek Shelter Trail to the north and 4.9 miles away on the parkway from Bearwallow Gap to the south (see Section 25).

Points of Interest

Sunset Field: a spacious area facing west on the Blue Ridge Parkway 0.3 mile south of the Trail *via* USFS 812. Its sweeping view of the Blue Ridge and the distant Allegheny Mountains is particularly attractive at sunset.

Apple Orchard Falls: 150-foot falls on the headwaters of North Creek National Recreation Trail; see separate description.

Black Rock: impressive outlook to north and west. See separate entry.

Bryant Ridge: noted for its diverse forest and large, multilevel Trail shelter.

Floyd Mountain: at 3,560 feet, high point of section.

Fork Mountain: with mature forest and scene of a hanging; see "Some Local History."

Jennings Creek: two old tragedies at the A.T. crossing at Panther Ford; see "Some Local History." Popular area for outdoor recreation.

Circuit Hikes

Two loops are suggested in this section. One is truly superb. Both involve Apple Orchard Falls and considerable change of elevation.

1. Apple Orchard Falls–Cornelius Creek: This outstanding circuit hike involves walking along two streams, two National Recreation Trails, by 150-foot Apple Orchard Falls, and over Backbone Ridge on a pleasant mix of trail, old woods roads, and former logging railroad bed. Numerous campsite possibilities enable a leisurely overnight trip. Two distances, and two elevation changes, are possible, depending on whether one connects the two main trails with a grassy logging road (total, 6.1 miles and 1,400-foot rise) or with the A.T. (total, 7.6 miles and 1,960-foot rise). Begin at the terminus of USFS 59 (see separate entries for Apple Orchard Falls Trail and Cornelius Creek Trail). Ascend the Cornelius Creek Trail, past the site of 1910 logging-railroad wreck; see "Some Local History." Once on top of Backbone Ridge, choose between the grassy logging road straight ahead (shorter) or the trail continuing up the ridge to the A.T. (longer), where one turns left (north) for 1.1

miles to the Apple Orchard Falls Trail. Now, descend left to Apple Orchard Falls and beyond to USFS 59 and starting point.

One could begin at Sunset Field, Blue Ridge Parkway milepost 78.4, but the length and elevation change are slightly greater and one must ascend (2,380 feet, total) to finish the day. If the day is clear and the hiker strong, a side trip of an additional 1.2 miles south on the A.T. to Black Rock, for exceptional views, might be considered.

2. *Apple Orchard Falls–Parkers Gap Road:* This 6.5-mile walk combines the National Recreation Trail, past Apple Orchard Falls and the cascades below (2.0 miles), with 4.5 miles of gently graded, gravel Forest Service roads. However, in this case, you ascend the stream and approach the falls from below, for a different perspective. To reach the starting point, from Sunset Field (Blue Ridge Parkway milepost 78.4), drive down USFS 812 for 2.8 miles to Parkers Gap, then turn sharp left on USFS 3034, Apple Tree Road. After 2 miles, reach terminus and parking area. Just ahead is the Apple Orchard Falls National Recreation Trail, on which you ascend to the left, past the falls, to the A.T. Turn left (north) on the A.T. for 350 feet to Parkers Gap Road, where you descend left again to Parkers Gap, turning left on USFS 3034, Apple Tree Road, to your car.

Road Approaches

The northern end of the section (limited parking available) is on Parkers Gap Road (USFS 812), 0.3 mile north of Sunset Field on the parkway, milepost 78.4. Ample parking is available at Sunset Field, which is 14.5 miles south of U.S. 501 and 7.6 miles north of the point where Va. 43 enters the parkway from Bedford. USFS 812 from the north is not a recommended road approach, because it winds nearly 10 miles through mountainous terrain from Va. 781 to the Trail.

Access to the A.T. in the middle of the section (limited parking available) is possible *via* short blue-blazed trail at the end of dirt-and-gravel Va. 714 (Middle Creek–North Creek Road). It can be approached from the Blue Ridge Parkway at Powell Gap (milepost 89.1). Follow Va. 618, turn right on Va. 614, and left on Va. 618 again to Va. 714, a total of 8.1 miles. This same point can also be reached from Exit 168 on I–81, *via* Va. 614 through Arcadia, left on Va. 618, and left on Va. 714, a total of 7.5 miles.

The southern end of the section (ample parking) is on Va. 614 along Jennings Creek at Panther Ford Bridge. It can be reached from the parkway at Powell Gap (milepost 89.1), where you follow Va. 618, then Va. 614, for a total of 5.8 miles to the Trail. From I–81 (Exit 168), take Va. 614 through Arcadia 4.6 miles to the A.T.

Maps

For route orientation, refer to ATC Glenwood–New Castle Districts Map. For area detail, refer to the following USGS topographic quadrangles: Peaks of Otter and Arnold Valley.

Shelters and Campsites

This section has two shelters:

Cornelius Creek Shelter: built by USFS in 1960 and maintained jointly by USFS and Natural Bridge Appalachian Trail Club; 2.7 miles from northern end of section on 0.1-mile side trail; accommodates six; water from unprotected springs. Campsites nearby.

Next shelter: north 5.3 miles (Thunder Hill); south (Bryant Ridge) 4.9 miles.

Bryant Ridge Shelter: built in 1992 in memory of Nelson Garnett, Jr., as a cooperative project of the Appalachian Trail Conference, Natural Bridge Appalachian Trail Club, USFS, the Garnett family, and several area firms, from a plan selected from submissions by Nelson's fellow Catholic University architecture students; 3.4 miles from southern end of section, accommodates sixteen; ample water.

Next shelter: north 4.9 miles (Cornelius Creek); south 7.0 miles (Cove Mountain, no water).

Camping is possible at several places in the section: from the northern end, at 1.4 miles near a small stream (unreliable in dry weather); at 4.4 miles in a major sag, with an unprotected spring on a 0.2-mile side trail; at 7.5 miles in a hemlock grove on Hamps Branch, at junction with side trail to Va. 714; and at 11.4 miles in wooded flat area at Jennings Creek, with water (pump), 0.3 mile south on Va. 614 at Middle Creek Picnic Area.

Regulations

The section lies entirely within Jefferson National Forest, where camping is permitted unless otherwise noted. The Forest Service has implemented the following rule in the Jennings Creek, Middle Creek, and North Creek areas: Camping and the building of fires, other than in stoves, grills, fireplaces, or fire rings provided for such purpose are prohibited within 300 feet of the following roads: Va. 614, Va. 618, Va. 714, USFS 59, USFS 768, and USFS 812.

Users of the Peaks of Otter Recreation Area are subject to parkway regulations. Camping and campfires are permitted in designated areas only. Leave all plant life, animal life, rocks, and minerals undisturbed.

Hitchhiking on the parkway is not permitted. Hikers walking on the parkway are cautioned to stay off the pavement, particularly in bad weather.

Note: All water is untested, except at Middle Creek picnic area and Peaks of Otter Campground.

Supplies, Services, and Public Accommodations

The northern end of the section has no services other than the Peaks of Otter Lodge, restaurant, and camp store (see "Points of Interest"), between mileposts 85.6 and 86 of the parkway, 7.6 miles south on the parkway from the northern end of the section.

USFS North Creek Campground (6 miles from the A.T. *via* Cornelius Creek Trail and USFS 59) is open year-round (fishing, drinking water). On Va. 618 (Middle Creek Road), A Wonderful Life Campground (1164 Middle Creek Road, Buchanan, VA 24066, (540) 254-2176), has camp store, coin laundry, showers, pay phone, rides to A.T. and will hold packages. Open all year; 0.5 mile side trail, 1.4 miles from Va. 714 terminus, 0.7 mile west from intersection of Va. 714 and Va. 618. It is also 1.5 miles from the southern end of the section: 0.3 miles south on Va. 614, then 1.2 miles east on Va. 618. There is also a campground at the Peaks of Otter Recreation Area (see entry above).

In an emergency, contact the Botetourt County sheriff's office, Fincastle, by calling 911 or (540) 473-8320.

Trail Description, North to South

Miles	Data

0.0   Descend from Parkers Gap Road, USFS 812, (3,430 feet) on
       southwest slope of Apple Orchard Mountain. In 350 feet,
       cross blue-blazed Apple Orchard Falls National Recre-
       ation Trail (3,364 feet).
       Parking is limited here, but, at Sunset Field, parkway mile-
       post 78.4, 0.3 mile to left, parking is ample. Blue-blazed trail
       leads left uphill 0.2 mile to Sunset Field, parkway milepost
       78.4, and right 1.0 mile to popular Apple Orchard Falls.
       Spring (unprotected) is 110 yards downhill to right at second
       switchback on blue-blazed trail. For circuit hike here, see
       section introduction. The cove below the A.T. here has been
       called Sugarland historically.

0.5   Reach second (larger) of two moss-covered rocky areas.

0.9   Descending, round shoulder of Rich Mountain to left,
       with winter view of Apple Orchard Mountain behind.
       Ramps, a species of wild onion, grow abundantly on Rich Mountain.

1.2   Bear sharp right at small sag. In 30 yards, blue-blazed
       Cornelius Creek National Recreation Trail (3,179 feet)
       enters on right. Ahead, cross over the top of Backbone
       Ridge.
       Cornelius Creek Trail goes downhill 3.0 miles to USFS 59 (North
       Creek Road). The creeklet beginning here is one of the headwaters of
       North Creek and has been called Bear Wallow Creek by natives. The
       gap above the Trail here has been called Bear Wallow Gap, not to be
       confused with Bearwallow Gap south of Cove Mountain on the
       parkway. For circuit hike, separate trail description, and "Some Local
       History," see section introduction.

1.4   After following small stream for 0.2 mile, bear right at old
       trail junction, and, in 45 feet, cross stream on log bridge.
       Possible **campsites** here. Ascend gradually.

1.8   Side trail right leads 200 feet to Black Rock (3,420 feet).
       Outstanding views west and north of Headforemost Moun-
       tain, Flat Top, Floyd Mountain, Pine Ridge, Pine Mountain,
       Big and Little House Mountains, Wildcat Mountain, and
       Backbone Ridge. This area is noted for its rhododendron.
       Winter views of Headforemost Mountain to left, and Floyd
       Mountain ahead.

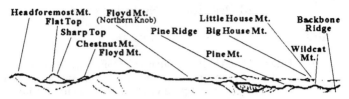

Headforemost Mt.   Floyd Mt.   Little House Mt.   Backbone Ridge
   Flat Top   (Northern Knob)   Big House Mt.
   Sharp Top   Pine Ridge
    Chestnut Mt.   Pine Mt.   Wildcat
     Floyd Mt.   Mt.

2.2   Switch back left, downhill.

2.4   Cross branch of Cornelius Creek in hemlock grove.

2.7   Cross second branch of Cornelius Creek. Seventy yards beyond, blue-blazed trail leads left 0.1 mile to **Cornelius Creek Shelter** and privy and water (unprotected) nearby. Trail bears north and west, leaving main Blue Ridge. Begin ascent of Floyd Mountain, leaving rhododendron and laurel.

      *Occasional views behind of Apple Orchard Mountain. Unmarked trail at rear of shelter leads 0.1 mile to fire road, which leads left 0.1 mile to Floyd Field at parkway milepost 80.4. To reach Peaks of Otter Lodge (with restaurant) and **Peaks of Otter Campground**, continue 5.5 miles south along parkway to mileposts 85.6 and 86, respectively.*

3.2   Cross saddle, and ascend south slope of Floyd Mountain.

3.3   Pass wooded crest of Floyd Mountain (3,560 feet), and begin 2,223-foot descent to Bryant Ridge Shelter.

3.8   Descending steeply through sag, reach crest of northern knob of Floyd Mountain (3,302 feet).

      Winter views ahead of Apple Orchard Mountain to right.

4.3   Curve left, 90 degrees, descending.

4.4   Reach major sag with dead chestnut trees on forest floor (2,935 feet).

      Blue-blazed trail leads right 0.2 mile downhill, to small, unprotected spring.

4.9   Turn left at first of six descending switchbacks.

5.4   Reach brief, 20-yard flat step in ridge.

5.6   Reach distinct sag (2,280 feet) between Floyd Mountain and Bryant Ridge. Then, ascend left, traversing around knob of Bryant Ridge (2,394 feet).

5.9   Join ridgecrest, and proceed over two rises.

      Bryant Ridge and Fork Mountain ahead were open and treeless in the 1930s.

6.2   Bear left, descending off ridgecrest.

6.5   Reach small saddle, briefly, and descend left.

6.7   Switch back to left.

7.1   After moving to northeast side of ridge, turn right on switchback where old trail continues straight.

7.3   Step down bank, and turn right onto old road. In 140 yards, turn left off road into hemlock grove, and follow Hamps Branch downhill.

7.5   At **campsite** and creeklet junction, reach blue-blaze trail left over "Button Hill" to Va. 714 terminus.
       After 0.5 mile side trail, take Va. 714 to junction with Va. 620 in 0.7 mile, and, in another 250 feet, turn right on Va. 618 0.7 mile to A Wonderful Life Campground.

7.6   Reach steps to **Bryant Ridge Shelter** and privy. Water from Hamps Branch in front of shelter.
       For "railroad" here at the shelter, see "Some Local History."

7.9   Bear left and cross Hamps Branch in hollow.
       In next 0.8 mile, encounter three switchbacks, followed by three small creeklets on or near the trail.

8.7   Step across creeklet on two large rocks.

9.2   After three switchbacks, pass blue-blazed side trail left 0.8 mile to Va. 714 terminus.
       Along the ridgecrest ahead, just before the summit, two men were hanged in the 1850s. See "Some Local History."

9.8   After two switchbacks, reach crest of Fork Mountain (2,042 feet) at cairn.

10.1   Cross gentle rise at end of level top, and begin 1,091-foot descent to Jennings Creek.

10.5   Pass distinct rocky outcropping on ridge to left, and, in 200 yards, cross left to south side of ridgeline.

10.8   Switch back left, and, in 130 yards, switch back right.

11.2   One hundred yards after crossing left across another rocky area, with Blue Spring Hill to left, bear right at intersection with old trail leading left.

11.4   At foot of hill, beyond hemlock grove, reach Va 614 and ample Trailhead parking, a few yards south of Panther Ford Bridge over Jennings Creek and end of section (951 feet).
       Thomas Jefferson passed here in September 1815 on his way from his Poplar Forest home, east of the Blue Ridge, to Natural Bridge, which he also owned, having purchased it in 1774 for

*twenty shillings. Water is available 0.3 mile south (left) on Va. 614 at Middle Creek picnic area, near junction with Va. 618. From picnic area, it is 1.2 miles to **A Wonderful Life Campground** on Va. 618. It is 5.8 miles south on Va. 614 and Va. 618 to Powell Gap on the Blue Ridge Parkway and 4.6 miles north on Va. 614 through Arcadia to I–81 (Exit 168).*

Trail Description, South to North

Miles   **Data**

0.0   A few yards south of Panther Ford Bridge (951 feet), where Va. 614 crosses Jennings Creek, the A.T. enters a hemlock grove and bears right uphill, beginning a 1,091-foot ascent of Fork Mountain.

*Thomas Jefferson passed here in September 1815 on his way from his Poplar Forest home, east of the Blue Ridge, to Natural Bridge, which he also owned, having purchased it in 1774 for twenty shillings. Ample parking at Trailhead. Water is available 0.3 mile south (left) on Va. 614 at Middle Creek picnic area, near junction with Va. 618. From picnic area, it is 1.2 miles to **A Wonderful Life Campground** on Va. 618. It is 5.8 miles south on Va. 614 and Va. 618 to Powell Gap on the Blue Ridge Parkway and 4.6 miles north on Va. 614 through Arcadia to I–81 (Exit 168).*

0.2   Pass intersection with old trail on right, and, in 100 yards, cross left over rocky area with Blue Spring Hill to right.

0.5   Switch back left, and, in 130 yards, switch back right.

0.8   Cross left to north side of ridgeline, and, in 130 yards, pass distinct rocky outcropping on ridge to right.

Fork Mountain and Bryant Ridge ahead were open and treeless in the 1930s.

1.3   Cross gentle false summit.

1.6   Reach crest of Fork Mountain (2,042 feet). Begin descent.

Along the ridgecrest just ahead, two men were hanged in the 1850s. See "Some Local History."

2.2   After two switchbacks, pass blue-blazed side trail leading right 0.8 mile to Va. 714 terminus.

2.7   After three switchbacks, step across creeklet on two large rocks.

In next 0.8 mile, encounter three more small creeklets, followed by three switchbacks.

3.5   Cross Hamps Branch in hollow and bear right.

3.8   Reach steps to **Bryant Ridge Shelter** and privy to left and water from Hamps Branch in front of shelter.
For "railroad" here, see "Some Local History."

3.9   Reach stream junction and **campsite** and blue-blazed side trail leading right over "Button Hill" 0.5 mile to Va. 714 terminus. Trail follows Hamps Branch uphill. Begin 2,223-foot ascent of Floyd Mountain.
*From Va. 714, it is 0.7 mile to junction with Va. 620 and, in another 250 feet, right 0.7 mile to **A Wonderful Life Campground**.*

4.0   Turn right onto old woods road, and, in 140 yards, turn sharp left up bank onto wide trail, as overgrown road continues ahead.
Ascend Bryant Ridge, sometimes by switchbacks, at other times skirting crest, first on southern, then on northern side of ridge.

4.3   Follow switchback to left where old trail comes in from right.

4.7   Switch back to right.

4.9   Reach small saddle, and angle uphill to the right.

5.2   Gain crest.

5.8   After leaving crest and traversing right around knob of Bryant Ridge (2,394 feet), reach distinct sag (2,280 feet) between Bryant Ridge and Floyd Mountain. Ascend along crest up Floyd Mountain.

6.0   Reach brief, 20-yard flat step in ridge, and bear to right of crest.

6.1   Turn sharp left at first of six switchbacks.

7.0   Reach major sag with dead chestnut trees on forest floor (2,935 feet).
Blue-blazed trail leads left, 0.2 mile downhill to small unprotected spring.

7.1   Turn right, 90 degrees, on wide switchback, and ascend steadily for 0.6 mile.
Winter views of Apple Orchard Mountain to left through trees.

7.6   Reach crest of knob of Floyd Mountain (3,302 feet). De-
        scend to sag, then steeply ascend northern slope of Floyd
        Mountain, regaining main Blue Ridge.

8.1   Pass wooded crest of Floyd Mountain (3,560 feet).

8.2   Reach saddle, and descend left, with occasional views of
        Apple Orchard Mountain.

8.6   Enter area of rhododendron and laurel.

8.7   Blue-blazed trail leads right 0.1 mile to **Cornelius Creek
        Shelter** and privy and water (unprotected) nearby. In 70
        yards, cross branch of Cornelius Creek at hemlock grove
        and rhododendron thicket.

        *Unmarked trail from rear of shelter leads 0.1 mile to fire road,
        which leads left 0.1 mile to Floyd Field at parkway mile 80.4.
        To reach Peaks of Otter Lodge (with restaurant) and **Peaks of
        Otter Campground**, continue south along parkway to mile-
        posts 85.6 and 86, respectively.*

9.0   Cross a second branch of Cornelius Creek in hemlock
        grove. Bear left, and ascend.

9.2   Bear right, ascending, with view of Floyd Mountain to
        rear and occasional views of Headforemost Mountain to
        right.

        This area is noted for its rhododendron.

9.6   Side trail leads left 200 feet to Black Rock (3,420 feet). A.T.
        gradually descends.

        *Outstanding views west and north of Headforemost Moun-
        tain, Flat Top, Floyd Mountain, Pine Ridge, Pine Mountain,
        Big and Little House mountains, Wildcat Mountain, and
        Backbone Ridge.*

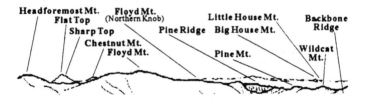

9.9   Cross stream on log bridge. In 45 feet, bear left at old trail
        junction, and follow small stream for 0.2 mile, possible

campsite here. Ahead, cross over the top of Backbone Ridge.

10.2   Blue-blazed Cornelius Creek National Recreation Trail (3,179 feet) enters on left. In 30 yards, the A.T. bears left sharply and ascends.

Blue-blazed trail leads downhill 3.0 miles to USFS 59 (North Creek Road). The creeklet beginning here is one of the headwaters of North Creek and has been called Bear Wallow Creek by local natives. The gap above the trail has been called Bear Wallow Gap, not to be confused with Bearwallow Gap below Cove Mountain on the parkway. For circuit hike, separate trail description and some local history, see section introduction.

10.5   Cross shoulder of Rich Mountain, to right, with winter view of Apple Orchard Mountain ahead.

Ramps, a species of wild onion, grow abundantly on Rich Mountain.

10.8   After brief descent, reach first (larger) of two moss-covered rocky areas.

The cove ahead, below the A.T., has been called Sugarland, historically.

11.3   Cross blue-blazed Apple Orchard Falls National Recreation Trail (3,364 feet), which leads right 0.2 mile to Sunset Field, parkway milepost 78.4, and left 1.0 mile to popular Apple Orchard Falls.

Spring (unprotected) is 110 yards downhill at second switchback on blue-blazed trail. For circuit hike here, see section introduction.

11.4   After short climb up wooden steps, reach Parkers Gap Road, USFS 812 (3,430 feet), and end of section. To continue on Trail, cross road, and ascend Apple Orchard Mountain (see Section 23).

Sunset Field at parkway milepost 78.4, is 0.3 mile right with ample parking.

Jennings Creek Road (Va. 614) to Bearwallow Gap (Va. 43)
Section Twenty–five
6.4 miles

Brief Description of Section

This section is noted for narrow ridges with picturesque stone outcrops that permit limited views north toward the James River Valley, Purgatory Mountain, and the Allegheny Mountains.

The lower Jennings Creek Valley is softer Hampton shale, but Cove Mountain is composed of hard Erwin quartzite. The Trail leaves Va. 614 close to a shale barren that has some interesting plants requiring this environment (shale-barren ragwort, prickly pear, shale-barren pussytoes, white-haired leather flower, and rocktwist), as well as gay wings, early saxifrage, bleeding heart, moss phlox, wild pink, and more.

The southern part of this section, known locally for many pink lady's-slippers (as many as one hundred in a good year), also has an impressive display of azaleas (pinxter and rose azalea) and mountain lily-of-the-valley, yellow star grass, wood betony, bird-foot violet, and vernal dwarf iris. In the dry pine woods, the understory also includes Catawba rhododendron and fetter bush.

A traverse of the section can be difficult from both directions, because of frequent elevation changes between peaks and sags. Southbound hikers must ascend to the main Blue Ridge by climbing 800 feet to the first crest of Cove Mountain (1,740 feet), then climbing across 10 knobs of increasing elevation to the 2,720-foot peak, before descending 490 feet to Bearwallow Gap (2,228 feet). Northbound hikers leave the main Blue Ridge at Bearwallow Gap, climb 490 feet to the 2,720-foot summit of Cove Mountain, and go over nine more knobs and sags, before descending to Va. 614 (951 feet). In the next 14 miles, before regaining the main Blue Ridge at Floyd Mountain, the northbound hiker faces a total of 4,925 feet in ascent and 3,666 feet in descent.

Cove Mountain should not be confused with the Cove Mountain farther south on the Trail in Roanoke and Craig counties. (Virginia alone has five Cove Mountains.)

The best water source is a well with a pump at the USFS Middle Creek picnic area, 0.3 mile from the Trail at the northern end of the section. This water is tested periodically to ensure its safety. Any water from Jennings Creek should definitely be boiled or treated before using.

Buchanan Trail

This 3.8-mile trail connects Va. 43, 1.8 miles from Buchanan, with the A.T. within yards of where the A.T. ascends to the northern crest of Cove Mountain from Jennings Creek at Panther Ford. For all but 0.2 mile at the upper end, treadway is shared with the Glenwood Horse Trail.

From the A.T. junction, 1.5 miles from Jennings Creek, descend 0.2 mile to a junction where the Glenwood Horse Trail joins the Buchanan Trail. This point is the present terminus of the Cove Mountain Trail, which the horse trail has ascended briefly and down which is located a small but steady, unprotected spring, 300 feet on the right. Ahead are winter views of the James River a half-mile below, with Purgatory Mountain beyond. Ignoring old trail to left, move right, crossing a ridge, enter switchbacks, and follow a gravel road for 0.6 mile. After another mile, more switchbacks bring you to Va. 43.

At the actual Trailhead on Va. 43, no parking is possible, so use the nearby Bearwallow Parking Area for the Glenwood Horse Trail. From Buchanan, after 1.6 miles on Va. 43, turn onto Va. 625, and, after 0.4 mile, turn left into parking area. An access trail leads 0.2 mile to the Glenwood Horse Trail, where you head left 0.2 mile to Va. 43 and the Buchanan Trail.

This trail, with the A.T., allows a two-car shuttle hike of 5.3 miles from Va. 614 at Jennings Creek or an 8.7-mile hike from Bearwallow Gap. It also allows fairly direct access to Buchanan for the A.T. hiker on Cove Mountain needing assistance.

Little Cove Mountain Trail

This attractive 2.8-mile trail, mostly along ridgeline, connects Va. 614 on Jennings Creek with the A.T., 1,500 feet above. It makes possible a two-car shuttle hike between Bearwallow Gap and Jennings Creek, as well as two fine circuit hikes.

Begin by crossing Jennings Creek on Va. 614 on a footbridge, passing the location of a former A.T. shelter on the left, then following Cove Creek and Little Cove Creek, crossing three times. After a mile, reach top of ridge, and cross old road. A half-mile beyond, after good winter views, cross gravel Yellowstone Road (Glenwood Horse Trail). The A.T., 1.0 mile farther, is reached on Cove Mountain at a point 1.8 miles from Bearwallow Gap.

From I–81, Exit 168, the Trailhead (limited parking) is reached by taking Va. 614 through Arcadia for 5.3 miles. The Trail's footbridge over Jennings Creek will be seen 0.4 mile after the junction of Va. 614 and Va. 618. It can also be reached from Powell Gap, Blue Ridge Parkway milepost 89.1, where you follow Va. 618, then Va. 614, for a total of 5.1 miles.

Some Local History

Bearwallow Gap is thought by some historians to be one of the major buffalo crossings of the Blue Ridge when that animal was plentiful in the East, even up to the mid-1700s. An Indian trail also is believed to have crossed here from the Buchanan area to the North Fork of Goose Creek on the east side. A road has been in the gap, passing from Buchanan through the Peaks of Otter Gap, since the late 18th century, moving "20 to 25 tons of lead" a year (Thomas Jefferson).

Below to the west, before paved roads and bridges, teamsters' wagons would get stuck in the mud at a creek-crossing north of the town of Buchanan. Other teams would hitch in tandem to extricate the vehicle. This happened so often that teamsters called it "going through Purgatory," hence the name of Purgatory Creek and the mountain where the creek rises, seen from the A.T. in this section.

A Buchanan and Bedford Turnpike Company worked for two years on a better road through Bearwallow Gap and between the Peaks of Otter. It was completed in September 1853.

During the 1850s, David Hunter Strothers, a young artist who used the name "Porte Crayon," crossed Bearwallow Gap after staying at the Peaks Hotel. He later remembered the road while chief of staff to Union General David Hunter, convincing Hunter that the best approach by which to attack Lynchburg from the Valley of Virginia was by way of the road through Bearwallow Gap and the Peaks of Otter. Thus it was that, on June 15,1864, the Army of West Virginia, 18,000 strong, marched all day up the hill from Buchanan, passed through Bearwallow Gap, and curved east toward the Peaks of Otter on an old road just below the present Blue Ridge Parkway.

An early legend claims a woman and her child were killed by a mountain lion while starting to cross Jennings Creek where the A.T. now crosses. The place came to be known as Panther Ford. Among natives, the Trailhead bridge crossing of Jennings Creek is still known as Panther Ford Bridge.

This entire A.T. section involves a traverse of a long, twisting ridge now called Cove Mountain. In the early 1900s, numerous maps call this ridge "Luna Mountain." On some maps, Luna Mountain is the southern section closest to Bearwallow Gap, and Boatland Mountain is the long, northeasterly ridge. Indeed, on John Lynch's 1811 survey, which shows family dwellings along the route, there is a place near Bearwallow Gap called "Luna's."

In a severe drought in 1930, a forest fire burned more than 10,000 acres for thirty days in this section. The fire swept the whole region in back of the Peaks of Otter from Harkening Hill, past McFall's Creek, over Cove Mountain to Bearwallow Gap. It burned both into Goose Creek Valley and down the length of Cove Mountain, to within a half mile of Arcadia.

Peaks of Otter Recreation Area

Near milepost 86 of the Blue Ridge Parkway, the National Park Service has set aside the 4,000-acre Peaks of Otter Recreation Area for the public's enjoyment. A.T. hikers may want to take advantage of the facilities, programs, and side trips to the interesting points in the area. The twin peaks, Sharp Top (3,875 feet) and Flat Top (4,002 feet), and a third peak, Harkening (or Hurricane) Hill, rise prominently above the valley at the headwaters of Otter River. Flat Top and Sharp Top are the sites of the northernmost large stand—more than 3,000—of Carolina hemlock. The programs, facilities, and activities of interest in the area are:

Peaks of Otter Lodge: motel with restaurant, coffee shop, and gift shop; open year-round (reservations required by mail: Peaks of Otter Lodge, Bedford, VA 24523).

Visitor Center and Ranger Station: nature exhibit, gas, and camp store (open May through October). Nature-study lectures and hikes. Phone available year 'round. Restrooms are open during warmer seasons.

Peaks of Otter Campground: open May through October (fee, water, fireplaces, and restrooms).

Flat Top Mountain: 4.4-mile trail over summit (1,500-foot climb and descent).

Sharp Top Mountain National Recreation Trail: 3.2-mile (round trip) trail to summit (1,300-foot climb and return). A historic attraction; Thomas Jefferson, who owned property in Bedford County east of the Peaks, climbed and measured Sharp Top in September 1815. A stone block from the top was used in 1851 in the construction of the Washington Monument.

Harkening Hill: 3.3-mile loop trail to summit (850-foot climb).

Johnson Farm: farm typical of 1920–39 period, on spur trail from Harkening Hill Trail.

Elk Run Loop Trail: 0.7-mile circuit hike behind visitor center.

Polly Woods Ordinary: restored early 19th-century log inn.

Falling Water Cascades National Recreation Trail: 250-foot-high, 0.3-mile-long cascade on 1.5-mile loop trail. Trail leaves parkway at milepost 83.1 (Wilkerson Gap).

Big Spring picnic area: across Va. 43 from campground.

Abbott Lake: between lodge and campground. Fishing allowed with permit; no swimming or boating.

The Appalachian Trail originally crossed the basin immediately west of Flat Top and Sharp Top (Peaks of Otter) but is now 6 miles away on the parkway and Cornelius Creek Shelter Trail, to the north, and 4.9 miles away on the parkway from Bearwallow Gap, to the south.

Points of Interest

Jennings Creek: two old tragedies at the A.T. crossing of Panther Ford; see "Some Local History," Section 24. Popular area for outdoor recreation.

Cove Mountain: a spur of the Blue Ridge extending five miles to the James River at Arcadia; interesting rock formations.

Bearwallow: a small, marshy area northwest of the intersection of the Blue Ridge Parkway and Va. 43. It has been reported that the area's cool mud makes it a favorite spot for bears in the summertime.

Circuit Hikes

Two fine circuit hikes are possible, both beginning at the northern end of the section at Panther Ford on Jennings Creek and both involving middle sections of some level walking. While both begin and conclude the same, the longer loop includes current A.T. on the ridgeline of Cove Mountain, while the shorter loop circles Cove Creek basin, briefly on former A.T.

1. Cove Mountain and Little Cove Mountain: This loop begins by walking south for 0.7 mile on Va. 614, from the A.T. Trailhead at Panther Ford on Jennings Creek. You then cross a footbridge over Jennings Creek and follow the 2.8-mile Little Cove Mountain Trail along Cove Creek, past the site of a former A.T. shelter, up an attractive ridge, and past Yellowstone Road (Glenwood Horse Trail) to the A.T. at a point 1.8 miles from Bearwallow Gap. Turning right (north) on the A.T., there are occasional views toward Buchanan and Purgatory Mountain. The Cove Mountain Shelter is passed, and, after another fine ridgewalk and a crossing of the Glenwood Horse Trail, a descent is made to Va. 614, for a total of 7.2 miles. For Trailhead directions, see "Road Approaches" for northern end of section.

2. Cove Creek Basin: This excellent loop hike is another example of the benefit to the hiker of the Glenwood Horse Trail. Begin by hiking south on the A.T. from the A.T. Trailhead on Va. 614, at Panther Ford on Jennings Creek. In 1.2 miles, turn left on the Glenwood Horse Trail at the barrier fences. For 0.6 mile, the horse trail basically utilizes former A.T. treadway before reaching the terminus of gravel Yellowstone Road. Winter views of the Jennings Creek basin, Fork Mountain, Blue Spring Hill, Bryant Ridge, and Floyd Mountain are enjoyed as a relatively level traverse is maintained around the Cove Creek basin. After 1.8 miles, cross Cove Creek headwaters, and, in 0.8 mile, bear right on road around ridge of Little Cove Mountain. Seven-tenths of a mile farther, after curving left around the ravine of Little Cove Creek, reach a road junction, with two gates, large Forest Service sign, and trail crossing with steps on right. Here, turn left on signed Little Cove Mountain Trail, just beyond gated road on left, descending to Va. 614. Little Cove Mountain Trail crosses an old road on ridgeline in 0.5 mile. At Va. 614, cross footbridge over Jennings Creek, and proceed left (north) on Va. 614 for 0.7 mile to A.T. Trailhead and starting point, for a total of 6.5 miles. For Trailhead directions, see "Road Approaches" for northern end of section.

Road Approaches

The northern end of the section (ample parking) is on Va. 614 along Jennings Creek at Panther Ford Bridge. It can be reached from the parkway at Powell Gap (milepost 89.1), where you follow Va. 618, then Va. 614, for a total of 5.8 miles to the Trail. From I–81 (Exit 168), take Va. 614, through Arcadia, 4.6 miles to the A.T.

The southern end of the section is at the junction of Va. 43 and Va. 695, milepost 90.9 of the parkway. It can be approached on Va. 43 from Buchanan, five miles north of the Trail, or on Va. 695 from Montvale on U.S. 221/460, 9.5 miles south of the Trail. Limited parking is available on Va. 43, just off the parkway.

Maps

For route orientation, refer to ATC Glenwood–New Castle Districts Map. For area detail, refer to the following USGS topographic quadrangles: Arnold Valley, Buchanan, and Montvale.

Shelters and Campsites

This section has one shelter:
Cove Mountain Shelter: Built by USFS in 1981 and maintained jointly by USFS and Natural Bridge Appalachian Trail Club; 3.2

miles from the northern end of the section, 200 feet east of the Trail; accommodates six; no convenient water. Originally (1960), this was the Marble Spring Shelter, moved here from just north of High Cock Knob because of establishment of the James River Face Wilderness.

Next shelter: north 7.0 miles (Bryant Ridge); south 6.4 miles (Bobblets Gap).

The best opportunity for camping is at the northern end of section, in the wooded flat area behind the Trailhead on Jennings Creek, Va. 614, at Panther Ford Bridge. Water is available at a pump 0.3 mile south on Va. 614, at Middle Creek Picnic Area. Note regulation below.

Regulations

This section lies within Jefferson National Forest, except for the 0.7 mile of Trail on parkway land at the southern end of the section. Although camping is generally permitted throughout the national forest, the Forest Service has implemented the following rule in the Jennings Creek, Middle Creek, and North Creek areas: Camping and the building of fires, other than in stoves, grills, fireplaces, or fire rings provided for such purpose, are prohibited within 300 feet of the following roads: Va. 614, Va. 618, Va. 714, USFS 59, USFS 768, and USFS 812.

Users of the Peaks of Otter Recreation Area are subject to parkway regulations. Camping and campfires are permitted in designated areas only. Leave all plant life, animal life, rocks, and minerals undisturbed.

Hitchhiking is not permitted on the Blue Ridge Parkway. Hikers using the parkway are cautioned to stay off the pavement, particularly in bad weather.

Note: All water is untested, except at Middle Creek Picnic Area and Peaks of Otter Campground.

Supplies, Services, and Public Accommodations

On Va. 618 1.5 miles from the northern end of section *via* Va. 614, **A Wonderful Life Campground** (1164 Middle Creek Road,

Buchanan, VA 24066, (540) 254-2176, has camp store, coin laundry, showers, pay phone, rides to A.T. and will hold packages. Open year-round.

The southern end is 4.9 miles from Peaks of Otter Recreation Area, *via* Blue Ridge Parkway, with campground, restaurant, limited supplies, and accommodations. See "Points of Interest." The southern end also is 4.9 miles from Buchanan (ZIP Code 24066), with grocery, restaurant, and coin laundry, *via* Va. 43.

In an emergency, contact the Botetourt County sheriff's office, Fincastle, by calling 911 or (540) 992-8230.

Trail Description, North to South

Miles   **Data**

0.0   From the Trailhead parking area on Va. 614, just south of Panther Ford Bridge over Jennings Creek (951 feet), the A.T. crosses the bridge and, 35 yards north of the bridge, turns left into the woods. Begin ascent of 1,769 feet up Cove Mountain.
       Water is available at the USFS Middle Creek Picnic Area, 0.3 mile south from the Trailhead. For circuit hikes here, see section introduction.

0.7   Cross small, intermittent stream in gully, then bear left, ascending, with winter views back to Fork Mountain, Blue Spring Hill, Bryant Ridge, and Floyd Mountain.

1.2   Cross Glenwood Horse Trail, then, in 30 yards, pass through two barrier fences, and switch back right, where old trail goes left downhill.

1.5   Reach crest of ridge on Cove Mountain (1,740 feet), where A.T. turns sharp left. In 300 feet, reach junction (1,780 feet) with Buchanan Trail, which leads right.
       Note interesting old A.T. sign on tree before sharp turn. A small spring (unprotected) is 0.2 mile down the Buchanan Trail and 300 feet right on Cove Mountain Trail.

1.9   Pass knob of Cove Mountain.
       This is first of ten knobs and nine sags, ranging from 1,944 feet to 2,692 feet, traversed in next 4.0 miles.

2.4   After two more knobs, cross sag with short section of narrow, elevated treadway.

2.7   Rising to cluster of small rocks with view of Jennings Creek Valley, cross to right side of ridge for first time.

3.1   Pass a rocky outlook on right with view of Buchanan area and Purgatory Mountain.

3.2   Reach side trail to **Cove Mountain Shelter** and privy, 200 feet left at low point in ridge (1,928 feet).

> *No water near shelter. Closest water involves a bushwhack steeply downhill 0.4 mile to the southeast, descending 500 feet to Cove Creek.*

4.0   After steep ascent, pass rocky outcrop on left, with winter view to right of Bearwallow Creek Valley.

4.4   Reach slight sag, with winter views to right of Bearwallow Gorge and to left of Cove Creek basin.

4.6   In mossy clearing, blue-blazed Little Cove Mountain Trail (2,563 feet) leads left 2.8 miles to Va. 614. In 300 feet, A.T. turns sharp right.

> *Behind is winter view of James River, with town of Buchanan and Purgatory Mountain beyond. For circuit hike here and separate trail description, see section introduction.*

5.0   Reach summit of Cove Mountain (2,720 feet), with two rock mounds to left. Winter views to left of Flat Top and Sharp Top (Peaks of Otter).

5.7   Cross secondary high point of Cove Mountain (2,682 feet), and descend.

> *The A.T. joins the Bedford–Botetourt county line here.*

6.2   Follow switchback right.

6.4   Reach Bearwallow Gap (2,228 feet) and end of section at Va. 43 near small parking area, 220 feet north of Blue Ridge Parkway overpass, milepost 90.9. To continue, walk downhill on Va. 43 for 150 yards.

> *Peaks of Otter Recreation Area, with lodge, restaurant, and **campground**, is 4.9 miles north on the parkway (milepost 86). To right on Va. 43, Buchanan is 5 miles.*

Trail Description, South to North

Miles   **Data**

0.0   From small parking area in Bearwallow Gap (2,228 feet), at Va. 43, 220 feet north of parkway overpass, milepost 90.9, ascend steadily through sparse woods.

The A.T. follows the Bedford–Botetourt county line for 0.6 mile, before entering Botetourt County. Peaks of Otter Recreation Area, with lodge, restaurant, and **campground***, is 4.9 miles north on the parkway (milepost 86). To left on Va. 43, Buchanan is 5 miles.*

0.2   Follow switchback left.

0.6   Reach false summit of Cove Mountain (2,682 feet).

Winter views to right of Sharp Top and Flat Top (Peaks of Otter).

1.4   Reach high point of Cove Mountain (2,720 feet), and begin 1,769-foot descent to Jennings Creek.

Trail traverses 5 miles of Cove Mountain ridge, going over a series of 10 knobs and 9 sags, ranging from 2,692 feet to 1,944 feet, before final descent to Jennings Creek.

1.8   Three hundred feet after A.T. makes sharp left turn, leaving main Blue Ridge, bear left on descending trail; blue blazed Little Cove Mountain Trail (2,563 feet) leads right 2.8 miles to Va. 614.

Beyond is winter view of James River, Buchanan, and Purgatory Mountain. Ridge of Cove Mountain veers west briefly at this point. For circuit hike here and separate trail description, see section introduction.

2.0   Reach slight sag, with winter views to left of Bearwallow Gorge and to right of Cove Creek basin.

2.4   Pass rocky outcrop on right, with another view to left of Bearwallow gorge.

3.2   Reach side trail to **Cove Mountain Shelter** and privy, right 200 feet, at low point in ridge.

No water near shelter. Closest water involves a bushwhack steeply downhill to southeast for 0.4 mile, descending 500 feet to Cove Creek.

3.3   Pass rocky outlook on left with view of Buchanan area and Purgatory Mountain.

3.7   Cross to right edge of ridge at cluster of small rocks, with view of Jennings Creek area. Descend slightly.

4.0   Cross sag with short section of elevated treadway followed by two more knobs.

4.5   Pass final knob of ridge.

4.9   Pass intersection with Buchanan Trail (1,780 feet) on left. In 300 feet, A.T. turns sharp right.

Note: interesting old A.T. sign on tree after sharp turn. A small spring (unprotected) is 0.2 mile down the Buchanan Trail and 300 feet right on Cove Mountain Trail.

5.2   Thirty yards after switchback left, where old trail heads right downhill, pass through two barrier fences, and reach Glenwood Horse Trail.

Winter views of Fork Mountain, Blue Spring Hill, Bryant Ridge, and Floyd Mountain ahead.

5.7   Cross small, intermittent stream in sag, then bear right.

6.3   Reach Va. 614, and turn right. In 300 feet, cross Jennings Creek on Panther Ford Bridge.

See "Some Local History."

6.4   Beyond bridge, on left, reach small Trailhead parking area on Va. 614 and end of section (951 feet).

*Water is available 0.3 mile ahead on Va. 614 at Middle Creek Picnic Area, near junction with Va. 618. From picnic area, it is 1.2 miles to **A Wonderful Life Campground** on Va. 618. It is 5.8 miles south on Va. 614 and Va. 618 to Powell Gap on the Blue Ridge Parkway (milepost 89.1) and 4.6 miles north on Va. 614, through Arcadia, to I–81 (Exit 168). For circuit hikes here, see section introduction.*

Bearwallow Gap (Va. 43) to
Black Horse Gap (USFS 186)
Section Twenty–six
8.1 miles

Brief Description of Section

The Blue Ridge narrows as it bends southward from Bearwallow Gap. Because of the steep terrain, construction of the Blue Ridge Parkway allowed little space for the Appalachian Trail that preceded it on the ridge. Consequently, the parkway crosses the Trail three times and abuts it at two places in the section, and hikers are seldom out of earshot of parkway traffic. Relocations are changing that. In the meantime, fine viewpoints from the A.T. are available at the parkway overlooks, several of which have picnic tables and benches (see "Points of Interest"). There are sweeping views to the east across the North Fork of Goose Creek Valley, 1,500 feet below, to the Peaks of Otter.

The Natural Bridge Appalachian Trail Club's 89.9 miles of A.T. responsibility extend from Black Horse Gap northward to the Tye River, in the George Washington National Forest. The Trail in this section presents no difficult climbs and averages 2,345 feet in elevation. Water (seasonal) is found 0.1 mile south of the northern end of the section, then at Bobblets Gap Shelter, and at the site of Mountain Gate Toll House, 0.4 mile east of Black Horse Gap on USFS 186 (off the A.T.) at the southern end of the section. In spite of efforts to clear the Trail regularly, hikers may encounter some heavy summer growth in spots.

From Bearwallow Gap to Black Horse Gap, the underlying rock is Unicoi quartzite. At times, the Trail passes through a forest of mixed hardwoods and conifers with a dense understory. Many wildflowers bloom in season on this section of the Trail, because it combines sunny and/or shady locations. In spring, mountain lily-of-the-valley, wood betony, pasture rose, yellow star grass, galax, and many others may be found. Later, look for thimbleweed, sundrops, goat's rue, spotted knapweed, skullcap, butter-and-eggs, and rattlesnake orchid. Blackberry lily, an Asian native, is well-established at Harveys Knob.

Hammond Hollow Trail

Three deep hollows, narrow ridge walking, beautiful galax, and nice treadway construction mark this 2.0-mile trail that connects Va. 645 west of the Blue Ridge with the A.T. 1,150 feet above. After 0.2 mile on an old road, the trail ascends the east side of Hanging Rock Hollow, before swinging up the sharp ridge north of Hammond Hollow. After the summit of a 2,136-foot knoll, the trail dips through a shallow saddle and then ascends the south wall of Tar Hollow to reach the A.T., 0.7 mile south of Bobblets Gap, where there is ample parking on Blue Ridge Parkway, milepost 93.1 . To reach Trailhead, south of Lithia between Buchanan and Troutville, turn east off Va. 640, and follow Va. 645 for 2.0 miles to trail sign on right at sharp turn, with limited parking. See "Circuit Hikes."

Spec Mines Trail

This trail circles around Iron Mine Hollow and Spec Mines Branch, above the 19th–century Spec Mines, as it drops 1,300 feet in 2.8 miles to Va. 645. Along the way, it passes a large pine tree the Forest Service has posted as a "designated wildlife tree," not to be cut. The upper end of Spec Mines Trail is on the western edge of the Blue Ridge Parkway 0.1 mile south of the Montvale Overlook, 50 yards south of milepost 96, and across the parkway from the A.T., 1.7 miles north of Black Horse Gap. The lower Trailhead, south of Lithia between Buchanan and Troutville, can be reached by turning east off Va. 640 onto Va. 645. After 0.4 mile on Va. 645, opposite the second (smaller) of two ponds, look for trail sign on right. See "Circuit Hikes."

Some Local History

Bearwallow Gap is thought by some historians to be one of the major buffalo crossings of the Blue Ridge, when that animal was plentiful in the East, even up to the mid–1700s. An Indian trail also is believed to have crossed here from the Buchanan area to the

North Fork of Goose Creek on the east side. A road has been in the gap, passing from Buchanan through the Peaks of Otter Gap, since the late 18th century, moving "20 to 25 tons of lead" a year (Thomas Jefferson).

"I have deposited in the County of Bedford about four miles from Buford's in an excavation or vault six feet below the surface of the ground the following articles...," reads Thomas Jefferson Beale's coded message, written in 1822. It then lists 2,921 pounds of gold, 5,100 pounds of silver, and valuable jewels in "Beale's Treasure," brought east from Indian and Spanish lands of the southwest and hidden in 1819 and 1821. Another coded message, left with a friend in Lynchburg, describing the exact location, has yet to be deciphered despite the best efforts of experts. Somewhere, probably east of the Blue Ridge crest in Goose Creek Valley, lies a tantalizing hoard (or hoax).

Black Horse Gap was mile ten on the fourteen-mile Fincastle and Blue Ridge Turnpike, chartered in 1830, completed in 1835, and running from Fincastle to Buford's, on the Lynchburg–Salem Turnpike. South of the gap on this road, also known as Old Sweet Springs Stagecoach Road and The Old Fincastle Road, was the Mountain Gate Toll House and spring. Using a horn, the gatekeeper signaled to Buford's, below in the valley, the number of guests arriving for dinner. (NBATC hikers in the 1930s found ruts worn in rocks by braking wheels as the coach rolled down the mountain.)

During the 1850s, David Hunter Strothers, a young artist who used the name "Porte Crayon," crossed Bearwallow Gap after staying at the Peaks Hotel. He later remembered the road as chief of staff to Union General David Hunter, convincing Hunter that the best approach by which to attack Lynchburg from the Valley of Virginia was by way of it. On June 15, 1864, the 18,000-man Army of West Virginia marched all day up the hill from Buchanan, passed through Bearwallow Gap, and curved east toward the Peaks of Otter on an old road just below the present Blue Ridge Parkway. See Section 25.

Hunter dispatched a large wagon train to West Virginia just before the Battle of Lynchburg: "Burn all wagons that break down.... Shoot all horses that give out." On June 18, 1864, 200 wagons filled with 130 sick and wounded, 142 prisoners, and "the families of refugees, white or colored," filed through Black Horse Gap. Among the loot transported was a bronze statue of George Washington, captured at the Virginia Military Institute. Intended for West Point, the statue got as far as West Virginia; the governor returned it to VMI in 1866.

Iron ore was mined in hollows on both sides of the narrow Blue Ridge here from about Civil War times until discovery in 1892 of the far richer and more easily worked ore of Minnesota's Mesabi Range.

The Buchanan Turnpike through Bobblets Gap was completed in 1855. Like many of his relatives in the area of the gap, Will Bobblet lived a hard life, working a small piece of land here for thirty-five years before moving his family to the valley. Among his last words were, "When I die, don't take me back to the mountains."

The original A.T. was largely eradicated by the construction of the Blue Ridge Parkway in the late 1930s and early 1940s in this section. The 1930 Trail in many places lay right along the center line of the current parkway or slightly to one side. However, three places where original tread is still followed are: about 0.2 mile south of Bobblets Gap, 0.4 mile around Harveys Knob, and about 0.2 mile north of Black Horse Gap.

On April 6, 1942, a farmer in Goose Creek Valley set one of his fields on fire to burn brush. A disastrous forest fire swept 10,300 acres, for 2.5 miles south of Bobblets Gap on both sides of the ridge. The main fire swept over backfire lines several times, before a crew of seven hundred men finally retreated three miles northward to establish another backfire line, stopping the fire after two days.

Sharp Top

Not able to experience the prominence of the Peaks of Otter from the fields of Bedford County, the A.T. hiker is offered the best glimpse of the distinctive matching mountains from the Trail crossings of the Blue Ridge Parkway overlooks. Of the two peaks, Sharp Top has always drawn the most attention, even though to many hikers Flat Top is the more satisfying climb. Due to its pointed summit, for years Sharp Top was erroneously thought to be not only the higher of the two, but the highest peak in the state.

Older maps simply label the mountain, "S. Knob" or "Peak." The first map showing "Sharp Top" was a 1917 map of the Natural Bridge National Forest. While today's throngs climb a single, partially tarred trail to the top, at least four other trails historically ascended from as many sides.

In September 1815, at age 72, Thomas Jefferson climbed Sharp Top "to take angles," measuring its height, while "exploring the sides for subjects botanical." The views from the crowning rocks have always been inspirational, especially at sunrise. A block of stone from the top was used in 1851 in the construction of the Washington Monument.

NBATC hikers in the 1930s refer to being able to purchase food and arrange primitive lodging at the stone summit house. For a few years, a fire tower accessible to the public capped the top.

Matched by Flat Top, yet a separate sentinel, Sharp Top has always had a profound emotional impact on the people of the region as a symbol of their beloved Blue Ridge.

Points of Interest

Parkway crossings or overlooks: Bearwallow Gap (milepost 90.9), see "Some Local History;" Mills Gap Overlook (milepost 91.8); Sharp Top Overlook (milepost 92.5), see separate entry; Bobblets Gap Overlook, with view of the Great Valley (milepost 93.1); Harveys Knob Overlook (milepost 95.3); Montvale and Goose Creek Valley Overlook (milepost 95.9); Taylors Mountain Overlook (milepost 97); and Black Horse Gap (milepost 97.7); see "Some Local History."

Circuit Hikes

Seven circuit hikes are possible in this section, involving the A.T., Hammond Hollow Trail, Spec Mines Trail, the parallel Glenwood Horse Trail on the southeast, and Forest Service roads on the northwest side of the ridge. Several of these are extended loops.

1. Spec Mines–Hammond Hollow: Park at the Montvale Overlook, Blue Ridge Parkway milepost 95.9, walk 0.1 mile left (south) on the parkway, and, 50 feet south of milepost 96, descend northwest on Spec Mines Trail for 2.0 miles. Turn right (northeast) on USFS 634 through Hanging Rock Hollow for 3.2 miles, being sure to turn sharp right after 1.4 miles (avoiding the road continuing 0.2 mile to Va. 645). Turn right (south) on Hammond Hollow Trail for 1.4 miles to the A.T., where you turn right (southwest) for 2.3 miles back to the Montvale Overlook, for a total of 9 miles.

2. *Spec Mines–Black Horse Gap:* Begin this loop by parking at the Montvale Overlook, parkway milepost 95.9, walking 0.1 mile left (south) on the parkway, and, 50 feet south of milepost 96, descending northwest on Spec Mines Trail for 2.0 miles. Turn left on USFS 634, passing gate in 0.5 mile, for 2.2 miles, to a junction with USFS 186, where you turn left (south) and, like the stagecoaches of old, climb for 2.2 miles to the A.T. at Black Horse Gap. Turn left (north) on the A.T. for 1.9 miles back to the Montvale Overlook, for a total of 8.4 miles.

3. *Bobblets Gap–Hammond Hollow:* After parking at Bobblets Gap Overlook, parkway mile 93.1, climb down informal trail to USFS 4008 (Glenwood Horse Trail), which goes through the gap. Turn right (north) on USFS 4008, past the A.T., noting the horse trail leaving the road in 1.0 mile. In 2.0 miles, reach junction with Va. 643, where you turn left for 0.1 mile. Turn left on USFS 634 for 2.2 miles through Chair Rock Hollow and Tar Hollow, to Hammond Hollow Trail, where you turn left (south) and ascend 1.4 miles to the A.T. Turn left (northeast) on A.T. for 0.7 mile to USFS 4008, where you turn right and climb back up to Bobblets Gap Overlook, for a total of 5.8 miles.

4. *Hammond Hollow–Black Horse Gap:* After parking at Montvale Overlook, parkway milepost 95.9, hike north of the A.T. for 2.3 miles to the Hammond Hollow Trail, where you turn left and descend 1.4 miles to USFS 634. Turn left (south) on USFS 634 for 5.4 miles, past the Spec Mines Trail, past sharp left turn (avoiding road 0.2 mile right to Va. 645), to a junction with USFS 186, where you turn left (south) and climb on the old Fincastle and Blue Ridge Turnpike for 2.2 miles to the A.T. Turn left (north) on the A.T. for 1.9 miles back to the Montvale Overlook, for a total of 13.2 miles.

5. *Bobblets Gap–Spec Mines:* Park at Bobblets Gap Overlook, parkway milepost 93.1, and climb down informal trail to USFS 4008 (Glenwood Horse Trail), which goes through the gap. Turn right (north) on USFS 4008, past the A.T. for 2.0 miles, noting the horse trail leaving the road in 1.0 mile, to junction with Va. 643, where you turn left for 0.1 mile. Turn left on USFS 634 for 5.4 miles, passing Chair Rock Hollow, Tar Hollow, the Hammond Hollow Trail, Hanging Rock Hollow, and sharp left turn (avoiding road 0.2 mile right to Va. 645), to the Spec Mines Trail, where you turn left

(southeast) and climb 2.0 miles to the parkway. Walk 0.1 mile north on the parkway to Montvale Overlook, and join the A.T. (north) for 3.0 miles to USFS 4008, where you turn right and climb back to Bobblets Gap Overlook, for a total of 12.5 miles.

The next two circuit hikes involve all the distance from Bobblets Gap to Black Horse Gap, on either the Glenwood Horse Trail (east) or Forest Service roads (west), and then a return *via* the A.T.

6. *Bobblets Gap–Glenwood Horse Trail–Black Horse Gap:* After parking at Bobblets Gap Overlook, parkway milepost 93.1, climb down informal trail to USFS 4008 (Glenwood Horse Trail), which goes through the gap, and turn left (south) on the road, crossing under the parkway. After 2.6 miles on USFS 4008, bear right where Glenwood Horse Trail leaves road and becomes trail. In 4.8 miles, reach the Glenwood Horse Trail's Day Creek Parking Area on USFS 186, and turn right (north) on USFS 186 for 2.3 miles, climbing past the site of the old Mountain Gate Toll House, with unprotected spring nearby, and crossing the parkway to the A.T. just beyond. Turn right (north) on A.T., and, in 4.9 miles, reach USFS 4008, where you turn right and climb back to the Bobblets Gap Overlook, for a total of 14.6 miles.

7. *Bobblets Gap–USFS 634–Black Horse Gap:* From the Bobblets Gap Overlook, parkway milepost 93.1, climb down informal trail to USFS 4008 (Glenwood Horse Trail), which goes through the gap, and turn right (north) on the road. Descend past the A.T. for 2.0 miles, noting the horse trail leaving the road in 1.0 mile, to junction with Va. 643, where you turn left for 0.1 mile. Turn left on USFS 634 for 7.6 miles, past Hammond Hollow Trail. Take sharp left turn (avoiding road 0.2 mile right to Va. 645) and Spec Mines Trail to junction with USFS 186. Here, you turn left, climb 2.2 miles to the A.T. at Black Horse Gap, and turn left on A.T. (north) for 4.9 miles to USFS 4008, where you turn right and climb back to the Bobblets Gap Overlook, for a total of 16.8 miles.

Road Approaches

The northern end of the section is on Va. 43, just off the Blue Ridge Parkway, at milepost 90.9 (ample parking). Bearwallow Gap is 4.9 miles from Buchanan (I–81 exits 162 and 167), by way of Va. 43, or 9.5 miles from Montvale, by way of mountainous Va. 695.

At the southern end of the section, parkway milepost 97.7 (limited parking available; do not block gate), the parkway itself provides access. USFS 186 (Old Fincastle Road), gated at the parkway, connects 2.2 miles to the east with USFS 634 and, 0.4 miles beyond, becomes Va. 606. U.S. 11 0.4 miles beyond, is 1.4 miles farther.

Six parkway overlooks provide parking adjacent to the Trail: Mills Gap, Sharp Top, Bobblets Gap, Harveys Knob, Montvale, and Taylors Mountain.

Maps

For route navigation, refer to ATC Glenwood–New Castle Districts Map. For more area detail, refer to the following USGS topographic quadrangles: Montvale and Villamont.

Shelters and Campsites

This section has one shelter:
Bobblets Gap Shelter: Built by USFS in 1961 and maintained jointly with Natural Bridge Appalachian Trail Club; 2.5 miles from northern end of section; accommodates six; unprotected spring may be low after long dry spells.

Next shelter: north 6.4 miles (Cove Mountain), south 7.3 miles (Wilson Creek).

This section does not have any recommended campsites.

Regulations

Most of the section lies within the Blue Ridge Parkway boundary, where camping or campfire-building is prohibited except at Bobblets Gap Shelter. Hitchhiking on the parkway is prohibited. Hikers using on the parkway should keep off the pavement, especially in bad weather. On parkway land, leave all plant life, animal life, rocks, and minerals undisturbed. *Note:* All water is untested.

Supplies, Services, and Public Accommodations

Peaks of Otter Lodge, restaurant, campground, and camp store (limited) are 4.9 miles north of Bearwallow Gap at parkway milepost 86 (see Section 25 for more information).

Bearwallow Gap is 4.9 miles south of Buchanan (ZIP Code 24066, groceries, restaurants, and coin laundry) on U.S. 11 and I–81 *via* Va. 43.

In an emergency, contact Blue Ridge Parkway rangers at (800)PARKWATCH.

Trail Description, North to South

Miles   **Data**

0.0   Follow Va. 43 downhill 150 yards from small parking area, just north of parkway overpass at milepost 90.9 (2,228 feet).

0.1   Turn left off Va. 43 at large brown sign (for Blue Ridge Parkway). In 15 yards cross seasonal creeklet. Begin 300 ft. climb with views back of Cove Mountain.
        The A.T. weaves along the Bedford–Botetourt county line from Bearwallow Gap to Black Horse Gap.

0.7   After four switchbacks, curve left at rock steps and reach flat top area of knoll.
        Much of this section is in deciduous woods with some pines, alternating with rhododendron.

1.4   High point of knoll at "Survey Marker Witness Post."

1.8   After passing side trail to picnic table, reach Mills Gap Overlook on Blue Ridge Parkway, milepost 91.8 (2,435 feet). Cross parkway diagonally and enter trees.
        To west, James River is 1,585 feet below. Ahead, winter views right of Buchanan and Purgatory Mountain.

2.5   Cross parkway diagonally at end of Sharp Top Overlook parking area, milepost 92.5 (2,344 feet). Enter woods.
        View of Sharp Top and Flat Top (see section introduction) is over North Fork Goose Creek Valley. Geologists call this valley a "breeched fenster," formed as a result of an overthrust fault during the folding of the Appalachians, followed by extensive weathering and erosion.

2.8   Join old road, and, in 80 yards, bear right off old road.

3.1   Bear left onto USFS 4008 (Glenwood Horse Trail).

3.2   Bear right from USFS 4008. In 30 feet, pass blue-blazed trail leading right 0.2 mile downhill to **Bobblets Gap Shelter** and privy and unprotected spring nearby, at head of Chair Rock Hollow.

> *Road ahead leads to parkway overpass at Bobblets Gap Overlook (2,123 feet), milepost 93.1, with view of the Valley of Virginia. For circuit hikes here, see section introduction.*

3.6   Reach second crest, then descend.

3.8   Follow overgrown roadway 70 feet, ascending.

4.0   Pass Hammond Hollow Trail (2,300 feet), which leads right 2.0 miles to USFS 645. A.T. bears right beyond Hammond Hollow Trail and parallels parkway on ridgecrest.

> *For circuit hikes here, and separate trail description, see section introduction.*

4.1   Begin descent from level traverse, and cross sag in rocky area, followed by small rise.

5.0   Pass low point in parkway retaining wall on left.

5.2   Bear right onto old road that circles around north side of Harveys Knob.

> *Old road becomes wide trail and, for 0.4 mile, is original 1930 A.T.*

5.6   Cross to south side of parkway, milepost 95.3, at Harveys Knob Overlook parking area (2,530 feet), with view of Peaks of Otter, and ascend.

5.7   Reach crest opposite overlook.

6.0   Bear left on gated road.

6.2   Reach Montvale Overlook parking area (2,433 feet), parkway milepost 95.9. Continue straight through parking area, and, in 80 yards, pass picnic table, and ascend through wood to crest.

> *For circuit hikes here, see section introduction.*

6.4   A few yards beyond top of first rise, across parkway from A.T. and 50 yards south of parkway milepost 96, Spec Mines Trail descends 2.8 miles around Iron Mountain Hollow to USFS 634.

> *For separate trail description, see section introduction.*

6.7   Pass low point by parkway embankment wall on right, in low area with heavy summer growth.

7.1   Reach crest.

7.3   Reach Taylors Mountain Overlook parking area (2,365 feet), parkway mile 97.0. Pass traffic island, and cross parkway diagonally.

7.7   Cross summit of first knob.

7.9   Cross rocky summit of second knob.

8.1   Reach Old Fincastle Road (USFS 186) at Black Horse Gap (2,402 feet), 110 feet west of parkway milepost 97.7, and end of section. A.T. continues across road.

To west, USFS 186 connects with USFS 634 in 2.2 miles and Va. 606 in another 0.4 mile. To east, it continues to Va. 697 and Montvale and passes unprotected spring in 0.4 mile. Traffic is barred on fire road. Mountain Gate Toll House on this old stagecoach turnpike was slightly to east; see "Some Local History." For circuit hikes here, see section introduction.

Trail Description, South to North

Miles   **Data**

0.0   Ascend slightly from Old Fincastle Road (USFS 186) in Black Horse Gap (2,402 feet), 110 feet west of parkway milepost 97.7.

To west, USFS 186 connects with USFS 634 in 2.2 miles and Va. 606 in another 0.4 mile. To east, it continues to Va. 697 and Montvale and passes unprotected spring in 0.4 mile. Traffic is barred on fire road. Mountain Gate Toll House on this old stagecoach turnpike was slightly to east; see "Some Local History." The A.T. weaves along the Bedford-Botetourt county line from Black Horse Gap to Bearwallow Gap. For circuit hikes here, see section introduction.

0.2   Cross rocky summit of first knob.

0.4   Cross top of second knob.

Much of ensuing 7.0 miles of this section is in deciduous woods with some pines alternating with rhododendron and other low growth.

0.7   Cross parkway diagonally at Taylors Mountain Overlook parking area (2,365 feet), parkway milepost 97.0, passing traffic island. Ascend through woods.

1.0   Reach crest.

1.4   Pass low point by parkway embankment wall on left, in low area with heavy summer growth.

1.7   A few yards before top of rise, across parkway from A.T. and 50 yards south of parkway milepost 96, Spec Mines Trail descends 2.8 miles around Iron Mountain Hollow to USFS 634.
        For separate trail description, see section introduction.

1.9   Reach Montvale Overlook parking area and picnic table (2,433 feet), parkway milepost 95.9. Continue 80 yards through overlook, then ascend into woods.
        For circuit hikes here, see section introduction.

2.4   Reach crest, opposite overlook.

2.5   Cross to north side of parkway, milepost 95.3, at Harveys Knob Overlook parking area (2,530 feet), with view of Peaks of Otter.
        Wide trail ahead for 0.4 mile is original 1930 A.T.

2.7   Trail becomes old road and curves around north side of Harveys Knob.

2.9   Bear left from old road, and go downhill.

3.1   Pass low point in parkway retaining wall on right, then cross small rise and sag in rocky area.

3.9   Begin ascent to short, level traverse.

4.1   Reach crest. Bear left away from parkway, descending. In 50 feet, Hammond Hollow Trail (2,300 feet) leads 2.0 miles left downhill to USFS 634.
        For circuit hikes here, and separate trail description, see section introduction.

4.3   Follow overgrown roadway 70 feet, and ascend.

4.4   Reach crest, then descend.

4.9   Blue-blazed side trail on left leads 0.2 mile downhill to **Bobblets Gap Shelter** and privy and unprotected spring nearby, at head of Chair Rock Hollow. Bear left onto USFS 4008 (Glenwood Horse Trail).
        To right, road goes under parkway at Bobblets Gap Overlook and parking area, milepost 93.1 (2,123 feet) from which there is a view of the Valley of Virginia. For circuit hikes here, see section introduction.

5.0   Bear right from USFS 4008, and ascend.

5.3   Join old woods road, and, in 80 yards, bear right off old road.

5.6   Cross parkway diagonally at Sharp Top Overlook parking
        area, milepost 92.5 (2,344 feet). Enter woods, and ascend.
        View of Sharp Top and Flat Top (see section introduction) is
        over North Fork Goose Creek Valley. Geologists call this
        valley a "breeched fenster," formed as a result of an overthrust
        fault during the folding of the Appalachians, followed by
        extensive weathering and erosion.

6.3   After winter views left of Buchanan and Purgatory Moun-
        tain, reach Mills Gap Overlook on Blue Ridge Parkway,
        milepost 91.8 (elevation 2,435 feet). Cross parkway diago-
        nally.
        As you enter trees, side trail right leads to picnic table.

6.7   High point of knoll at "Survey Marker Witness Post."

7.4   Leaving flat top area of knoll, curve right at rock steps and
        descend. Four switchbacks ahead.
        During 300 foot descent, views ahead of Cove Mountain.

8.0   Fifteen yards after crossing seasonal creeklet, reach Va. 43
        at large brown sign (for Blue Ridge Parkway) and ascend
        right on road.

8.1   Hiking 150 yards uphill on Va. 43, reach small Trailhead
        parking area on left at Bearwallow Gap, just north of
        parkway, milepost 90.9 (2,228 feet), and end of section.
        Trail continues up wooded slope to north (see Section 25).
        Peaks of Otter Recreation Area with lodge, restaurant, and
        ***campground** is 4.9 miles north on the parkway (milepost 86).*
        Ahead on Va. 43, Buchanan is 5 miles.

Black Horse Gap (USFS 186) to U.S. 220 and Va. 816
Section Twenty–seven
13.6 miles

Brief Description of Section

The original route of the A.T. along the crest of the Blue Ridge was displaced by the Blue Ridge Parkway. In 1948–49, USFS and the Roanoke A.T. Club reconstructed the Trail within a newly acquired area of Jefferson National Forest. For the next 85.9 miles, the Trail is the responsibility of the Roanoke A.T. Club.

The A.T. now traverses the northern slope of the Blue Ridge near Fullhardt Knob (2,676 feet) and descends into the narrow Valley of Virginia, where the Trail weaves across roads and farmland.

For its northern five miles, the Trail in this section follows graded trail through rhododendron, with occasional outlooks and wild, dense forest growth. The Trail then follows the crest by footpath and fire road, skirting Fullhardt Knob and descending some 1,100 feet to the valley. From north to south, the way is mostly downhill.

This section generally has ample water.

History

The northern terminus of this section begins on Old Fincastle Road (USFS 186, a continuation of Va. 606). This road was a turnpike in the 1700s that settlers used in heading west. This was believed to be one of the easier routes over the mountains.

Points of Interest

Fullhardt Knob (2,676 feet): views of surrounding peaks and valleys.

Valley of Virginia: the most prominent of the several major valleys that are part of a major geological feature that stretches from the Hudson River in New York to northern Alabama. The A.T. crosses these valleys in New Jersey, Pennsylvania, and twice in Virginia (at the southern end of the section and in southwestern Virginia, near Groseclose). The Shenandoah, Roanoke, and Tennessee valleys are all linked by this feature.

Road Approaches

The northern end of the section is on USFS 186, 110 feet west of milepost 97.7 of the Blue Ridge Parkway in Black Horse Gap (ample parking). The road is gated at the parkway but may be ascended in good weather from U.S. 11, 4 miles to the west.

The southern end of the section is on U.S. 220, about 0.5 mile northwest of Exit 150 of I–81, about 10 miles north of Roanoke. A park-and-ride lot is located 0.2 mile south of the A.T. crossing of U.S. 220, at Va. 816.

Salt Pond Road (USFS 191, which turns off Va. 711) provides access to the center of the section from U.S. 11 and Va. 640, approximately 5 miles downhill to the west. In the other direction, the road continues uphill from the A.T. 1.1 miles to the Blue Ridge Parkway, where it is gated. A Trailhead parking lot is located at the U.S. 11 crossing, two miles north of Exit 150 of I–81.

Maps

For route orientation, refer to ATC Glenwood–New Castle Districts Map 4. For area detail, refer to the following USGS topographic quadrangles: Villamont and Daleville.

Shelters and Campsites

This section has two shelters:

Wilson Creek Shelter: built by Roanoke Appalachian Trail Club and ATC's Konnarock Trail crew in 1986; maintained jointly by USFS and RATC; 2.4 miles from the northern end of the section; accommodates six; camping below shelter; water from creek.

Next shelter: north 7.3 miles (Bobblets Gap); south 6.2 miles (Fullhardt Knob).

Fullhardt Knob Shelter: built by USFS in the 1960s and maintained jointly by USFS and RATC; 5.0 miles from southern end of section; accommodates six; water from cistern (unreliable); spring is 0.4 mile north on A.T and 350 feet on left.

Next shelter: north 6.2 miles (Wilson Creek); south 14.3 (Lamberts Meadow).

Regulations

The northern 11.5 miles of the section, from Black Horse Gap to Va. 652, lie within the Jefferson National Forest, where camping and campfires are permitted unless specifically noted otherwise. No designated campsites are located in this section, though Trail shelters are surrounded by campsites. Between Va. 652 and U.S. 220, the southern 2.1 miles of this section, the Trail is on National Park Service A.T. corridor lands, where camping is not permitted due to the narrowness of the corridor.

Supplies, Services, and Public Accommodations

There are no services convenient to the north end of this segment. Troutville (ZIP Code 24175, with groceries) is 0.5 mile north on U.S. 11 from A.T. crossing. Cloverdale is 2.3 miles south on U.S. 220 and U.S. 11 at the southern end of the section (ZIP Code 24077; groceries, restaurant, and motels). Daleville is 1.0 mile north on U.S. 220. Showers are available at a truck stop just east of the end of the section at junction of U.S. 11 and U.S. 220. Restaurants and lodging are on both sides of I–81. Roanoke, 10 miles south *via* U.S. 11 or I–81, offers a full range of supplies and services.

Trail Description, North to South

Miles   **Data**

0.0   From Old Fincastle Road (USFS 186),110 feet west of the Blue Ridge Parkway (2,402 feet), follow narrow, graded footpath across northern slope through rhododendron.

0.3   Cross north-facing spur with views north. One-third mile farther, cross another spur.

1.1   Cross third spur, with view to right of rocky knob known as Shirleys Knob. One-half mile farther, cross another spur.

2.0   Pass ledge with unreliable spring. Five hundred feet beyond, cross fifth spur, and begin long, steady descent through dense forest with limited views.

2.4   Blue-blazed trail leads right 150 feet to **Wilson Creek Shelter** and privy. Soon, come to second blue-blazed trail, also leading to shelter. Trail begins descent to Wilson Creek. Water from stream 200 yards in front of shelter.

3.1   Descend short series of steps, and cross Wilson Creek. Trail ascends.

4.3   Cross branch of Little Wilson Creek, and ascend steeply.

4.6   Pass through gap between Grindstone Knob and unnamed 2,516-foot peak, then descend steadily, with views north.

5.0   Cross Curry Creek in mature forest. Just before, Curry Creek Trail leads right approximately 2.5 miles to Va. 640. Beyond, A.T. ascends very steeply on switchbacks.

5.8   Cross Salt Pond Road (USFS 191) where road bears sharply south. Road leads left 1.1 miles to Blue Ridge Parkway, milepost 101.5 (where road is gated) and right to Va. 711 and Va. 640 and U.S. 11. A.T. follows level footpath along crest of ridge for about 2 miles.

6.4   Cross high point of ridge (2,529 feet) and, 0.3 mile farther, another knob. The Trail then descends steadily along narrow crest with views of Fullhardt Knob ahead.

7.7   Trail turns sharply left onto Fullhardt Knob fire road and ascends steadily. To the right, road leads downhill 0.15 mile to Salt Pond Road (USFS 191), which descends to Va. 711, Va. 640, and U.S. 11. In the Trail section ahead are a number of unblazed trails that intersect with the A.T.

8.2   Unblazed trail to right descends 350 feet to water source.

8.3   Unblazed trail to left leads 60 feet to limited view of valley below.

8.6   Trail veers to right, leaving fire road, and begins to descend on arm of ridge. Blue-blazed trail continues straight ahead on fire road, ascending to **Fullhardt Knob Shelter** and privy in 465 feet.

9.2   Trail turns sharply to right and shortly begins a section of long graded switchbacks descending to "Tollhouse Gap." Blue-blazed trail to left leads 250 feet to view of valley below.

10.0   Reach "Tollhouse Gap," a saddle between Fullhardt Knob and main spine of Blue Ridge. Graded Trail section is briefly interrupted by the gap but begins again as Trail skirts southern and western slopes of Fullhardt Knob. An unblazed trail comes into the gap at left.

10.6   Trail descends rock steps and switches back to the left. This is the first of a half-dozen switchbacks to be encountered in the next 0.4 mile as the Trail descends Fullhardt Knob, proceeding toward the Va. 652 crossing.

11.0   Trail descends rock steps and switches back to the right. Shortly, graded trail section comes to an end.
         No camping is permitted from this point to southern end of section.

11.1   Trail enters open field. View ahead and slightly to left is Tinker Mountain.

11.3   Trail reaches old farm lane, turns to the right onto the lane, and ascends slightly.

11.5   Trail turns to the right, crosses stile, and skirts open field. Shortly, Trail crosses second stile, and reaches Va. 652. Trail continues ahead, directly across road. Upon crossing road, Trail passes around gate and, shortly, in 115 feet, crosses bridge and enters open field. In another 270 feet, Trail turns left, dips, and crosses intermittent stream. Trail then ascends steeply toward top of knoll.

11.7   Reach crest of knoll, with views ahead and to left of Tinker Mountain, Julias Knob, and McAfee Knob; view behind of Fullhardt Knob. Trail begins gradual descent to right and, in 100 yards, crosses stile and enters woods.

12.0   Trail turns slightly to the right, reaching old road. Follow old road straight ahead for 130 feet, before turning left and crossing Norfolk Southern Railroad tracks.
         This is a busy rail line: be very careful when crossing.

12.1　Reach busy U.S. 11. Cross with caution. Trail continues directly across highway, turns slightly to left, and crosses Buffalo Creek on bridge.
　　　Troutville is 0.8 mile north along highway.

12.3　Trail crosses bridge and ascends slightly.

12.4　Trail turns left onto Va. 779, following shoulder of road, and shortly passes under I–81.

12.5　Trail turns sharply to the left as it leaves Va. 779 and ascends bank *via* log steps. Shortly, Trail turns sharply to right and crosses stile into apple orchard.

12.7　Cross bridge, and ascend steps.

13.1　Trail crosses stile, leaving orchard, and soon passes under utility line.

13.3　Trail passes through old fence, entering grove of white pine and cedar.

13.6　Trail descends bank and reaches U.S. 220. Trail continues across highway and slightly to right, ascending gradually (see Section 28).
　　　Daleville is right (north) 1.2 miles on U.S. 220. To left (south) is I-81/U.S. 220/11 interchange area, with many services. Cloverdale is 2.3 miles south via U.S. 220/11.

Trail Description, South to North

Miles　　　　　　　　　　　　**Data**

0.0　Having crossed U.S. 220, Trail ascends bank and soon enters grove of white pine and cedar.
　　　At Trailhead, Daleville is left (north) 1.2 miles on U.S. 220. To right (south) is I-81/U.S. 220/11 interchange area, with many services. Cloverdale is 2.3 miles south via U.S. 220/11.

0.3　Trail passes through old fence, leaving pines.

0.5　Trail passes under utility line and, shortly, crosses stile, entering apple orchard.

0.9　Descend steps, and cross bridge.

1.1　Trail crosses over stile, leaving orchard. Trail soon turns to left and descends log steps to Va. 779. Trail turns right, follows shoulder of road, and shortly passes under I–81.

1.2　Trail turns to right, leaving Va. 779, and ascends slightly.

1.3   Trail descends slightly and crosses over bridge.

1.5   Trail crosses wooden bridge over Buffalo Creek and reaches busy U.S. 11. After crossing the highway, Trail continues straight ahead and slightly to the right, ascending slightly to the crossing of Norfolk and Southern Railroad tracks in about 200 feet. Immediately after crossing tracks, Trail turns to right onto old road.

   This is a busy highway and rail line; be careful when crossing. Troutville is 0.8 mile north along the highway.

1. 6   Trail leaves old road, veering to left and ascending slightly. Shortly, Trail switches back to the left, ascending for short distance before switching back to right and ascending as it skirts side of hill.

1.8   Trail crosses stile and enters open pasture area. Trail continues to ascend slightly to left and just below top of knoll. From top of knoll, views ahead are of Fullhardt Knob and, to right and behind, of Tinker Mountain, Julias Knob, and McAfee Knob. Trail then descends steeply toward Va. 652.

2.1   Trail crosses intermittent stream, and, after climbing bank, turns to right. Shortly, Trail crosses bridge and enters wooded area. Just ahead, Trail passes around gate and reaches Va. 652. Trail continues ahead, directly across road, crossing over stile. Trail turns to right, skirts open field, and ascends slightly to second stile. Upon crossing second stile, Trail turns sharply to left onto old farm lane and continues slight ascent.

2.3   Trail descends and turns to right. Trail soon turns to left, leaving old farm lane.

2.5   Trail leaves open field and enters wooded area. View behind and slightly to the right is of Tinker Mountain. Trail becomes graded as it begins ascent of side of Fullhardt Knob. From here to end of section, Trail is on National Forest Land, where **camping** is permitted.

2.6   Trail switches back to the left and ascends rock steps. This is the first of a half-dozen switchbacks to be encountered in the next 0.4 mile as the Trail ascends toward "Tollhouse Gap."

3.0   Trail switches back to the right and ascends rock steps.

3.6   Reach "Tollhouse Gap," a saddle between Fullhardt Knob and main spine of the Blue Ridge. Graded trail section is briefly interrupted by the gap but begins again shortly as Trail ascends toward crest of Blue Ridge. An unblazed trail enters the gap at right.

4.4   Trail turns sharply to left and continues gradual ascent toward ridgecrest and Fullhardt Knob Shelter on mostly ungraded trail along ridge arm. Blue-blazed trail straight ahead leads 250 feet to view of valley below.

5.0   Trail veers to left onto Fullhardt Knob fire road and begins steady descent. In the Trail section ahead along the fire road are a number of unblazed trails that intersect with the A.T. Blue-blazed trail to right along fire road ascends to **Fullhardt Knob Shelter** and privy in 465 feet.

5.3   Unblazed trail to right leads 60 feet to limited view of valley below.

5.4   Unblazed trail to left descends 350 feet to water source.

5.9   Trail turns sharply to right, leaving fire road and, shortly, begins to ascend slightly. Fire road continues ahead down hill 0.15 mile to Salt Pond Road (USFS 191), which descends to Va. 711, Va. 640, and U.S. 11.

6.9   Cross knob, and, 0.3 mile farther, cross a second knob (2,529 feet), highest point on ridge. Beyond knob, descend.

7.8   Cross Salt Pond Road (USFS 191), and descend very steeply by switchbacks. Road leads right 1.1 miles to parkway, milepost 101.5 (where road is gated), and left to Va. 711, Va. 640, and U.S. 11.

8.6   Curry Creek. Just beyond, Curry Creek Trail leads left 2.5 miles to Va. 640. Ascend steeply, with views north.

9.0   Reach gap between Grindstone Knob and unnamed 2,516-foot peak, and descend steeply.

9.3   Cross branch of Little Wilson Creek.

10.5   Cross Wilson Creek, and soon climb series of steps. Trails ascends slightly.

11.2   Blue-blazed trail leads left 100 feet to **Wilson Creek Shelter** and privy. Soon, come to second blue-blazed trail, also leading to shelter. Water from stream 200 yards in front of shelter.

11.6   Pass ledge with intermittent water.

12.5   Cross spur with view left of small rocky knob known as Shirleys Knob. Begin traversing northern slope of ridge through rhododendron with limited views.

13.1   Cross spur, and, 0.2 mile farther, cross another spur.

13.6   Reach Old Fincastle Road (USFS 186, a continuation of Va. 606),110 feet west of parkway at milepost 97.7 (2,402 feet). To continue on Trail, cross road into woods (see Section 26). A spring is across parkway, 0.4 mile down dirt Old Fincastle Road .

The Roanoke–Blacksburg Area
Valley of Virginia (U.S. 220)
to New River (U.S. 460)

This part of the A.T. leaves the Valley of Virginia and ascends to and follows a series of long, parallel northeast- to southwest-trending mountain ridges, descending only to cross the valleys between the crests. It traverses Tinker, Catawba, Cove, Brush, Sinking Creek, Johns Creek, Salt Pond, Potts, and Big mountains, reaches the Allegheny Front at Peters Mountain, then descends into the New River Valley. Along the way, it passes spectacular Tinker Cliffs, McAfee Knob, the monolith of Dragon's Tooth, Wind Rock, and the meadows of Symms Gap on Peters Mountain.

In the Tinker Mountain, Catawba Mountain, and Sinking Creek areas, the Trail is on National Park Service A.T. corridor lands. The remainder primarily traverses the Jefferson National Forest: the New Castle Ranger District on Cove Mountain and the New River Ranger District from Cove Mountain south to Pearisburg.

Originally, the A.T. followed the eastern edge of the Blue Ridge from the vicinity of Roanoke south to the Tennessee line. The area was fairly inaccessible and included the scenic Pinnacles of Dan, Dan River Gorge, and Fisher Peak. Roads in the area were improved, the Blue Ridge Parkway was built, and travel increased. It became clear that the Blue Ridge south of Roanoke was no longer a suitable location for a backcountry trail. The Appalachian Trail Conference in 1940 proposed a reroute for the Trail far to the west in Jefferson National Forest. World War II delayed the project. The Roanoke Appalachian Trail Club began scouting, locating, clearing, and marking the new route in 1951. By 1955, it was completed.

Two clubs are responsible for this part of the Trail. The Roanoke Appalachian Trail Club maintains the Trail from U.S. 220 to Stony Creek Valley, and the Outdoor Club at Virginia Tech maintains it from Stony Creek Valley to the New River. The USFS provides assistance in the Jefferson National Forest.

This section has many shelters, but they are at irregular intervals, some a long day's hike apart. Shelters and some public accommodations are listed in individual sections.

Water sources are scarce or nonexistent on the ridgecrests in this area. Hikers should carry ample water.

Trail Route in the Roanoke–Blacksburg Area

This part of the Trail begins in the Valley of Virginia just west of I–81 on U.S. 220. The Trail climbs to and follows the narrow crest of Tinker Mountain northward to Scorched Earth Gap, with views of Brushy Mountain and Carvins Cove Reservoir. It ascends from Scorched Earth Gap to Tinker Cliffs, with a breathtaking view of Catawba Valley and the mountains beyond. At the Botetourt–Roanoke County line, the name of the ridge changes to Catawba Mountain.

The Trail ascends to the summit and McAfee Knob, an overhanging rock ledge with spectacular views of both the Catawba and Roanoke valleys, as well as mountain ridges to the north and west. The Trail passes over the sharp teeth of Sawtooth Ridge before crossing Catawba Valley. It traverses the narrow rock crest of a spur of Cove Mountain and reaches the crest of the ridge at the dramatic monolith known as Dragon's Tooth, with panoramic views into Millers Cove below and the ridges beyond. The Trail turns sharply north at the Tooth and follows the rocky, hook-shaped crest of Cove Mountain for four miles, descending at the ridge's western end to cross Trout Creek near Trout Creek Gorge.

From Trout Creek, the Trail rises again, to the crest of Brush Mountain, follows the crest for about 1.5 miles, passing a monument to Audie Murphy before descending to Craig Creek Valley, crosses Craig Creek, climbs to the crest of Sinking Creek Mountain (part of the eastern continental divide), and follows it for some five miles through deep woods, with occasional outlooks.

The Trail crosses Sinking Creek Valley, seven miles east of Newport, then ascends onto a spur of Johns Creek Mountain, which it follows until descending into Johns Creek Valley.

From the remote upper reaches of Johns Creek, the Trail climbs to the flat, wooded summit of Salt Pond Mountain, traversing about 4.5 miles of the Mountain Lake Wilderness, where hikers might see a variety of wildlife. It traverses the crest of Potts Mountain (4,128 feet), passes Wind Rock, a viewpoint overlooking Stony Creek Valley, and then descends across the northern slope of Big Mountain.

The route crosses Stony Creek Valley near Interior, parallels the creek for a short distance, and then climbs to the crest of Peters Mountain (3,800 feet), passing a stand of large hemlocks in a swampy depression known as Pine Swamp. About 5.8 miles of the Trail lie near the boundary of the Peters Mountain Wilderness. The Trail then follows the crest of Peters Mountain—roughly the West Virginia–Virginia border—for more than 12 miles, crossing Symms Gap Meadow in the center of the ridge and later Rice Field, with views of the farmland and mountains to the west in West Virginia. The Trail passes several powerline rights-of-way with similar views. Leaving the ridge, the route descends steadily to the New River and U.S. 460, just west of Pearisburg.

Wildflowers

Within these sections of Trail can be found examples of most of the plants common to the valleys and mountains of the southwest Appalachians. In the Blacksburg area, a few moisture-loving plants give way quickly to those of the dry ridgetops. Brambles fill open areas under powerline crossings.

Spring flora include bellwort, bloodroot, buttercup, chickweed, colts foot, columbine, dwarf iris, fire pink, hepatica, lily-of-the-valley, lady's-slipper, ragwort, Solomon's seal, spring beauty, squawroot, trailing arbutus, trillium, trout lily, violets (several varieties), wild ginger, and wintergreen.

Summer flora include cinquefoil, jack-in-the-pulpit, ox-eye daisy, spotted wintergreen, wild geranium, and viper's bugloss.

Autumn flora seen along the Trail are black-eyed Susan, boneset, cardinal lobelia, goldenrods, grass of parnassus, great blue lobelia, Indian pipes, Joe-pye weed, marsh pinks, milkweeds, pokeweed, Queen Anne's lace, stiff genetian, and jewelweed.

Flowering trees and shrubs include pinxter and flame azalea, blueberry, brambles, dogwood, redbud, sarvice berry, and rhododendron maximum. Some of the many species of trees are oak, hickory, maple, tulip poplar, hemlock, and white and Virginia pine.

The lower areas along the many creeks abound in numerous varieties of fungi. These are exceedingly fascinating, but only the expert should investigate beyond viewing the specimens.

Wildlife

Several species of animals typical of this part of Virginia can be found. Avoid direct contact with all wild animals, due to the risk of rabies. Rabbits, squirrels, skunk, raccoon, opossum, chipmunk, mice, deer, beaver, turkey, and grouse have all been seen along the Trail.

U.S. 220 and Va. 816 to Va. 624
Section Twenty-eight
25.5 miles

Brief Description of Section

In this section, as the A.T. follows the rocky, twisted backbone of Tinker Ridge for some 13 miles, it crosses a series of sandstone outcrops with spectacular views of farms and orchards in the Valley of Virginia and Catawba Valley, of North Mountain, of the jagged shore of Carvins Cove Reservoir, and of the towering ridges encircling it. The route follows the crest of Catawba Mountain for eight miles, with considerable variation in elevation.

Near the middle of this section, the Trail follows Tinker Cliffs for half a mile. These sheer rock cliffs overlook Catawba Valley and the mountain ridges beyond. For much of their length, the cliffs overhang, and the Trail is very close to the edge. *Hikers should be cautious.*

Farther south, the Trail ascends Catawba Mountain, created millions of years ago by the collision of continental plates, to McAfee Knob, with spectacular views of both the Catawba and Roanoke valleys. A side trail follows this massive overhanging rock ledge for 200 yards, forming a loop with the Trail. *Exercise extreme caution at all times here, but especially during wet or icy conditions.*

The North Mountain Trail (see page 236) intersects the A.T. at Scorched Earth Gap and at Va. 624. This 14.0-mile trail (the former A.T.) forms a loop trail with the A.T. of about 29.5 miles. The Andy Layne Trail begins at Scorched Earth Gap and is the northern connector of the North Mountain Trail, ending at Va. 779.

Geology

This section of the Trail started as swampy mud flats during the Paleozoic Period, where shales and limestones together formed the Martinsburg formation. Five hundred million years ago, Virginia lay near the equator, with Africa attached to the east. When Africa drifted away, inland seas arrived. East of here, over millions of years, tall mountain ranges came and went as the seas covered the landscape. On these mud flats, sand and silt collected and compacted. This tremendous weight bowed the flats down to an incredible depth of 40,000 feet (seven times that of the Grand Canyon!).

Sixty million years ago, Africa crashed back into Virginia. These compacted mud flats, now stone layers, rippled and cracked. Africa left yet again, and, after the seas receded, uplifting began throughout the land. The high rocks were exposed to streams and weather.

Catawba and Tinker mountains are the front edge of a huge rock block known as the Pulaski Fault. The hooked shape of Tinker Mountain is due to the shearing, dragging effect of the advancing rock face's smearing across its stationary neighbor.

Among the many reminders of Silurian sandstone in this section are Hay Rock, Tinker Cliffs, Devil's Kitchen (atop Catawba Mountain), Snack Bar Rock, and McAfee Knob.

History

In this part of Virginia, evidence of inhabitants dating back to about 9500 B.C. has been found. In this Paleoindian period, the land was changing from the last glaciation and resembled a tundra environment. Native Americans hunted mammoth and mastodon and developed stone tools.

The Archaic Period (8000 B.C. to 1200 B.C.) saw a gradual warming of the environment and the disappearance of the larger animals. Deer, bear, and turkey were the hunter's sustenance, and the tools changed to reflect this. Hardwood forests began to develop as well.

The Woodland Period (1200 B.C. to 1600 A.D.) brought the beginning of land-clearing by native Americans. Spearhead points evolved into arrowheads, marking development of the bow and arrow. Agriculture developed, as did some ceramic production.

European settlement began in this part of Virginia in the early 1700s. Fort Lewis, near Salem, provided protection to the early settlers in the region. Some may have lived on the north side of Tinker Mountain as early as 1730. Later, they headed west toward Catawba and Craig creeks.

In the late 1800s, stagecoach travel brought more settlers through the area. These coaches had horns that might be heard at great distances. According to legend, one driver on the Fincastle, Va.–

Lewisburg, W.Va., line would blow his horn while crossing Catawba Mountain, so tavern keepers might begin preparing meals for hungry travelers.

Points of Interest

Valley of Virginia: the most prominent of the several major valleys that are part of a major geological feature that stretches from the Hudson River in New York to northern Alabama. The A.T. crosses these valleys in New Jersey, Pennsylvania, and twice in Virginia (at the northern end of the section and in southwestern Virginia, near Groseclose). The Shenandoah, Roanoke, and Tennessee valleys are all linked by this feature.

Tinker Mountain: Name comes from legend that a number of deserters in the Revolutionary War hid here, making pots and pans, hence they were called "tinkers."

Hay Rock: views of Carvins Cove Reservoir and the Valley of Virginia.

Tinker Cliffs (3,000 feet): half-mile-long rock wall overlooking Catawba Valley.

McAfee Knob (3,197 feet): overhanging rock ledge with views of Catawba and Roanoke valleys.

Road Approaches

The northern end of this section is just west of I-81 Exit 150, at the Trail's intersection with U.S. 220. Parking is available at a park-and-ride lot on Va. 816, 0.2 mile south of the A.T. crossing of U.S. 220.

The southern end of the section is on Va. 624, 0.3 mile west of its intersection with Va. 311 (limited parking).

The A.T. crosses Va. 311, 5.9 miles from the section's southern end, 8 miles north of Salem, 12 miles north of downtown Roanoke (*via* Va. 419 and U.S. 460, or Va. 311, I-81, and I-581), and 14 miles south of New Castle. A parking lot is on the southern side of Va. 311.

Paved Va. 785 intersects the Trail in Catawba Valley, 1.6 miles from the southern end of the section (limited roadside parking).

Maps

For route navigation, refer to ATC Glenwood-New Castle Districts Map 4. For area detail, refer to the following USGS topographic quadrangles: Daleville, Catawba, Salem, Glenvar, and Looney.

Shelters and Campsites

This very popular section has four shelters and three primitive campsites (camping is restricted to shelters and designated campsites):

Lamberts Meadow Shelter: built in 1974 and maintained by Roanoke A.T. Club; 9.3 miles from northern end of section; accommodates six; water from nearby stream.

Next shelter: north 14.3 miles (Fullhardt Knob); south 6.1 miles (Campbell).

Campbell Shelter: built in 1989 by ATC's Konnarock Trail crew and Roanoke A.T. Club, maintained by latter; 10.1 miles from southern end of section; accommodates six; water from nearby spring.

Next shelter: north 6.1 miles (Lamberts Meadow); south 2.2 miles (Catawba).

Catawba Mountain Shelter: built in 1984 by Konnarock Trail crew and Roanoke A.T. Club, maintained by latter; 7.9 miles from southern end of section, accommodates six; water from nearby spring.

Next shelter: north 2.2 miles (Campbell); south 1.0 mile (Boy Scout).

Boy Scout Shelter: maintained by Roanoke A.T. Club; 6.9 miles from southern end of section; accommodates ten; seasonal spring in front of shelter, usually dry in summer.

Next shelter: north 1.0 mile (Catawba); south 12.9 miles (Pickle Branch, on a 0.5-mile side trail).

One primitive campsite is 0.2 mile north of Lamberts Meadow Shelter on Sawmill Run. The second, the Pig Farm Campsite (pigs were raised in this area as recently as 1982), is 0.6 mile north of McAfee Knob and 0.1 mile south of the Campbell Shelter. The third one is 0.1 mile north of Catawba Mountain Shelter.

Regulations

This section is on National Park Service A.T.-corridor land. Camping and campfires are permitted only at shelters and designated campsites, unless specifically noted otherwise.

Supplies, Services, and Public Accommodations

Daleville (ZIP Code 24083, 1.2 miles west) and Cloverdale (ZIP Code 24077, 2.3 miles east) are near the northern end of this section at the junction with U.S. 220. Supermarkets, restaurants, motels, and other services are within 0.2 mile of the Trailhead.

A truck stop off I-81 at Exit 150 (U.S. 220) has hot showers. Roanoke, 10 miles south on U.S. 11 or I-81, has a complete range of supplies, services, and accommodations.

A store on Va. 311 is 0.4 mile from the southern end of the section. From the Va. 311 crossing, 5.9 miles from the southern end of section, it is 1.0 mile west to Catawba (ZIP Code 24070; grocery; restaurant open Thursday–Sunday).

Trail Description, North to South

Miles   **Data**

0.0   After crossing U.S. 220, Trail ascends gradually through old fruit orchard.
         Daleville is right (north) 1.2 miles on U.S. 220. To left (south) is I-81/U.S. 220/11 interchange area, with many services. Cloverdale is 2.3 miles south via U.S. 220/11.

0.2   Trail veers to the left and enters open field.

0.3   Trail turns to the right, descending through old fruit orchard. Unmarked trail (old Trail route) to left leads in 0.2 mile to commuter parking lot near intersection of U.S. 220 and Va. 816.

0.4   Trail turns to right onto old road and continues with gradual descent onto Tinker Creek floodplain, passing grove of white pines on left.

0.5   Trail crosses concrete bridge over Tinker Creek, and, shortly, curves to right around overgrown field

0.6   Trail turns to left and crosses railroad spur. After crossing tracks, Trail continues to ascend gradually off Tinker Creek floodplain. Shortly, Trail crosses gas line right-of-way and reenters pine grove.

0.8   Trail passes under powerline and enters area of mixed conifer and deciduous growth. Trail continues to follow old road and shortly enters small ravine with intermittent stream to left.

1.1   Trail turns sharply to right and steeply ascends 155 feet to sign board.

1.2   Trail switches back sharply to right, leaving old woods road, and, in 260 feet, passes under powerline.

1.6   Trail switches back to left. This is the first of a series of seven relatively long and sharp switchbacks in the next 0.4 mile as the Trail ascends toward the crest of Tinker Ridge.

2.0   Trail climbs rock stairs and switches back to the left. In 100 feet, Trail bends to the right, away from private road. In the next 370 feet, Trail undergoes a number of directional changes on relatively short switchbacks as it ascends to crest of ridge.

2.1   Trail turns sharply to right onto old tower access road and ascends steeply for 70 feet, to crest of Tinker Ridge. Immediately after crossing under powerline and gaining ridgecrest, large rock just to the right of Trail affords view of Daleville–Cloverdale area of the Great Valley of Virginia below and of Fullhardt Knob and Blue Ridge across valley.

2.7   View of Carvins Cove and surrounding ridges and peaks.

2.8   Pass under powerline.

4.0   Reach Hay Rock, a massive fragment of the tilted sandstone layer that forms the backbone of Tinker Ridge. A climb to the top provides good views. Continue along ridge, soon passing Balanced Rock, then Chimney Rocks.

4.5   Enter old road. Soon, where road bears to right and descends, continue straight along ridge.

4.7   Pass under powerline, and descend.

5.1   Reach Angels Gap, where a gasline right-of-way leads down both sides of ridge. From the gap, the A.T. ascends steeply northwest along crest.

5.4   Reach top of Ruckers Knob (2,200 feet); pass under powerline.

8.5   In second gap (2,100 feet), turn left, and descend. The ridge ahead (no trail) leads 1.5 miles to cliffs of Julius Knob.

8.9   Red-blazed trail leads left, descending about 2 miles to picnic area on Carvins Cove Reservoir.

9.1   **Lamberts Meadow primitive campsite** is 100 feet to right of Trail, just before it crosses Sawmill Run. In 100 yards, A.T. turns sharply right. Blue-blazed trail to left rejoins the A.T. at Brickey's Gap (mile 12.3) after 1.7 miles, bypassing Tinker Cliffs.

9.3   Cross stream, and ascend sharply, though only briefly. After 0.1 mile, side trail descends left 50 yards to **Lamberts Meadow Shelter** and privy with water from stream 50 yards below. (Roof of shelter is barely visible from A.T. in summer.)

10.0   Reach Scorched Earth Gap. The A.T. continues to ascend to the left, soon coming to a series of switchbacks.
        Yellow-blazed Andy Layne Trail to right leads to Va. 779 in 3.1 miles, and North Mountain Trail continues up and southward from there, along North Mountain ridge for 10.4 additional miles, until it descends onto Va. 311. It rejoins A.T. on Va. 624 for a total of 14.0 miles. With the A.T., it forms a loop trail of 29.5 miles. (See next chapter for full description.)

10.4   Reach Lunch Box Rock, with views of Purgatory Mountain and the Blue Ridge. Trail bends sharply to right.

10.5   Reach northern end of Tinker Cliffs (3,000 feet) at The Well, a natural hole in the rocks resembling a dug well. Turn left, and follow edge of cliffs, with views of Dragon's Tooth, McAfee Knob, North Mountain, and other, more distant mountains. *Use caution in wet or icy weather.*

11.0   Reach end of cliffs.

12.3   After steep descent, reach Brickey's Gap in large, open field. Blue-blazed trail to left leads 1.7 miles north to Lamberts Meadow and rejoins A.T. at mile 9.1. Old road to right leads to Va. 779. A.T. ascends toward ridgecrest.

12.4   Regain ridgetop.

13.1   Reach rock outcropping; views left of Carvins Cove, Peaks of Otter, and Tinker and Apple Orchard mountains; view to right is of McAfee Knob. Within next 0.1 mile, A.T. descends on rocky ridge. *Use caution when Trail is wet or icy.*

13.5   Pass Rock Haven, an overhanging rock.

13.7   Pass between two very large rocks known as Snack Bar Rock.

14.0   Bear right onto remnant of old road.

14.7   Turn right, leaving road and ascending.

15.4   Blue-blazed trail leads 100 feet **to Campbell Shelter** and privy on left. In 100 yards, turn slightly right onto old road.

15.5   Reach **Pig Farm campsite** with picnic table, fire grate, and views of Roanoke Valley to left of Trail. Blue-blazed trail leads 0.1 mile left to spring.

15.6   Old road ends. Soon, continue ascent, on series of steeper switchbacks.

16.0   Reach area atop Catawba Mountain of room-sized rock blocks known as Devil's Kitchen. Be careful in following A.T.; unmarked side trails are complex in this area.

16.1   Reach small clearing at end of old road. This is top of McAfee Knob (3,197 feet). A.T. continues left on old road and begins descent. Side trail to right leads to cliffs. On clear days, there are magnificent views from cliffs. *Use caution in wet and icy conditions.*

16.2   Continue ahead on old road. Second side trail to right leads to cliffs. Soon, reach another area of large rock blocks. Unmarked side-trail pattern is complex here, too. Be careful to stay on A.T.

16.3   Turn right, leave old road, and continue descent. Rock outcroppings to right of Trail for next 0.8 mile have views in winter of Catawba Valley, Gravelly Ridge, and North Mountain.

17.1   Trail bends back sharply to left and soon crosses under powerline.

17.3   Cross road, and continue descent.

17.5   Turn sharp right onto old woods road. **Primitive campsite** is 100 feet to left.

17.6   Blue-blazed trails, both here and shortly ahead, lead left to **Catawba Mountain Shelter** and privy. Not far beyond second blue blazed trail, cross stream, intersect blue-blazed trails leading right to spring (undeveloped water source; treat before using), then enter old road again, ascending slightly.

17.7   Turn left, leaving old road. For next 1.5 miles, Trail parallels ridgecrest, with minor ascents and descents. Winter and late-fall views to left of Fort Lewis Mountain.

18.6   Metal **Boy Scout Shelter** and privy, is 100 feet to left of Trail. Seasonal spring in front of shelter is usually dry in summer.

19.2   Turn sharp right (bulletin board on right). Soon, turn left onto old woods road, turn left again, leaving road, and ascend along rock ridgecrest.

19.3   Turn left onto old woods road again, and begin descent.

19.4   Leave road to left, and descend on switchbacks. Pass under two utility lines as Trail approaches highway.

19.6   Cross Va. 311. *Be extremely cautious crossing highway here; southbound traffic has limited visibility.* Trail passes through right side of parking lot and begins gradual ascent.

         Catawba is 1.0 mile to right (west) on Va. 311, with post office, store, and restaurant.

19.9   Side trail leads left to view of Fort Lewis Mountain.

20.0   For next 2.9 miles, ascend and descend, sometimes fairly steeply, over several steep knobs that give this section of mountain its local name, Sawtooth Ridge. Views of Fort Lewis Mountain to left, Cove and North mountains to right.

22.9   Pass rock outcropping and pine grove. Begin descent on switchbacks.

23.2   Cross stile.

23.4   Enter open field, and continue descent. Blazes are on wooden utility poles. Views in clear weather of Cove Mountain and Dragon's Tooth (above and to right of powerline towers).

23.6   Beckner Gap is noticeable to left. Cross intermittent stream on small bridge and stile in 100 feet. Follow left bank of Catawba Creek.

23.8   Cross another stile and, in 100 yards, wooden bridge over Catawba Creek. Ascend hill in open field toward highway.

23.9   Cross stile, and immediately cross Va. 785, then second stile slightly to left. Bear right at intermittent stream.

        At road crossing, lodging is 0.1 mile right (north)

24.0   Trail approaches fence and turns sharp right before crossing intermittently wet area. Follow right side of fence.

24.1   At fence corner, continue straight toward blazed post on top of hill. In 50 yards, reach top of open hill, and begin slight descent, crossing stile in another 50 yards.

24.2   Begin slight ascent, staying to left of small sinkhole. Sawtooth Ridge visible to right.

24.3   Descend back to old woods road, and bear sharp left onto road. Pass remains of old dam on right. Follow left side of stream for next 0.3 mile.

24.6   Cross bridge over stream, and begin ascent on old woods road through pine grove.

24.8   Bear sharply off old woods road through hardwood forest.

24.9   Cross old woods road (barely recognizable), and ascend gradually through overgrown pasture.

25.0   Cross stile near top of Sandstone Ridge, and begin descent on switchbacks.

25.5   Cross stream on culverted driveway. Cross Va. 624 (1,790 feet) at end of section (see Section 29).

        Yellow-blazed North Mountain Trail leads right to Va. 311 in 0.3 mile and to store 0.1 mile farther. It traverses North Mountain, joins Andy Layne Trail, and rejoins A.T. at Scorched Earth Gap in 14.0 miles, making a loop hike with the A.T. of 29.5 miles (see next chapter).

Trail Description, South to North

Miles   **Data**

 0.0   Cross Va. 624 (1,790 feet). Cross stream on culverted driveway. Begin slight ascent to left.

Yellow-blazed North Mountain Trail follows Va. 624 to left, reaching Va. 311 in 0.3 mile and store 0.1 mile farther. That trail traverses North Mountain, and in 14.0 miles, joins A.T., making a loop hike with the A.T. of 29.5 miles (see next chapter).

0.1   Turn back sharply to right, beginning a series of eight switchbacks over next 0.4 mile.

0.5   Turn sharp left, and cross stile near top of Sandstone Ridge. Soon, begin slight descent through overgrown pasture.

0.6   Cross old woods road (barely recognizable), and enter thickly wooded area.

0.7   Follow old woods road to right.

0.8   Rejoin and follow old woods road, continuing descent through pines.

0.9   Cross bridge over stream. Follow stream to left, downhill.

1.2   Pass remains of an old dam on left. Climb bank to right, leaving old woods road, and enter pasture. View of Sawtooth Ridge to left. Ascend ahead, slightly to right.

1.3   Begin slight descent; stay to right of small sinkhole.

1.4   Cross stile, and, in 50 yards, reach top of open hill with blaze on post. In another 50 yards, pass fence corner, and continue slight descent to left of electric fence.

1.5   Turn sharp left just beyond low, intermittently wet area, leaving fence. Follow intermittent stream toward road.

1.6   Cross stile, approach and cross Va. 785. Just to left, cross second stile. Ascend slightly, skirting to left of hilltop before descending onto the floodplain of Catawba Creek.
        Lodging 0.1 mile left from road crossing (north).

1.7   Cross bridge over Catawba Creek, and turn sharp left. Cross stile in 50 yards.

1.9   Cross second stile, and, in 100 feet, cross small bridge over intermittent stream. Beckner Gap is visible to the right.

2.1   Leave open area, and continue ascent. Nice views here, to rear, of Cove Mountain and Dragon's Tooth (above and to right of powerline towers) on clear day.

2.2   Turn back sharply to right. Begin series of five switchbacks and four sets of log steps over next 0.3 mile.

2.3   Cross stile.

2.6   Reach rock outcroppings and pines at crest of Sawtooth Ridge. For next 2.9 miles, descend and ascend, sometimes fairly steeply, over several steep knolls that give the ridge its name. Take care to follow blazes along this section. A number of views of Fort Lewis Mountain are to right; of Cove Mountain and North Mountain to left.

5.5   Gradually descend toward Va. 311.

5.6   Side trail to right leads to view of Fort Lewis Mountain.

5.9   Reach parking area at Va. 311. *Be extremely cautious crossing highway here;* southbound traffic has limited visibility. Soon, pass under two utility lines, and turn left to begin series of switchbacks, ascending to crest of ridge.
        Catawba is 1.0 mile to left (west) on Va. 311, with post office, store, and restaurant.

6.1   At ridgecrest, turn slightly to right, and ascend on old woods road.

6.2   Leave old woods road, and follow rocky ridgecrest to right. Soon, descend. Turn slightly to right, and rejoin old woods road to right, before turning right again, leaving old woods road. A bulletin board is to the left of the Trail.

6.3   Turn sharp left, and parallel ridgecrest, with minor ascents and descents, for 1.5 mile. Fall and winter views to right of Fort Lewis Mountain.

6.9   **Metal Boy Scout Shelter** and privy is 100 feet to right of Trail. Seasonal spring in front of shelter is usually dry in summer.

7.8   Turn right onto old road, and descend. Soon, reach junction with blue-blazed trails leading left to spring. Cross stream.

7.9   Blue-blazed trails here and just ahead lead right to **Catawba Mountain Shelter** and privy.

8.0   Turn sharp left, leaving old woods road, and ascend. **Primitive campsite** is 100 feet to right.

8.2   Cross road, and enter area of thick laurel undergrowth.

8.4   Pass under powerline. Soon, turn sharp right. Begin ascent to McAfee Knob. Rock outcroppings to left of Trail have winter views of Catawba Valley, Gravelly Ridge, and North Mountain.

9.2   Turn left onto old road, and continue ascent through area of large rock blocks. Many trails cross this area; take care to follow A.T. route.

9.3   Continue on old road. Side trail to left leads to cliffs, with good views; *treacherous footing in wet and icy weather. Use extreme caution.*

9.4   Reach McAfee Knob (small clearing at end of road). Side trail left leads to cliffs, with magnificent views on clear day.

9.5   Descend rock steps into Devil's Kitchen, area of large rock blocks. Many crossing trails; take care to follow A.T. route. Soon, descend on series of steep switchbacks.

9.9   Join old road, and continue descent.

10.0 Reach **Pig Farm campsite**; picnic tables, fire grate, and views of Roanoke Valley to right. Blue-blazed trail leads 0.1 mile right to spring. In 100 yards, turn sharp left; leave old road.

10.1 Blue-blazed trail leads 100 feet to **Campbell Shelter** and privy on right. Water available at nearby spring.

10.8 Begin to follow old road to left.

11.5 Bear left; leave remains of old road. Begin short ascent

11.8 Pass between two large rocks known as Snack Bar Rock.

12.1 Pass Rock Haven, an overhanging rock.

12.3 Begin ascent on rock ridge. *Take extra precautions in wet and icy conditions.*

12.4 Rock outcropping, with views to right of Carvins Cove, Tinker Mountain, Peaks of Otter, and Apple Orchard Mountain. View to left of McAfee Knob.

13.1 Leave ridge, and descend old road.

13.2 Reach Brickey's Gap in large open field. Blue-blazed trail to right leads 1.7 miles to Lamberts Meadow and rejoins A.T. at mile 16.4, bypassing Tinker Cliffs. Old road to left leads to Va. 779. Begin steep ascent.

14.5 Reach southern end of Tinker Cliffs. Follow edge of cliffs for next 0.5 mile. Views of Dragon's Tooth, McAfee Knob, North Mountain, and distant mountains. *Take extra precautions in wet and icy conditions.*

15.0 Reach end of cliffs at The Well, a natural hole in the rocks.

15.1   Reach Lunch Box Rock, with views of Purgatory Mountain and the Blue Ridge. Bear sharply to left, and descend on switchbacks.

15.5   Reach Scorched Earth Gap (2,360 feet). Yellow-blazed Andy Layne Trail leads left 3.1 miles to Va. 779 and North Mountain Trail and, in another 10.9 miles, rejoins the A.T. at Va. 624 (see next chapter). A.T. continues to descend to right.

16.1   Side trail descends right 50 yards to **Lamberts Meadow Shelter** and privy and water from stream 50 yards below. (Roof of shelter is barely visible from A.T. in summer.) From shelter side trail, A.T. descends steeply.

16.2   Cross stream, and ascend gently through woods.

16.4   Turn left. Blue-blazed trail straight ahead leads back 1.7 miles to rejoin the A.T. at mile 13.2 in Brickey's Gap. Beyond junction, reach stream in Lamberts Meadow. One hundred feet to left is area used for **primitive camping**.

16.6   Red-blazed trail leads right and descends into valley. A.T. ascends back toward Tinker Ridge.

17.0   Reach gap (2,100 feet) on Tinker Ridge. To left, ridge (no trail) leads 1.5 miles to cliffs of Julias Knob. A.T. leads right, following narrow, winding Tinker Ridge for next 6.4 miles, with frequent views to left of nearby subdivisions, orchards, farms, and mountains beyond James River. To left are views of Carvins Cove Reservoir and Brushy Mountain.

20.1   Pass under powerline, and reach top of Ruckers Knob (2,200 feet). Beyond, descend steeply along crest.

20.4   Reach Angels Gap, where a gasline right-of-way leads down both sides of the ridge. Ascend southeast along crest.

20.8   Pass under powerline. Trail levels somewhat.

20.9   Enter old road. Road soon ends. A.T. continues straight ahead along ridge, soon passing Chimney Rocks, then Balanced Rock.

21.5   Reach Hay Rock, a massive fragment of tilted sandstone layer that forms backbone of Tinker Ridge. A climb to top provides good views.

22.7   Pass under powerline.

22.8   View of Carvins Cove and surrounding mountains.

23.4   Immediately before crossing under powerline, large rock just to left of Trail has view of Daleville–Cloverdale area of Valley of Virginia below and of Fullhardt Knob and Blue Ridge ahead across valley. Trail passes under powerline and begins to descend steeply on old tower access road . In 70 feet, Trail turns sharply to left, leaving access road and entering area of young, piney growth. In the next 370 feet, Trail undergoes a number of directional changes on relatively short switchbacks as it descends toward private road.

23.5   Trail bends to left, away from private road, and continues descent of ridge in a series of seven longer, sharper switchbacks for the next 0.4 mile, beginning in 100 feet. Trail moves into an area of mixed conifer and deciduous growth.

23.9   Trail switches back to the right.

24.3   Trail passes under power line and in 260 feet, switches back sharply to left, coming onto old woods road.

24.4   Reach signboard. Trail descends steeply and, in 155 feet, turns sharply left onto more noticeable old road in a small ravine. A paralleling, intermittent stream soon becomes noticeable to right of Trail.

24.7   Trail passes under powerline and enters pine grove.

24.9   Trail leaves pine grove, and, in 195 feet, crosses gasline right-of-way. Shortly, Trail crosses railroad spur. Just beyond tracks, Trail curves to the right around overgrown field on Tinker Creek floodplain.

25.0   Trail crosses concrete bridge over Tinker Creek. Trail continues straight ahead on old road and passes to the left of old field replanted with pines, ascending gradually toward a more mature grove of white pines as it climbs off the floodplain.

25.1   Trail turns to left, leaving old road, and, in 250 feet, begins to ascend more steadily through old fruit orchard.

25.2   Trail turns to left and soon passes through open field. Unmarked trail (old Trail route) straight ahead leads in 0.2 mile to commuter parking lot near intersection of U.S. 220 and Va. 816.

25.3   Trail veers to right, reenters old fruit orchard, and soon
        begins gradual descent toward U.S. 220.

25.5   Reach U.S. 220 and end of section. Trail continues across
        highway and slightly to right, with ascent of bank just to
        the right of private driveway (see Section 27).

        *At Trailhead, Daleville is left (north) 1.2 miles on U.S. 220.
        To right (south) is I-81/U.S. 220/11 interchange area, with
        many services. Cloverdale is 2.3 miles south via U.S. 220/11.*

North Mountain Trail and Andy Layne Trail
14.0 miles

The yellow-blazed North Mountain Trail and the Andy Layne Trail (also blazed yellow) form a loop hike with the A.T. (Section 28) of 29.5 miles. These two trails follow an old A.T. route that was used after the Trail was removed from Sawtooth Ridge and Catawba Mountain in the 1970s. When the present Trail route was reestablished on these ridges in the 1980s, this old route was designated as the North Mountain Trail. After a permanent corridor was obtained for the northern 3.1 miles of this trail, the Roanoke Appalachian Trail Club renamed this section the Andy Layne Trail, in memory of a former overseer of the section of the Trail here across the Catawba Valley.

From the intersection with the A.T. at Scorched Earth Gap, the Andy Layne Trail descends south to Catawba Creek. Across this stream, the trail continues to a parking area just off Va. 779. Across Va. 779, opposite this parking area, the North Mountain Trail begins and ascends to the crest of North Mountain, which it follows for nine miles.

Va. 779 (in the Catawba Valley) serves as a southern trailhead for the Andy Layne Trail and as a northern trailhead for the North Mountain Trail. Ample parking is available here. Limited parking for the North Mountain Trail is found near its southern end on Va. 311.

These trails do not have shelters, but a seasonal spring provides water for camping 6.1 miles from the northern end. The 3.1 miles between Scorched Earth Gap and Va. 779 are on private land where neither camping nor campfires are permitted. The rest of the route is in Jefferson National Forest.

Trail Description, North to South

Miles   **Data**

0.0   From Scorched Earth Gap (2,460 feet), yellow-blazed Andy
        Layne Trail descends from the A.T. into Catawba Valley,
        beginning on graded switchbacks.
            *For the first 0.5 mile of this trail is on A.T.-corridor land. The
            remainder of the trail is on land owned by Roanoke Cement
            Company.*

1.0   Ungraded trail descends quite steeply down nose of ridge,
        with private property to left and deep gully on right.

1.2   Reach saddle, and begin gradual ascent.

1.3   Reach top of wooded hill, and begin descent on old road
        with views of cement plant and North Mountain to right.

1.6   Bear left off road and, in 100 feet, bear left again on another
        old road.

1.7   Pass around right end of gate and continue to descend on
        dug trail.

2.1   Cross fence on ladder stile, and enter pasture area. De-
        scend through pasture toward creek.

2.2   Cross Catawba Creek on bridge. Bear right, and follow
        creek downstream at edge of pasture, with views of rock
        cliffs across creek.

2.3   Cross fence on ladder stile near huge, double-trunked
        sycamore tree. Turn left, and follow fence through pas-
        ture.

2.4   Cross Little Catawba Creek on bridge. In 100 feet cross
        fence on ladder stile. Bear right, and, in 50 feet, make sharp
        turn to left.

2.6   With views of Little Catawba Creek on left, descend to
        flood plain on steps. For next 500 feet, trail follows creek
        bank.

2.7   Begin gradual ascent through semi-open pasture. In places
        bedrock appears at the earth's surface.

2.8   Reach gap in open, grassy area. Bear left, and ascend quite
        steeply.

3.0   Reach wooded hilltop and descend westward. In 200 feet,
        cross fence on ladder stile. Andy Layne Trail bulletin
        board is to right of trail just beyond stile.

3.1   Reach gravel parking lot off Va. 779. This is the end of the
      Andy Layne Trail. The North Mountain Trail (also yellow-
      blazed) begins on opposite side of Va. 779, ascending
      gently on old logging road.

3.6   Enter dense stand of young hardwoods.

3.9   Ascend rock steps with small stream at base. Beyond,
      climb steeply on sometimes rough, rocky footpath.

4.5   Turn left, follow crest of North Mountain. Side trail leads
      right 4.5 miles to Stone Coal Gap. For next 9.0 miles, the
      trail follows the crest of North Mountain, frequently climb-
      ing and descending.

6.1   Side trail descends steeply left 250 yards to unreliable
      spring.

6.8   Descend 15 feet of naturally layered rock steps.

7.3   In sag, Turkey Trail (often obscured by growth) leads
      right, approximately 1.5 miles, to USFS 224.

10.1 In sag, Grouse Trail leads right about one mile to USFS 224.

11.1 In gap, Deer Trail (often obscured by growth) leads right
      about one mile to USFS 224.

12.3 Pass small rock outcrop with views to right of Sinking
      Creek Mountain and Craig Creek Valley and, to the left,
      part of Cove Mountain.

12.6 Descend northern end of North Mountain. In 0.1 mile,
      pass rock outcrop with limited views, then cross sloping
      summit, and continue descent, sometimes by switchbacks.
      Huckleberries abound in late summer.

13.5 Reach Va. 311(1,780 feet), in narrow gap between North
      and Cove mountains. Turn left, and follow Va. 311.

13.6 Pass gas station and grocery store on right.

13.7 Turn right onto Va. 624.

14.0 Trail ends at intersection with A.T. (1,790 feet). See Section
      28.

Va. 624 (North Mountain Trail) to Craig Creek Valley (Va. 621)
Section Twenty-nine
14.6 miles

Brief Description of Section

The Trail in this section offers great variety. It traverses the ridgecrest forming the great rocky hook of Cove Mountain. The spur and the crest of the mountain, culminating in the spectacular monolith of Dragon's Tooth (3,050 feet), offer splendid views. The Trail also crosses the lower end of Trout Creek Gorge and then ascends to the crest of Brush Mountain, where it passes the Audie Murphy Monument before descending to Craig Creek.

Points of Interest

Viewpoint Rock, Devils Seat, Rawies Rest, Hemlock Point: scenic outlooks.

Dragon's Tooth: a spectacular monolith with good views near the summit of Cove Mountain.

Cove Mountain: long, sweeping ridge.

Audie Murphy Monument: site of 1971 plane crash that killed the most decorated U.S. soldier of World War II, later a film star. Scenic overlook behind monument affords excellent views of Sinking Creek Mountain and upper Craig Creek Valley.

Road Approaches

The northern end of the section is on Va. 624, 0.3 mile west of Va. 311, 12 miles north of Salem, 16 miles north of Roanoke, and 10 miles south of New Castle. A parking lot is on Va. 311, 0.4 mile west of intersection of Va. 311 and Va. 624. Two blue-blazed trails lead from the parking lot to the A.T.

The southern end of the section (small parking lot) is on Va. 621 in Craig Creek Valley, 6.5 miles west of the junction of Va. 311 and

Va. 621. From this junction, it is 12 miles south to I-81 and 8 miles north to New Castle *via* Va. 311 .

The Trail also crosses dirt Va. 620 (rough, but passable by automobile) 7.0 miles from the northern end of the section. In 1.1 miles, Va. 620 intersects hard-surfaced Va. 621, 3 miles west of Va. 311.

Maps

For route navigation, refer to ATC Glenwood–New Castle Districts and Blacksburg Area maps. For area detail, refer to the following USGS topographic quadrangles: Glenvar and Looney.

Shelters and Campsites

This section has one shelter:
Pickle Branch Shelter: built by USFS and maintained jointly by USFS and Roanoke A.T. Club; moved to its current location in 1980; 6.0 miles from the northern end of section; 0.5 mile off A.T. on blue-blazed side trail; accommodates six; ample water.

Next shelter: north 12.9 miles (Boy Scout); south 9.9 miles (Niday).

Regulations

Most of this section lies within Jefferson National Forest, where camping and campfires are permitted unless specifically noted otherwise. The northern 7 miles are in the New Castle Ranger District. The Trail from Trout Creek south to the New River is in the Blacksburg Area of the New River Ranger District.

Supplies, Services, and Public Accommodations

At the northern end of the section, the yellow-blazed North Mountain Trail passes a grocery store and camping area, 0.4 mile west on Va. 624 at Va. 311. It is 2.5 miles east to Catawba (ZIP Code 24070; groceries; lodging; restaurant open Thursday–Sunday) on Va. 311.

Trail Description, North to South

Miles   **Data**

0.0   Cross Va. 624 (1,790 feet), and ascend through pine grove. *Yellow-blazed North Mountain Trail follows Va. 624 to left, reaching Va. 311 in 0.3 mile and store 0.1 mile farther. That trail traverses North Mountain, and in 14.0 miles, joins A.T., making a loop hike with the A.T. of 29.5 miles (see previous chapter).*

0.4   Blue-blazed trail on right leads to stream, 0.2 mile, and to USFS parking lot on Va. 311, 0.4 mile. Blue-blazed trail forks at sign board: To the right is the parking lot; the other leads back to A.T. (mile 1.5) in 1.5 miles.

0.8   Reach narrow ridge.

1.0   Ridge narrows to scenic, knife-like, rocky rim known as Rawies Rest, with good views. Proceed cautiously, ascending along crest of spur.

1.3   Reach Viewpoint Rock, with a view of gap between North and Cove mountains. Turn sharp left. After another 0.2 mile, crest widens.

1.4   Pass to right of Devils Seat, a rocky outlook on the southern edge of the spur, with views of Catawba Valley and mountain.

1.5   Begin descent into sag known as Lost Spectacles Gap, where blue-blazed trail on right leads 1.5 miles to USFS parking lot on Va. 311.

1.6   Begin ascent from sag; climb gradually across eastern slope of Cove Mountain, with occasional views over Catawba Valley to left.

2.1   Cross rock slope on narrow ledge.

2.5   Soon, after sighting Dragon's Tooth ahead, ascend steeply through rocks to crest of Cove Mountain (3,020 feet). At crest, the A.T. turns sharp right and follows the giant sweep of Cove Mountain's crest. Blue-blazed trail leads left 200 yards to Dragon's Tooth, a monolith with views of Catawba Valley, McAfee Knob, and Tinker Cliffs. On a clear day, the Peaks of Otter are visible to the east. Dragon's Tooth can be climbed to its sharp crown *via* a crack. *Use extreme caution when attempting this climb, particularly in wet or windy weather.*

2.6	Pass over summit of Cove Mountain (3,050 feet), with outstanding views. Follow wooded ridge with steep slopes on either side.
3.8	Go to left of rocks.
4.1	Pass Hemlock Point, a rocky outcrop 100 feet to right, obscured by slight rise, where there are views of North Mountain and valley.
4.2	Bear left, bypassing an unnamed knob on right (2,600 feet).
4.4	Regain crest, with views of Millers Cove to left.
5.8	Pass through rocks with sharp drop-off to right and first good view to west over Sinking Creek Valley. Just beyond, bear left, descending. In 150 yards, turn sharp right, soon descending on steep, rocky trail.
6.0	Blue-blazed trail leads left 0.5 mile to **Pickle Branch Shelter** and privy, with water (treat before using) from stream below shelter.
6.2	Descend gradually along small ridge in pine woods. Pass under powerline. Turn left; descend long slope into Trout Creek Gorge.
7.0	Cross wooden footbridge over Trout Creek. Just beyond, reach Va. 620, which leads right 1.1 miles to Va. 621 and left through Trout Creek Gorge to Catawba Valley. The A.T. crosses Va. 620 and, in 100 feet on right, passes Trail registration box. Please sign register. Trail turns sharp right and begins ascent with a short series of switchbacks.
7.3	Trail junction. Old A.T. route continues straight ahead; current A.T. route continues to left, ascending.
7.9	Trail switches back sharply to left.
8.2	Short series of steps ascends as Trail jags back to left. Within the next 0.2 mile, the Trail crosses a firebreak and turns to the right to join the firebreak for a short distance, before it veers to the left and again crosses firebreak.
8.4	Short series of steps ascends as Trail jags back to left.
8.5	Trail crosses firebreak.

8.6   Vista to left. Nice view of Cove Mountain, North Mountain, and Mason's Cove. Top of Dragon's Tooth can be seen toward right end of Cove Mountain.

8.7   Short series of steps ascends as Trail jags back to left. Just ahead, as Trail turns back to right, is a vista to the left. In addition to previous sights, there are nice views of Sinking Creek Mountain and Craig Creek Valley.

9.2   Trail begins to follow along rocky spine and crosses it several times within the next 0.3 mile.

9.7   Trail descends slightly on rock steps.

9.8   Trail joins old woods road and begins ascent.

10.0   Trail begins slight descent, at the bottom of which a road is more recognizable. With minor ascents and descents, Trail roughly follows ridgecrest for another 1.4 miles.

10.8   Blue-blazed trail to right ascends and reaches Audie Murphy Monument in about 200 feet, then continues for another 100 feet to rock outcrop and lovely vista.

11.4   Trail leaves road to the right and begins descent toward Va. 621.

11.6   Trail descends on rock steps, switching back to the right. Shortly, there is a vista to the left with nice views of Sinking Creek Mountain and Craig Creek Valley.

11.7   Switch back to left.

11.9   Trail switches back sharply to right.

12.3   Trail descends log steps, switching back to right six times in the next 1.2 miles.

13.6   Trail crosses bridge.

13.7   Trail crosses another bridge.

14.1   Trail crosses third bridge and ascends log stairs. Trail soon crosses intermittent stream twice more.

14.2   Trail junction. Old A.T. route ascends sharply to right. Trail continues straight ahead.

14.4   Trail crosses bridge over intermittent stream, with bridge over Craig Creek just ahead.

14.6   Shortly after passing bridge, Trail turns to right onto old road and follows road to Va. 621(1,540 feet) immediately ahead, the end of the section. To continue on Trail, cross highway, and enter small parking lot, before bearing left into woods (see Section 30).

Trail Description, South to North

Miles	Data

Miles　　　　　　　　　　　　**Data**

0.0	From Va. 621 (1,540 feet), Trail turns left and soon passes bridge.
0.2	Cross bridge over Craig Creek (plus another bridge over intermittent stream) just ahead.
0.4	Trail junction. Old A.T. route ascends sharply to left; current A.T. route continues straight ahead, bears slightly to right, and soon crosses intermittent stream (twice).
0.5	Trail descends log stairs and crosses bridge.
0.9	Trail passes over bridge.
1.0	Trail crosses another bridge.
1.1	Trail ascends log steps and switches back to left six times within the next 1.2 miles.
2.7	Trail switches back sharply to left.
2.9	Switch back to right.
3.0	Vista to right. Nice view of Sinking Creek Mountain and Craig Creek Valley. Soon, Trail ascends on rock steps and switches back to left.
3.2	Trail turns left onto old road at top of mountain. With minor ascents and descents, Trail roughly follows crest of ridge for another 1.4 miles.
3.8	Blue-blazed trail to left ascends and reaches Audie Murphy Monument in about 200 feet, then continues for another 100 feet to rock outcrop and lovely vista.
4.6	Old road, which has become less recognizable as a road, reaches top of ascent. Trail now begins descent toward Va. 620.
4.9	Trail ascends slightly on rock steps.
5.4	Trail leaves rocky spring it has crossed several times within the last 0.3 mile.
5.9	Trail descends on short series of steps.
6.0	Vista to right. Nice view of Cove Mountain, North Mountain, and Mason's Cove. Top of Dragon's Tooth can be seen toward right end of Cove Mountain.
6.1	Trail crosses firebreak.

6.2   Short series of steps descends as Trail jags back to right. Within the next 0.2 mile, Trail crosses firebreak several times and even joins it for a short distance.

6.4   Short series of steps descends as Trail jags back to right.

6.7   Trail switches back sharply to right.

7.3   Trail junction. Old A.T. route comes in from left. Trail turns to right, descends.

7.6   Trail passes left of register box (please sign register), and, in 100 feet, reaches Va. 620. Va. 620 leads left 1.1 miles to Va. 621 and right through Trout Creek Gorge to Catawba Valley. Cross Va. 620, then cross Trout Creek on a wooden footbridge, turn left, and ascend just beyond.

8.0   Pass under powerline.

8.4   Traverse low ridge in pine woods, then ascend across steep slope on footway.

8.6   Blue-blazed trail leads right 0.5 mile to **Pickle Branch Shelter** and privy, with water from stream below shelter.

8.7   Ascend on steep, rocky trail.

8.8   Turn sharp left, uphill. In 50 feet, reach crest of mountain with sharp drop-off to left and view of Sinking Creek Valley to west. For the next 3.3 miles, follow the giant sweep of Cove Mountain, mostly in woods, with occasional rock formations.

10.2   Descend right to bypass unnamed knob ahead (2,600 feet).

10.4   Regain crest.

10.5   Pass Hemlock Point, a rocky outlook 100 feet to left (obscured by slight rise), which has good views of North Mountain and Valley. Ahead, crest narrows, and Trail becomes rough and rocky at times, with steep slopes on either side.

10.8   Pass to right of large rock outcrop. Woods begin to thin to small pines.

12.0   Pass over summit of Cove Mountain (3,050 feet), with outstanding views.

12.1   Reach junction where A.T. turns sharp left, leaving crest, while blue-blazed trail proceeds straight. Blue-blazed trail leads 200 yards to Dragon's Tooth, a monolith with views of Catawba Valley, McAfee Knob, and Tinker Cliffs. On a clear day, Peaks of Otter are visible to the east. The Tooth can be climbed to its sharp crown by way of a crack. *Use great caution, particularly in wet and windy weather.* From crest, A.T. descends steeply through rocks for 100 yards, then bears left and descends less steeply along eastern slope of Cove Mountain.

12.5   Cross rock slope on narrow ledge. Continue descending with occasional views of Catawba Valley to right.

13.0   Pass through sag known as Lost Spectacles Gap, between Cove Mountain and adjacent spur, then bear right, uphill. In 100 yards, reach crest of spur, bearing left. Blue-blazed trail on left leads to USFS parking lot on Va. 311 in 1.5 miles and, in another 0.4 mile, back to A.T. at mile 14.2.

13.2   On right, pass Devils Seat, a rocky outlook on southern edge of spur with views of Catawba Valley and mountain. (Deep gap to east is Beckner Gap.)

13.3   Spur begins to narrow at Viewpoint Rock, with a view of gap between Cove and North mountains. Turn right from ledge and descend.

13.6   Reach scenic Rawies Rest, where ridge narrows to knife-edged rock rim.

13.9   Veer to left of hill with view of Cove opening to left. With little change in elevation, bear right around hill.

14.2   Blue-blazed trail on left leads to stream, 0.2 mile, and to USFS parking lot on Va. 311, 0.4 mile. Blue-blazed trail forks at signboard; trail to left leads to parking lot, trail straight ahead and turning back to right leads back to A.T. mile 13.0 in 15 miles.

14.6   Descend through pine grove, and Cross Va. 624 (1,790 feet); reach end of section (see Section 28).

   Yellow-blazed North Mountain Trail leads right to Va. 311 in 0.3 mile and to store 0.1 mile farther. It traverses North Mountain, joins Andy Layne Trail, and rejoins A.T. at Scorched Earth Gap in 14.0 miles, making a loop hike with the A.T. of 29.5 miles (see previous chapter).

Craig Creek Valley (Va. 621) to Sinking Creek Valley (Va. 42)
Section Thirty
11.3 miles

Brief Description of Section

The Trail in this section follows the rocky and sometimes narrow crest of Sinking Creek Mountain, with views into Sinking Creek Valley and east into Craig Creek Valley. It passes through deep woods with occasional outlooks, scenic ledges, rocky outcrops, and open fields. Except for the climb or descent from the ridge at either end, the Trail gains and loses little elevation. The ascent of Sinking Creek Mountain for the southbound hiker is steep and strenuous, while the climb is much more gradual for the northbound hiker. The footway is, at times, rocky and uneven, making walking difficult.

No water is available on the mountain crest. Side trail near middle of section leads to Sarver Cabin (shelter available beginning in fall 2001) and spring.

Points of Interest

Sinking Creek Mountain: long ridgewalk along eastern continental divide, with several views, from rock outcrops, of Craig Creek Valley and Sinking Creek Valley. Several large piles of rocks along the ridge originated from farmers stacking them aside in order to farm the land. The name arises from a creek's disappearing underground near Hoges Chapel on Va. 42. The record of settlers along the stream dates from 1757.

Keffer Oak: one of the largest standing blazed trees on the Trail.

Road Approaches

The northern end of the section is on Va. 621 in Craig Creek Valley, 6.5 miles west of Va. 311. The intersection of Va. 621 and Va. 311 is 12 miles north of I-81 and 8 miles south of New Castle.

The southern end of the section is in Sinking Creek Valley on Va. 42, approximately 7 miles northeast of Newport, 1.6 miles south-west of Twin Oaks, and 21 miles southwest of New Castle.

Maps

For route navigation, refer to ATC Blacksburg Area Map. For area detail, refer to the following USGS topographic quadrangles: Waiteville, Craig Springs, McDonalds Mill, and Newport.

Shelters and Campsites

Two shelters and one primitive campsite are in this section:

Niday Shelter: built by USFS and maintained jointly by the Jefferson National Forest and the Roanoke A.T. Club; moved to present location by Marine Corps Reserves in 1980; 1.3 miles from the northern end of the section; accommodates six; water from nearby stream.

Next shelter: north 9.9 miles (Pickle Branch); south 6.0 miles (Sarver Cabin).

Sarver Cabin (New shelter available beginning Fall, 2001): 7.3 miles from the northern end of the section on a 0.3-mile side trail; currently, shed in poor condition providing primitive shelter; water from nearby spring. An old cemetery nearby possibly dates to the late 1800s.

Next shelter: north 6.0 miles (Niday); south 6.3 miles (Laurel Creek).

The campsite is on Cabin Branch (reliable water), 2.0 miles from the northern end of the section.

Regulations

The Trail passes through Jefferson National Forest and National Park Service lands. Camping and campfires are permitted anywhere, unless specifically noted otherwise. Campfires must be attended at all times and completely extinguished when leaving campsite.

Supplies, Services, and Public Accommodations

No supplies or services are near either end of this section.

Trail Description, North to South

Miles	Data
0.0	From small parking area on northern side of Va. 621 (1,540 feet), bear left (northwest), uphill, with stream on right.
0.1	Turn right along small ridge; ascend less steeply.
0.5	Bear left, downhill.
0.6	Reach stream; follow it to right.
0.7	Cross stream.
1.3	Begin steep ascent of Sinking Creek Mountain. Blue-blazed trail leads 50 feet left to **Niday Shelter** and privy. Water is from stream to right of A.T (treat before using).
2.0	Unblazed trail leads left downhill 150 yards to **primitive campsite** by Cabin Branch.
3.4	Pass small sinkhole in slight sag.
3.5	Enter laurel thicket. Views left of Craig Creek Valley.
3.7	Turn left onto crest of Sinking Creek Mountain. (Blue-blazed trail leads right 2.5 miles to USFS 209, Old Hall Road. Old Hall Road leads 1.5 miles left to Va. 42 and 3.5 miles right to Va. 621.) Trending southwest on crest, A.T. crosses several slanting rock ledges in next 1.3 miles, with good views of Craig Creek Valley and the ridges beyond.
7.3	Blue-blazed trail descends steeply left 0.3 mile to spring and **Sarver Cabin** (shelter and privy available beginning fall 2001).
8.1	Reach junction with former A.T., entering from the left.

8.3   Pass under powerline.

8.9   Descend crest of Sinking Creek Mountain.

9.6   Leave woods. In 100 yards pass under powerlines and reenter woods.

9.7   Make sharp right turn. In 100 yards, cross stile.

9.8   Cross second stile. Bear left though pasture.

9.9   Cross third stile, bear right along fence. In 200 feet, cross a fourth stile beside giant "Keffer Oak."

10.1   Turn sharp left and descend old farm road.

10.3   Cross wooden bridge over small stream.

10.4   Turn right on Va. 630 (limited parking). Cross Sinking Creek on road bridge.

10.5   Turn sharp left off road, cross stile, and ascend open hill. Sinking Creek on left.

10.8   Reach top of hill, with views. Begin gradual descent.

10.9   Cross fence on stile, enter small patch of woods, and reenter open field in 100 yards, descending.

11.2   Cross fence on stile, and, in 50 feet, reach Va. 42. Trail continues across highway (see Section 31).

Trail Description, South to North

Miles   **Data**

0.0   After crossing Va. 42, Trail crosses stile and begins ascent past utility pole in open pasture.

0.3   Enter woods. In 100 yards, cross fence on stile, and reenter open pasture. Continue gradual ascent.

0.5   Reach top of hill, with views. Begin steep descent.

0.8   Descend to fence. Sinking Creek on right. Turn right on Va. 630. Cross creek on road bridge.

0.9   Turn left shortly after road bridge. Leave road (limited parking), and ascend Sinking Creek Mountain.

1.0   Cross wooden bridge over small stream.

1.2   Trail turns sharp right (south) before an old farm shed.

1.4   Cross stile beside giant "Keffer Oak." In 200 feet, cross second stile. Turn sharp left, uphill.

1.5   Cross third stile, making a sharp right turn.

1.6   Cross fourth stile, reenter woods, bear right. In 100 yards, turn sharp left.

1.7   Pass under powerline. In 100 yards, reenter woods.

2.4   Reach crest of Sinking Creek Mountain. Bear left, following old ridgetop road.

2.9   Pass under powerline.

3.2   Reach junction with former A.T., entering from right.

3.9   Enter small field with scattered apple trees and limited views to right.

4.0   Blue-blazed trail descends steeply to right 0.3 mile to spring and **Sarver Cabin** (shelter with privy available beginning fall 2001).

4.2   Cross slanting rocks, and continue on crest with little change in elevation.

6.4   Pass over first of several slanting rock ledges in next mile, with views to right over Craig Creek Valley and mountain ridges beyond.

7.6   Leave crest, and descend steeply to right (northeast) on rough, uneven footway. (Blue-blazed trail ahead leads 2.5 miles to USFS 209, Old Hall Road. This road leads right 3.5 miles to Va. 621 and left 1.5 miles to Va. 42.)

7.9   Pass small sinkhole in slight sag. Soon, circle headwaters of Cabin Branch; never cross stream.

9.3   Side trail leads right, downhill, 150 yards to Cabin Branch **primitive campsite**, with water available from stream. A.T. descends steadily ahead.

10.0   Blue-blazed trail leads 50 feet right to **Niday Shelter** and privy. Water is available from stream on left of A.T.

10.2   Bear right, downhill.

10.5   Cross stream, follow its left side a short distance, then turn left, uphill.

10.8   Turn right down ridge.

11.1   Bear left, leave ridge, and descend more steeply.

11.3   Pass through pines, and enter small parking lot with stream on far side. Reach hard-surfaced Va. 621(1,540 feet), the end of section. To continue on Trail, cross road, and enter woods (see Section 29).

Sinking Creek Valley (Va. 42) to Johns Creek Valley (USFS 156)
Section Thirty-one
7.4 miles

Brief Description of Section

From the northern end of the section, the Trail climbs the wavy, inclining, northeast ridge of Johns Creek Mountain. The A.T. then follows a fairly level route around the curving Johns Creek Mountain rim and finally descends to Johns Creek Valley.

Big Pond, 3.8 miles from the northern end of the section, is the only source of water on the mountain. It is a stagnant pond and not recommended as a source of drinking water. Water is available, however, from Laurel Creek, about two miles from the northern end of the section, and at the southern end in Johns Creek Valley.

Points of Interest

Views from rock ledges: Sinking Creek Valley and Johns Creek Valley.

Road Approaches

The northern end of this section is in Sinking Creek Valley on Va. 42, approximately 7 miles northeast of Newport, 1.6 miles southwest of Twin Oaks, and 21 miles southwest of New Castle.

The southern end of this section is at the junction of War Branch Trail and USFS 156 in the upper part of Johns Creek Valley. It is 25 miles from New Castle *via* Va. 311, Va. 658, and Va. 632 (continuation of USFS 156). The southern end of the section can also be reached from Va. 42 near Simmonsville (10 miles east of Newport) by following Va. 658 north about 4 miles, then turning left on Johns Creek Valley Road (Va. 632) and following it for 4.2 miles. A small parking lot (four to six cars) is located at this end.

Two miles from the southern end of the section, the Trail crosses dirt Va. 601 (USFS 10721). Limited roadside parking is available.

Maps

For route navigation, refer to ATC Blacksburg Area Map. For area detail, refer to the following USGS topographic quadrangles: Waiteville and Newport.

Shelters and Campsites

This section has one shelter:

Laurel Creek Shelter: moved from Big Pond in 1988, maintained jointly by USFS and Roanoke A.T. Club; 2.4 miles from the northern end of the section; accommodates six.

Next shelter: north (Niday) 12.3 miles (6.3 after new Sarver Cabin—shelter is complete in fall 2001); south 5.8 miles (War Spur).

Regulations

This section of the Trail lies within Jefferson National Forest or on National Park Service Trail-corridor lands. Camping and camp-fires are permitted unless specifically noted otherwise. Campfires should be attended at all times and completely extinguished when you leave the campsite.

Supplies, Services, and Public Accommodations

No services or supplies are near either end of this section.

Trail Description, North to South

Miles	Data
0.0	After crossing Va. 42 (2,150 feet), Trail descends driveway and turns left to cross stile. (Hikers may park vehicles along side of driveway but *must not* block either driveway or farm lane in front of stile. After crossing stile, Trail

heads across active pasture toward bridge, in 350 feet, and second stile beyond. This pasture can be very wet at times.

0.1   Cross stile. Trail turns sharply to left and, in 250 feet, crosses over "hot" electric fence on step stile. Trail then turns to right onto farm lane and follows it for 70 feet before veering to right and beginning to slab up hillside through cedars and pines. A number of cattle paths are on this hillside, so care should be taken to follow blazing.

0.4   Trail passes by opening in fence line to right and parallels fence line (hikers should stay to left of fence) for 240 feet before turning sharply to left and continuing to slab up hillside in open pasture. View ahead is of Johns Creek Mountain. High point to the right of powerline is Kelly Knob.

0.6   Trail reaches second fence line, turns to right, and crosses stile. In 250 feet, Trail turns to left and begins to slab down hillside. View is of Johns Creek Mountain and, to extreme right, of Sinking Creek Mountain.

0.8   Trail passes through stile and enters wooded area.

1.4   Pass spring just off Trail to left, in small clump of rhododendron.

1.9   Leave old road, and pass barbed-wire fence to right of Trail.

2.2   Descend steeply into gorge, and cross first prong of Laurel Creek.

2.3   Cross main prong of Laurel Creek in cove of rhododendron and hemlocks. Trail begins ascending toward Kelly Knob.

2.4   Blue-blazed trail to left leads 100 feet to **Laurel Creek Shelter** and privy. Water is available from Laurel Creek.

3.3   Reach Kelly Knob (3,742 feet). Turn right, away from edge of cliff and former A.T. route.

3.6   Trail begins gradual descent toward Big Pond. Blue-blazed trail leads left 100 yards to White Rock, with views of Salt Pond Mountain.

3.8   Trail to the right leads 200 yards to a large bog known as Big Pond.

4.8   Reach former site of firetower (3,788 feet). Beyond site, enter woods road, and begin descent. In 300 feet, Johns

Creek Mountain Trail leads to the right approximately 3.5 miles along crest to Maggie Road (Va. 658). A.T. continues ahead, descending, with views across Johns Creek Valley to War Spur, Salt Pond Mountain, and Potts Mountain. As Trail turns left, there is a view of Clover Hollow Mountain, Johns Creek Mountain, and Sinking Creek Valley.

5.4   Cross dirt Va. 601 (USFS 10721) in Rocky Gap (3,264 feet). Beyond, descend steadily over rocky footpath.

5.8   Pass large cliffs on left, with view of Potts and Peters mountains and soil-conservation pond on right. Trail becomes less rocky but continues steady descent.

6.4   Cross small creek (may be dry in summer).

7.0   Pass through stand of small pines, and descend more gradually.

7.4   Cross Johns Creek in rhododendron thicket. One hundred yards farther, reach USFS 156 (Va. 632) and end of section (2,080 feet). Trail continues on other side of road and crosses small stream and rutted road (see Section 32).

Trail Description, South to North

Miles   **Data**

0.0   From USFS 156 (Va. 632; 2,080 feet), head southeast into woods. In 100 yards, cross Johns Creek on bridge in area covered with dense rhododendron growth.

0.4   Pass through stand of small pines. Ascent becomes steeper.

1.0   Cross small stream (may be dry in summer).

1.6   Pass large cliffs on right, with view of Potts and Peters mountains and soil-conservation pond on left. Trail ascends steadily over rocky footpath.

2.0   Cross Va. 601 (USFS 10721) in Rocky Gap (3,264 feet); ascend beyond on old woods road. Where Trail bears right, there are views of Clover Hollow Mountain, Johns Creek Mountain, and Sinking Creek Valley. Soon, there are views back across Johns Creek Valley to War Spur, Salt Pond Mountain, and Potts Mountain.

2.5   Johns Creek Mountain Trail leads left approximately 3.5 miles along crest to Maggie Road (Va. 658). A.T. leads ahead 300 feet to former site of firetower, then continues along crest of high, curving arm of Johns Creek Mountain.

3.6   Trail to left leads 200 yards to large bog known as Big Pond.

3.8   Blue-blazed trail to right leads 100 yards to White Rock with views of Salt Pond Mountain.

4.1   At top of Kelly Knob (3,742 feet), turn left, away from edge of cliff, pass old A.T. route, and begin long descent.

5.0   Blue-blazed trail to right leads 100 feet to **Laurel Creek Shelter** and privy. Water is available from Laurel Creek.

5.1   In 100 yards, cross main prong of Laurel Creek in beautiful cove of rhododendron and hemlocks.

5.2   Cross second prong of Laurel Creek, and begin steep ascent out of gorge.

5.6   Pass barbed-wire fence to left. Turn right shortly on old road, and descend.

6.0   Pass spring just off Trail to right, in clump of rhododendron.

6.7   Trail passes through stile and turns to left, entering open pasture. Trail veers to right and begins to slab up open hillside toward treeline. View ahead is of Sinking Creek Mountain.

6.9   Trail turns to right, and, in 220 feet, crosses over stile into open pasture. After crossing stile, Trail turns to left and begins to slab downhill toward second fenceline. View ahead is of Sinking Creek Mountain. As Trail approaches second fenceline, two fence posts with double blazes are visible; Trail heads toward the leftmost post.

7.2   Trail reaches second fenceline and turns sharply to right to follow it for 240 feet before coming to an opening in the fenceline. Trail now begins to veer to the right, away from fenceline, and shortly begins to slab down hillside through cedars and pines. A number of cattle paths are on this hillside, so care should be taken to follow blazes.

7.3   Trail comes onto farm lane, and, turning to left, follows it for 70 feet before turning sharply to left and crossing over "hot" electric fence on step stile. In 250 feet, Trail turns sharply to right and crosses stile into active pasture. Trail heads across pasture toward bridge and, beyond that, a second stile. This pasture can be very wet at times.

7.4 Trail crosses stile and reaches farm lane. Trail turns to left, then immediately to right, ascending driveway onto Va. 42. Trail continues ahead across Va. 42 (see Section 30). Hikers may park their vehicles along the side of the driveway here but *must not* block either the driveway or the farm lane in front of the stile.

Johns Creek Valley (USFS 156) to Stony Creek Valley
Section Thirty-two
13.2 miles

Brief Description of Section

The Trail in this section crosses the broad, wooded ridge of Salt Pond Mountain (4,054 feet), traverses part of the crest of Potts Mountain (4,128 feet), and crosses the heavily wooded northern slope of Big Mountain. Wind Rock, on Potts Mountain overlooking Stony Creek Valley, provides the best view. The Trail crosses wild terrain. Deer frequent the swampy area on Salt Pond Mountain, as do grouse and possibly bear elsewhere. The Trail lies within the Mountain Lake Wilderness between War Spur Shelter and Salt Sulphur Turnpike.

For the southbound hiker, the 2,000-foot ascent in 3.3 miles from Johns Creek Valley to Lone Pine Peak is the most strenuous part of the section though a recent relocation has improved the grade. For the northbound hiker, the 1,100-foot ascent in one mile of Big Mountain from Stony Creek Valley is the most strenuous. Other grades are gradual.

Points of Interest

Salt Pond Mountain: above 4,000 feet, early settlers took their cattle to a depression for salting. They reported that the continuous tramping of cattle closed an outlet in the floor of the depression, forming Mountain Lake. This report led to mountain's name.

Wind Rock: views over Stony Creek Valley toward Fork and Peters mountains.

Mountain Lake Wilderness: Trail passes through this beautiful, 11,172-acre wilderness area for about 4.5 miles.

Stony Creek: A.T. parallels turbulent creek for a short distance.

Road Approaches

The northern end of the section is at the junction of War Branch Trail and USFS 156 (Va. 632) in the upper part of Johns Creek Valley. The Trailhead is 25 miles from New Castle *via* Va. 311, Va. 658, and Va. 632 (USFS 156). A parking lot that accommodates 4 to 6 cars is available. The northern end of the section also may be reached from Va. 42 near Simmonsville (10 miles east of Newport) by following Va. 658 north about 4 miles, then turning left, and following Johns Creek Valley Road (Va. 632) for 4.2 miles.

The southern end of the section is just off Va. 635 at the end of the Pine Swamp Branch access road, 10 miles east of U.S. 460. The junction of Va. 635 and U.S. 460 is five miles east of Pearisburg.

Gravel Salt Sulphur Turnpike (Va. 613) intersects the A.T. on the crest between Potts and Big Mountains. It leads north 2.2 miles to the community of Kire on Va. 635, 5 miles east of the southern end of the section. It leads south 5.5 miles to Mountain Lake and 11 miles to U.S. 460, 2 miles west of Newport. A large parking lot is located at the Va. 613 crossing. Va. 635 crosses the Trail 2.1 miles from the southern end (limited parking). From here, it is 11.5 miles to U.S. 460.

Maps

For route navigation, refer to ATC Blacksburg Area Map. For area detail, refer to the following USGS topographic quadrangles: Waiteville and Interior.

Shelters and Campsites

This section has two shelters:

War Spur Shelter: built by USFS in the 1960s and maintained jointly by USFS and Roanoke A.T. Club; 0.8 mile from northern end of section; accommodates six; water from War Branch.

Next shelter: north 5.8 miles (Laurel Creek); south 8.8 miles (Bailey Gap).

Bailey Gap Shelter: built by USFS in the 1960s and maintained jointly by USFS and Roanoke A.T. Club; 3.6 miles from southern end of section; accommodates six; water from spring 0.2 mile south on A.T.

Next shelter: north 8.8 miles (War Spur); south 3.9 miles (Pine Swamp Branch).

The only water sources are at the two shelters, a couple of seasonal springs 1.5 miles south of War Spur, and a spring on Potts Mountain.

Regulations

This section lies within Jefferson National Forest, where camping and campfires are permitted unless specifically noted otherwise. Campfires should be attended at all times and completely extinguished when you leave the campsite.

Supplies, Services, and Public Accommodations

No supplies, services, or accommodations are near this section.

Trail Description, North to South

Miles	Data
0.0	From USFS 156 (Va. 632; 2,080 feet), walk northwest on War Branch Trail, crossing stream and rutted road. In 70 yards, enter partially open field, and bear left.
0.2	Trail skirts to left of boggy area and begins gradual ascent.
0.8	Cross War Branch. Pass **War Spur Shelter** and privy on right. Treat water from stream. Begin ascent.
2.3	Pass seasonal spring.
2.5	Pass rock field on right and spring.
2.8	Ascend right at junction. War Branch Trail leads left 1.5 miles to Salt Sulphur Turnpike, 2.0 miles south of A.T. crossing.
3.3	Cross to right (north) of Lone Pine Peak (4,054 feet), an inconspicuous rise to left of Trail.

3.9   On broad, flat, wooded crest of Salt Pond Mountain, pass through swampy area. To left is Little Stony Creek Valley; to right, Johns Creek Valley.

4.0   Turn sharp left. Old trail straight ahead leads 150 yards to Potts Mountain Trail.

4.5   Pass spring to left of Trail. In 100 feet, pass semi-open area that offers good **campsites**.

4.8   Cross old woods road. Potts Mountain Trail is 100 yards to right.

5.7   Pass Wind Rock (4,100 feet) on right. Good views north over Stony Creek Valley, toward Fork and Peters mountains.

5.9   Cross gravel Salt Sulphur Turnpike (Va. 613). Gradually descend rocky trail across heavily wooded northern slope of Big Mountain.

7.0   Pass overhanging rock ledge, which can be used for emergency shelter, on right.

9.3   Turn right to join Bailey Gap Trail, which leads 0.4 mile left to Bailey Gap.

9.6   Pass **Bailey Gap Shelter** and privy on right. Seasonal spring, directly across the Trail from shelter, may be dry in summer. Continue to descend steadily on the northern slope of Big Mountain.

9.8   Blue-blazed trail leads 125 yards left to spring.

10.0   Cross gravel fire road (Va. 734), which leads left along a circuitous route to Interior and right across the northern slope of Big Mountain to Salt Sulphur Turnpike, 1.5 miles north of Trail crossing.

11.0   Cross woods road.

11.1   Cross paved Va. 635 (2,450 feet), and enter woods. In 100 feet, cross Stony Creek on wooden bridge.

11.4   Pass through open meadow, then reenter woods, leaving stream bank.

10.7   Begin ascending Sarton Ridge.

11.9   Reach top of Sarton Ridge. Bear left, and descend spine of ridge.

12.0   Bear right, and, in 100 yards, turn right onto old road along Dismal Branch.

12.1   Bear left off old road. On log-and-board bridge, cross Dismal Branch. Ascend briefly, cross small tributary, and continue downstream until Trail bears right onto old railroad grade along Stony Creek. Trail soon bears right off railroad grade, but still parallels Stony Creek.

12.7   Cross small tributary of Stony Creek.

13.0   Follow switchback to left, descend 300 yards, then turn right along Stony Creek.

13.1   Cross Pine Swamp Branch.

13.2   Enter clearing beside Va. 635 bridge over Stony Creek, and parallel highway for 40 yards. Reach end of section. Small parking area is to left on Va. 635.

Trail Description, South to North

Miles   **Data**

0.0   Wooden sign indicates that Pine Swamp Branch access road is closed to vehicles. At sign, turn left off road, and parallel Va. 635 and Stony Creek.

0.1   Cross Pine Swamp Branch. Turn left soon, and climb two switchbacks.

0.5   Cross small tributary of Stony Creek. Ascend soon, then descend steeply.

0.7   Follow Stony Creek on old railroad grade. Bear left upstream, crossing a tributary of Dismal Branch.

1.1   On log-and-board bridge, cross Dismal Branch, then turn right onto dirt road.

1.2   Turn right off old road, and ascend Sarton Ridge.

1.3   Bear left up spine of Sarton Ridge.

1.4   Bear right, off Sarton Ridge, descending steeply in places.

1.6   Trail levels in valley bottom.

1.8   Cross meadow, and reenter woods near Stony Creek.

2.1   Cross wooden bridge over Stony Creek and, in 100 feet, cross Va. 635 (2,450 feet).

2.2   Cross woods road, and ascend steadily.

3.2   Cross gravel fire road (Va. 734), which leads right along a circuitous route to Interior and left across the northern slope of Big Mountain to Salt Sulphur Turnpike, 1.5 miles north of the Trail crossing.

3.4   Blue-blazed trail leads right 125 yards to spring.

3.6	Pass **Bailey Gap Shelter** and privy on left. Seasonal spring, directly across Trail from shelter, may be dry in summer.
3.8	Turn left, and ascend gradually on sometimes rocky trail across heavily wooded northern slope of Big Mountain. Bailey Gap Trail continues ahead 0.4 mile to Bailey Gap on crest of Big Mountain.
6.2	Pass overhanging rocks on left, which can be used for emergency shelter.
7.3	Cross gravel Salt Sulphur Turnpike (Va. 613). Follow woods road, ascending.
7.6	Pass Wind Rock (4,100 feet), which has good views north over Stony Creek Valley toward Fork and Peters mountains on left. Trail bears to right.
8.4	Cross old woods road. Potts Mountain Trail is 100 yards to the left.
8.7	Pass through semi-open area, which offers good campsites. In 100 feet, pass spring to right of Trail.
9.2	Turn sharp right. Old trail to left leads 150 yards to Potts Mountain Trail.
9.3	On broad, flat, wooded crest of Salt Pond Mountain, pass through swampy area. To right is Little Stony Creek Valley, and, to left, Johns Creek Valley.
9.9	Cross left (north) side of Lone Pine Peak (4,054 feet), an inconspicuous rise to right of Trail, and descend.
10.4	Descend left at junction. War Branch Trail leads right 1.5 miles to Salt Sulphur Turnpike, 2 miles south of A.T. crossing.
10.7	Pass rock field on left, and spring.
10.9	Pass seasonal spring.
12.4	**War Spur Shelter** and privy is 50 feet on left. Treat water from stream. Turn right and cross War Branch in 75 yards.
13.0	Trail skirts to right of boggy area.
13.1	Bear left across partially open field.
13.2	After crossing rutted road and stream, reach USFS 156 (Va. 632; 2,080 feet) and end of section. To continue on Trail, proceed into woods, and soon cross Johns Creek (see Section 31).

Stony Creek Valley to New River (U.S. 460)
Section Thirty-three
19.4 miles

Brief Description of Section

A traverse of Peters Mountain, an imposing ridge marking the edge of the Allegheny Plateau along the West Virginia–Virginia border, dominates this section, with a few long upright rocks, placed post-Civil War, to mark the border. Following the mountain's crest for about 12.5 miles, the A.T. gently rises and falls across ridgetop knobs and through chestnut-oak/red-maple forests. Just west of a knob 0.2 mile south of the Allegheny Trail intersection, the Trail reaches its highest point in this section, at 3,860 feet. The mountain ridgecrest has good seasonal views west into West Virginia and east toward prominent Appalachian ridges. Best are the open views from Symms Gap Meadow, in the center of the ridge, and from the Rice Fields, an extensive pasture 6.4 miles to the south.

A 1,300-foot climb in 2.6 miles on the northern end, from Va. 635 to the ridgecrest swale where the Pine Swamp is located, is the most significant climb in the section, although the Trail generally has a gentle grade and numerous switchbacks. The southern end of the section, between U.S. 460 and the crest, is rough and broken.

Several side trails intersect the A.T. in the section. The yellow-blazed Allegheny Trail, which extends from West Virginia to the Mason-Dixon line, intersects the A.T. on the crest of Peters Mountain. Two blue-blazed trails provide access to the crest. One leads to the southeast from Dickinson Gap to Va. 635, and the other, the Groundhog Trail, leads to the northwest off the ridge to W.Va. 219/24. Peters Mountain has little or no water along its ridgecrest, and hikers should be prepared to carry sufficient amounts, especially if they plan to camp on the ridge. Several seasonal springs are on the southern end of Peters Mountain. All water should be treated before use. Water from Stony Creek and Stillhouse Branch should *not* be used.

264

Hikers crossing the Senator Shumate Bridge on U.S. 460 at the southern end of the section need to observe caution, use the pedestrian lane, and read the note at mile 19.0 in the north-to-south trail description. The large industrial site on the western side of the bridge is owned by Hoescht Celanese, a manufacturer of industrial fibers and a major employer in the region. Pine Swamp Branch Shelter is the dividing point of Trail responsibility between the Roanoke A.T. Club (to the north for 85.9 miles) and the Outdoor Club at Virginia Tech (for 19.1 miles south to the New River).

Points of Interest

New River: Trail crosses this geologically ancient river (second oldest on Earth to the Nile, some say) at the U.S. 460-Senator Shumate Bridge. These waters, unlike others in the region that feed the Atlantic Ocean, eventually reach the Mississippi River after flowing northwesterly toward the Ohio River basin.

Pine Swamp: a swampy depression at the northern end of the Trail route on Peters Mountain. Source of Pine Swamp Branch and the location of a fine hemlock stand.

Symms Gap Meadow: cleared area on site of old orchard in center of Peters Mountain Trail route, with sweeping views of West Virginia.

Rice Field: extensive open pasture with rock outcroppings located on southern end of Peters Mountain. Trail route features far-reaching westward views.

Peters Mountain: commanding, lengthy ridge, the crest of which is the West Virginia-Virginia state line.

Peters Mountain Wilderness: federally designated 3,300-acre wilderness area containing about six miles of the A.T.

Allegheny Trail: yellow-blazed long-distance trail leading from A.T. on Peters Mountain crest north (with one major incomplete section) through West Virginia to Mason-Dixon Line.

Groundhog Trail: blue-blazed trail leading from A.T. on Peters Mountain crest to road access on W.Va. 219/24.

Maps

For route navigation, refer to ATC Blacksburg Area Map. For area detail, refer to the following USGS topographic quadrangles: Interior, Lindside, Peterstown, and Narrows.

Road Approaches

The northern end of the section is on paved Va. 635 nine miles northeast of U.S. 460 from an intersection five miles east of Pearisburg, marked for USFS White Rocks Recreation Area. Small, unimproved parking area, for one or two cars, is available near this end of the section on Va. 635. This road not heavily traveled, so be wary of vandalism.

The southern end of the section is at the eastern end of the Senator Shumate Bridge, where U.S. 460 crosses the New River near the Celanese industrial site. Parking is not permitted at Celanese plant. A large commercial parking lot is across U.S. 460 from the A.T. Hikers should seek permission from the grocery store to leave cars in the lot.

A small parking area is about two miles from the southern end of the section, where the A.T. crosses Va. 641 (Stillhouse Branch Road).

Cars also may be parked at a small lot on W.Va. 219/24 at the Groundhog Trail crossing. The road to W.Va. 219/24 from U.S. 219 is marked with blue blazes, and there is a small sign at the parking area.

Shelters and Campsites

This section has two shelters:

Pine Swamp Branch Shelter: three-walled stone lean-to with chimney, fireplace, bunks, and picnic table, 0.3 mile from northern end of section; accommodates 8; water from Pine Swamp Branch 150 yards northeast. The shelter was constructed and is maintained with funds donated by the family of the late Robert Trimpi.

Next shelter: north 3.9 miles (Bailey Gap); south 12.5 miles (Rice Field).

Rice Field Shelter: built in 1996 and maintained jointly by the USFS and the Outdoor Club at Virginia Tech; 6.8 miles from southern end of section; accommodates eight; water from spring 0.5 mile behind shelter.

Next shelter: north 12.5 miles (Pine Swamp Branch); south 14.9 miles (Doc's Knob).

Primitive campsites without water are located along the ridge of Peters Mountain, with seasonal water between Va. 641 and the ridgecrest on the southern end.

Regulations

Camping and campfires are prohibited on the southern part of this section for 1.8 miles between Va. 641 and U.S. 460, where the A.T. crosses private land.

The northern 17.6 miles of the section lie in the Jefferson National Forest, where camping and campfires are permitted, unless noted otherwise.

Supplies, Services, and Public Accommodations

No supplies or services are near the northern end of this section. The USFS White Rocks Campground is located about five miles east, off Va. 635, with restrooms, tentsites, and water.

A supermarket is 0.1 mile southwest of the New River on U.S. 460 at the southern end. Pearisburg, one mile east, has a variety of services and facilities (ZIP Code 24134), supermarkets, hostel, equipment/hardware store, motel, restaurant, shoe repair, coin laundry, hospital, taxi and other service).

Trail Description, North to South

Miles   **Data**

0.0   From a USFS parking area on the west side of Va. 635, pass to the right of the Forest Service information display, and intersect the A.T. in about 100 feet. Turn left on the Trail, and ascend gradually on old road.

0.3   **Pine Swamp Branch Shelter** and privy is just to left of Trail. Privy is uphill and behind the shelter. Water is from a stream 150 yards north of the shelter.

0.4   Graded trail bears left away from creek and begins a series of long, gradual switchbacks toward crest of Peters Mountain.

0.9   A.T. bears right and crosses stream. (*Caution:* Old A.T. route is still visible straight ahead. Do not follow.) After crossing stream, A.T. turns sharply left uphill.

2.6   Trail levels and descends into shallow swale of Pine Swamp. Area has a hemlock stand and is plentiful with rhododendron. A large yellow poplar indicates an unmarked trail that leads right to a possible water source in the wet times of the year.

2.8   Yellow-blazed Allegheny Trail intersects A.T. from right.

2.9   Reach crest of Peters Mountain (3,740 feet). Trail veers southwest of 3,956-foot knob. The forested ridge ahead provides an abundant spring–summer wildflower display.

4.7   Rocky Trail regains ridgecrest and descends toward Dickinson Gap. Red wilderness area boundary markers appear with frequency for the next few miles.

5.2   Pass through Dickinson Gap, with stone marker (now painted bright red) on right. Blue-blazed trail joining from left descends steeply 1.4 miles to Va. 635, 7.4 miles north of U.S. 460. A.T. follows ridgecrest, ascending and descending over knobs.

6.7   Blue-blazed Groundhog Trail, leading 2 miles northwest to W.Va. 219/24, joins A.T. from the right.

7.7   Reach old road, and enter meadow in Symms Gap. Ascend thorough meadow on grassy path.

7.8   Excellent **campsite** (no water) under large oak tree to left of Trail. Trail follows ridgecrest on old roads.

11.2   Trail left leads 150 feet to small spring.

11.9   Reach powerline access road, and turn right. Soon, reach powerline right-of-way with view to south of Angels Rest and the shear face of Pearis Mountain, a peak climbed by the A.T. south of Pearisburg.

12.2   Pass television antenna on right.

12.6	Cross stile, and enter a large, open pasture known as the Rice Field, with numerous weathered rock outcroppings and sweeping westward views of the West Virginia hills.
12.8	Reach side trail to **Rice Field Shelter** and privy (3,400 feet). Water is 0.5 mile behind shelter.
13.0	Cross stile, and reenter woods on old road.
13.5	Pass under powerline.
13.7	Cross pipeline right-of-way.
13.9	Cross larger pipeline right-of-way.
15.3	Bear sharply left, and begin descent of Peters Mountain on rocky trail.
15.4	Cross small stream with pipe for spring. Excellent **campsite** just beyond to right of trail.
16.4	Turn sharp right, and, in 30 yards, turn sharp left across stream. Just beyond, turn right, downhill.
16.5	Bear downhill onto old road.
16.7	From saddle of spur, turn off old road, and ascend over prominent spur knobs.
16.8	Descend steeply *via* switchbacks.
17.0	Turn sharp right off spur, and bear right, downhill at fork. Enter dirt access road.
17.2	Join another dirt access road, and, in 90 yards, bear off road.
17.3	Cross under powerline.
17.4	Cross tributary of Stillhouse Branch; recross several times in succession.
17.6	Turn left onto dirt access road, and, in about 40 yards, reach small USFS parking area on the west side of Va. 641 (Stillhouse Branch Road). Diagonally cross road, and ascend high bank beyond. At top of bank, Trail turns sharply right.
17.8	Bear right off broad spur, and descend steeply to gully. For next 0.4 mile, cross series of small spurs and gullies.
18.2	Cross sulfurous creek (unsafe for drinking), and ascend spur.
18.4	Turn left, descend spur, and cross another series of small spurs and gullies in the next 0.3 mile.
18.6	Descend two switchbacks.

18.7   Diagonally cross dirt road, then turn sharp right, and ascend spur.

18.9   Turn right, and begin gradual descent.

19.0   Turn right onto gravel road. Then turn right onto paved road. Turn left and follow pedestrian lane across the Senator Shumate Bridge (U.S. 460) over New River. *Note: Upon completion of the replacement westbound lanes of the Shumate Bridge, the Trail will take the hiker under U.S. 460, ascend steps to bridge level and follow a new separated walkway on the new bridges across both the railroad and the river. This safety improvement by VDOT eliminates the dash across four-lane U.S. 460.*

19.4   At eastern end of Senator Shumate Bridge (1,600 feet), cross U.S. 460 and reach end of the section. To continue on the Trail, proceed into woods at the end of the bridge on the right side of the road. (See *Appalachian Trail Guide to Southwest Virginia*.)

Trail Description, South to North

Miles   **Data**

0.0   From eastern end of Senator Shumate Bridge across the New River (1,600 feet), turn right, cross U.S. 460 and follow pedestrian lane across bridge. Turn right onto paved road on opposite side. Follow road 80 yards, turn left onto gravel road, then turn left up bank *See the note at mile 19.0 in north-to-south Trail description.*

0.5   Turn left, and begin gradual descent.

0.7   Turn sharp left, then diagonally cross road.

0.8   Ascend two switchbacks.

1.0   Turn right, and cross series of small spurs and gullies in the next 0.3 mile.

1.2   Cross sulfurous creek (unsafe for drinking). For next 0.4 mile, cross another series of small spurs and gullies.

1.6   Ascend steeply from gully; bear left off broad spur.

1.8   Cross Stillhouse Branch. Just beyond, diagonally cross Stillhouse Branch Road (Va. 641). A small USFS parking area for about four cars is located next to the Trail. Turn onto dirt road and into woods toward tributary of branch. Cross tributary several times in succession.

2.1	Cross under powerline.
2.2	Turn onto dirt access road. In 90 yards, bear uphill off road.
2.5	Reach broad spine of spur, and ascend several switchbacks .
2.7	Cross knob of spur to saddle, and turn onto old road.
3.0	Trail bears off old road, begins a steep, rocky ascent parallel to stream, and crosses it in 150 yards.
4.0	Reach good **campsite** to left of Trail. Water from small stream is just beyond campsite.
4.1	Reach eastern summit of Peters Mountain, turn sharp right, and follow ridgeline.
5.5	Cross pipeline right-of-way.
5.7	Cross smaller pipeline right-of-way.
5.9	Pass under electric transmission lines.
6.4	Cross stile, and enter open pasture known as the Rice Field. Enjoy sweeping views over numerous rocky outcroppings.
6.6	Reach side trail to **Rice Field Shelter** and privy (3,400 feet). Water is 0.5 mile behind shelter.
6.8	Cross stile, and reenter woods. Trail continues to follow narrow ridgeline.
7.2	Pass television antenna. Later, enter large powerline right-of-way with view to south of the shear face of Pearis Mountain and the A.T. south of Pearisburg.
8.2	Unmarked trail to the right leads 50 yards to a small spring.
11.3	Trail follows woods road. Enter the southern part of Symms Gap meadow.
11.6	Excellent **campsite** to right of Trail under large oak (no water).
11.7	Reach Symms Gap. Bear left, and descend on old road. Then, turn off road, and ascend over rocky trail.
12.7	Blue-blazed (unmaintained) Groundhog Trail, leading 2 miles northwest to W.Va. 219/24, joins A.T. from the left. The mileage sign here is inaccurate; it was placed before a relocation farther north was completed.

14.2   Reach Dickinson Gap with historical stone marker now painted bright red (or orange) on left. Unmaintained blue-blazed trail that joins A.T. from right descends 1.4 miles to Va. 635, 7.4 miles from U.S. 460. A.T. ascends over rocky trail through uplifted rock formations and upland hardwoods.

16.5   Trail veers southwest of knob (3,956 feet). Forested ridge provides an abundant spring-summer wildflower display.

16.6   A.T. bears right. Yellow-blazed Allegheny Trail intersects A.T. from the left.

16.8   Trail descends into shallow swale of Pine Swamp. This area has a hemlock stand and is plentiful with rhododendron. A large yellow poplar indicates an unmarked trail that leads left to a possible water source in wet times of the year.

17.1   Trail begins descent of Peters Mountain over switchbacks on graded trail.

18.4   Turn sharply right, and cross the rocky streambed of Pine Swamp Branch. Turn sharply left, and descend on graded trail.

19.1   Reach **Pine Swamp Branch Shelter** with privy, uphill just to the right of the Trail. Privy is farther uphill behind the shelter. Water is available from Pine Swamp Branch, 150 yards to the left.

19.4   Reach end of section. A.T. bears left up Stony Creek (see Section 32). Trailhead leads 100 feet to USFS parking area and display on Va. 635, 9 miles northeast of U.S. 460.

Important Addresses

Appalachian Trail Conference
P.O. Box 807
Harpers Ferry, WV 25425
(304) 535-6331

ATC Regional Office
P.O. Box 10
Newport, VA 24128
(540) 544-7388

Blue Ridge Parkway
Superintendent
700 Northwestern Bank Bldg.
Asheville, NC 28801
(704) 259-0718

Blue Ridge Parkway
Assistant Virginia Ranger
Rural Route 3, Box 39-D
Vinton, VA 24179
(540) 982-6458

Blue Ridge Parkway
James River District
Route 1, Box 17
Vesuvius, VA 24483
(828) 298-0281or
(800) PARKWATCH

Forest Supervisor
George Washington and
Jefferson National Forests
5162 Valleypointe Parkway
Roanoke, VA 24019
(540) 265-5100
(888) 265-0019

Jefferson National Forest
New River Valley
   Ranger District
Blacksburg Office
110 Southpark Drive
Blacksburg, VA 24060
(540) 552-4641

George Washington
   National Forest
Glenwood and
   Pedlar Ranger Districts
P.O. Box 10
27 Ranger Lane
Natural Bridge
   Station, VA 24579
(540) 291-2188

Jefferson National Forest
Mt. Rogers National
   Recreation Area
Route 1, Box 303
Marion, VA 24354

Jefferson National Forest
New Castle Ranger District
P.O. Box 246
New Castle, VA 24127
(703) 864-5195

Jefferson National Forest
Wythe Ranger District
1625 W. Lee Highway
Wytheville, VA 24382

Natural Bridge A.T. Club
P.O. Box 3012
Lynchburg, VA 24503

Old Dominion A.T. Club
P.O. Box 25283
Richmond, VA 23260

Outing Club at Virginia Tech
P.O. Box 538
Blacksburg, VA 24063

Roanoke A.T. Club
P.O. Box 12282
Roanoke, VA 24024

Tidewater A.T. Club
P.O. Box 8246
Norfolk, VA 23503

Summary of Distances

<table>
<tr><td>**North to South (read down)**</td><td></td><td>**South to North (read up)**</td></tr>
<tr><td>0.0</td><td>Rockfish Gap, U.S. 250, I-64</td><td>224.8</td></tr>
<tr><td>5.0</td><td>**Paul Wolfe Shelter**</td><td>219.8</td></tr>
<tr><td>5.1</td><td>Mill Creek</td><td>219.7</td></tr>
<tr><td>10.6</td><td>Humpback Mountain</td><td>214.2</td></tr>
<tr><td>14.2</td><td>Laurel Springs</td><td>210.6</td></tr>
<tr><td>14.6</td><td>Blue Ridge Parkway, Dripping Rock parking area</td><td>210.2</td></tr>
<tr><td>15.1</td><td>Cedar Cliffs</td><td>209.7</td></tr>
<tr><td>18.8</td><td>Blue Ridge Parkway, Three Ridges parking area</td><td>206.0</td></tr>
<tr><td>19.4</td><td>Reeds Gap, Va. 664;
Blue Ridge Parkway, milepost 13.6</td><td>205.4</td></tr>
<tr><td>21.1</td><td>**Maupin Field Shelter** side trail</td><td>203.7</td></tr>
<tr><td>21.5</td><td>Bee Mountain</td><td>203.3</td></tr>
<tr><td>23.1</td><td>Hanging Rock</td><td>201.7</td></tr>
<tr><td>23.6</td><td>Three Ridges summit</td><td>201.2</td></tr>
<tr><td>25.3</td><td>Chimney Rocks</td><td>199.5</td></tr>
<tr><td>27.3</td><td>**Harpers Creek Shelter** side trail</td><td>197.5</td></tr>
<tr><td>29.8</td><td>Tye River</td><td>195.0</td></tr>
<tr><td>29.9</td><td>Va. 56</td><td>194.9</td></tr>
<tr><td>31.2</td><td>Cripple Creek</td><td>193.6</td></tr>
<tr><td>34.2</td><td>The Priest summit</td><td>190.6</td></tr>
<tr><td>34.7</td><td>**The Priest Shelter** side trail</td><td>190.1</td></tr>
<tr><td>35.6</td><td>Crabtree Farm Road, Va. 826</td><td>189.2</td></tr>
<tr><td>36.4</td><td>Cash Hollow Road</td><td>188.4</td></tr>
<tr><td>37.7</td><td>Cash Hollow Rock</td><td>187.1</td></tr>
<tr><td>38.5</td><td>Main Top Mountain</td><td>186.3</td></tr>
<tr><td>38.8</td><td>Spy Rock side trail</td><td>186.0</td></tr>
<tr><td>39.3</td><td>Fish Hatchery Road</td><td>185.5</td></tr>
<tr><td>40.1</td><td>Porters Ridge</td><td>184.7</td></tr>
<tr><td>40.5</td><td>Porters Field</td><td>184.3</td></tr>
<tr><td>41.6</td><td>**Seeley-Woodworth Shelter**</td><td>183.2</td></tr>
<tr><td>42.3</td><td>Elk Pond Branch</td><td>182.5</td></tr>
</table>

44.4	Wolf Rocks	180.4
45.4	Greasy Spring Road (USFS 1176A)	179.4
47.1	Salt Log Gap (north), USFS 63 (ext. of Va. 634)	177.7
48.4	Tar Jacket Ridge	176.4
49.3	Hog Camp Gap (USFS 48)	175.5
50.6	Cold Mountain	174.2
51.8	**Cow Camp Gap Shelter** side trail	173.0
52.8	Bald Knob	172.0
54.7	USFS 507 & USFS 520	170.1
55.6	Long Mountain Wayside, U.S. 60	169.2
57.4	**Brown Mountain Creek Shelter**	167.4
59.4	Pedlar Lake Road, USFS 38	165.4
61.5	Pedlar Dam	163.3
61.8	USFS 39	163.0
63.6	Rice Mountain	161.2
65.5	Robinson Gap Road (Va. 607)	159.3
65.8	Blue Ridge Parkway crossing, milepost 51.7	159.0
66.2	**Punchbowl Shelter**	158.6
66.7	Punchbowl Mountain	158.1
67.8	Bluff Mountain	157.0
69.3	Saltlog Gap (south)	155.5
71.9	Big Rocky Row	152.9
72.9	Fullers Rocks, Little Rocky Row	151.9
75.0	**Johns Hollow Shelter**	149.8
75.6	USFS 36 (Va. 812), Hercules Road	149.2
76.7	U.S. 501, Va. 130	148.1
76.9	James River Foot Bridge	147.9
78.9	**Matts Creek Shelter**	145.9
80.8	Big Cove Branch	144.0
81.6	Sulfur Spring Trail	143.2
84.4	Marble Spring, **campsite**	140.4
85.4	High Cock Knob	139.4
86.6	Petites Gap Road, USFS 35; Blue Ridge Parkway, milepost 71.0	138.2
88.0	Harrison Ground Spring	136.8
88.7	Thunder Ridge	136.1
89.9	Thunder Ridge Overlook; Blue Ridge Parkway, milepost 74.7	134.9
90.3	Lower Blue Ridge Parkway crossing, milepost 74.9	134.5
91.3	**Thunder Hill Shelter**	133.5

91.6	Upper Blue Ridge Parkway crossing, milepost 76.3	133.2
92.2	The Guillotine	132.6
92.5	Apple Orchard Mountain	132.3
93.9	Parkers Gap Road (USFS 812)	130.9
95.1	Cornelius Creek National Recreation Trail	129.7
95.7	Black Rock side trail	129.1
96.6	**Cornelius Creek Shelter** side trail	128.2
97.2	Floyd Mountain	127.6
101.4	Side Trail to Va. 714	123.4
101.5	**Bryant Ridge Shelter**	123.3
103.7	Fork Mountain	121.1
105.3	Va. 614, Jennings Creek	119.5
106.5	Glenwood Horse Trail	118.3
108.5	**Cove Mountain Shelter** side trail	116.3
110.3	Cove Mountain summit	114.5
111.7	Bearwallow Gap. Va. 43; Blue Ridge Parkway, milepost 90.9	113.1
113.5	Mills Gap Overlook	111.3
114.2	Sharp Top Overlook; Blue Ridge Parkway crossing, milepost 92.5	110.6
114.9	**Bobblets Gap Shelter**	109.9
115.7	Hammond Hollow Trail	109.1
117.3	Harveys Knob Overlook; Blue Ridge Parkway crossing, milepost 95.3	107.5
117.9	Montvale Overlook; Blue Ridge Parkway, milepost 95.9	106.9
119.0	Taylors Mountain Overlook; Blue Ridge Parkway crossing, milepost 97.0	105.8
119.8	Black Horse Gap, USFS 186; Blue Ridge Parkway, milepost 97.7	105.0
122.2	**Wilson Creek Shelter** side trail	102.6
124.8	Curry Creek	100.0
125.6	Salt Pond Road (USFS 191)	99.2
128.4	**Fullhardt Knob Shelter** side trail	96.4
129.8	Tollhouse Gap	95.0
131.3	Va. 652	93.5
131.9	U.S. 11	92.9
132.2	Va. 779 and I-81	92.6
133.4	U.S. 220, I-81/U.S. 220/11	91.4

135.5	Tinker Ridge	89.3
137.4	Hay Rock	87.4
138.5	Angels Gap	86.3
138.8	Ruckers Gap	86.0
142.5	**Lamberts Meadow primitive campsite**	82.3
142.7	**Lamberts Meadow Shelter** side trail	82.1
143.4	Scorched Earth Gap, Andy Layne Trail	81.4
143.8	Lunch Box Rock	81.0
143.9	Tinker Cliffs	80.9
145.7	Brickey's Gap	79.1
147.1	Snack Bar Rock	77.7
148.8	**Campbell Shelter**	76.0
148.9	**Pig Farm Campsite**	75.9
149.4	Devil's Kitchen	75.4
149.5	McAfee Knob	75.3
151.0	**Catawba Mountain Shelter**	73.8
152.0	**Boy Scout Shelter**	72.8
153.0	Va. 311	71.8
157.2	Catawba Creek	67.6
158.9	Va. 624, North Mountain Trail	65.9
159.9	Rawies Rest	64.9
160.2	Viewpoint Rock	64.6
160.4	Lost Spectacles Gap	64.4
161.4	Dragon's Tooth side trail	63.4
161.5	Cove Mountain	63.3
164.9	**Pickle Branch Shelter**	59.9
165.9	Trout Creek, Va. 620	58.9
169.7	Audie Murphy Monument side trail	55.1
173.5	Craig Creek Valley, Va. 621	51.3
174.8	**Niday Shelter** side trail	50.0
175.5	**Cabin Branch primitive campsite**	49.3
177.2	Sinking Creek Mountain (north crest)	47.6
180.8	**Sarver Cabin** (Shelter, fall 2001) side trail	44.0
183.9	Va. 630	40.9
184.8	Va. 42, Sinking Creek Valley	40.0
187.1	Laurel Creek, main prong	37.7
187.2	**Laurel Creek Shelter** side trail	37.6
188.6	Big Pond side trail	36.2
190.2	Rocky Gap (USFS 10721, Va. 601)	34.6

192.2	Johns Creek Valley (USFS 156)	32.6
193.0	**War Spur Shelter**	31.8
197.9	Wind Rock	26.9
198.1	Salt Sulfur Turnpike, Va. 613	26.7
201.8	**Bailey Gap Shelter**	23.0
203.3	Va. 635 (north crossing)	21.5
205.4	Stony Creek Valley, Va. 635	19.4
205.7	**Pine Swamp Branch Shelter**	19.1
208.3	Peters Mountain crest (north end)	16.5
213.1	Symms Gap Meadow	11.7
218.2	**Rice Field Shelter**	6.6
223.0	Stillhouse Branch Road, Va. 641	1.8
224.8	U.S. 460, Senator Shumate Bridge (southeast end), New River	0.0

Index